The Successful Entrep[reneur] Bible [6 in 1]

A Collection of Ideas, Businesses, Strategies, and Tricks that Will Make You Big Money in 2021

By

Nespy Online Marketing

for clarifying purposes only and are the owned by the owners themselves, not affiliated with this document.

Author: NESPY ONLINE MARKETING

THE GOLDEN

INNER CIRCLE

The Golden Inner Circle is an elitist group business incubator. It's a way to speed yourself up with far fewer setbacks. If you are already on track follow these enlighten entrepreneurs to take you to the next level of your potential.

Get the support you need to:

- free yourself from negative limiting beliefs

- develop a marketing strategy that works

- discover the Golden Method to improve your skills

- realize the dream of being able to work in complete autonomy

- create passive income with low-budget investments form your home.

The Golden Inner Circle is the movement that is leading hundreds of people to find a real strategy to achieve great results in the most profitable businesses such as Youtube, Instagram, Airbnb...

This series of over 20 books called "Clever Entrepreneurs in the XXI Century" is a step-by-step program that will take you from zero to the highest level of success.

The information contained within will help you to raise the dormant leader inside you, develop the King Midas' touch and to embody the NEW Golden YOU.

Table of Contents

Private Label Crash Course

Youtube, Tik-Tok and Instagram Made Easy

Short Stays Real Estate with No (or Low) Money Down

The Golden Ratio Trading Algorithm

Deducting | The Right Way

Private Label Crash Course

Build Your First 6-Figure Business Supported by a Collection of 9+1 Profitable Strategies. Find the Best Products, Build an Enlighten Team and Start Your Personal Brand

By

NESPY ONLINE MARKETING

Table of Contents

Introduction

A private label is where a person or corporation paying another business to make a commodity without its name, emblem, etc. The person or business then applies to the packaging their name and design. So, what sorts of items should be labeled privately? From skincare and dietary treatments and infant essentials, pet products, and kitchen utensils, pretty much all under the sun. The benefit of private labeling is that nothing innovative needs to be produced or developed by you. You can add your mark on it as long as it's not a proprietary commodity and label it yours. For the last ten years, private labels have risen by at least double the number of popular household products. In reality, there is a lot of conversation about the rise of private labels or retail brands around the world these days. Or we need to claim private brands, maybe since they are indeed labels by the end of each day. Opportunities to have ever-better-value offerings for both of us as consumers. Possibilities for everyone to push the main factors transforming the world of today and tomorrow. Yes, it's not the Private Label curse. It could well, in truth, be a present. A blessing that pushes us all to question the status quo again. A gift that pushes one to step positively with some of the main big forces that form the world of today to collaborate together more successfully and collaboratively. A blessing that is increasingly important to all of us, whether in the United Kingdom, the United States, China, or Scandinavia. If we like it or not, Private Label will soon have a single category of quick products in the country. In the last ten years, private labels have risen at least double the amount of popular consumer packaged goods brands. How did the Private Label expand at the above remarkable pace, and what lessons does it give players in the more narrowly established markets of fast-moving consumer goods? We like to think of it as a food event, but it's increasingly a complete experience of consumption. Flavors' globalization, marketers, and individuals have made Private Label a global fact. More and more, Private Label is the face of today's retailer. Comprehend it. This isn't going to go away. Act about it. Perhaps we should name them PRIVATE Companies from now on. Perhaps we might create very different tactics to survive if we began naming them brands instead of labels. Brands are concerned about combating their closest competing brand. Will they behave as though their closest advertised rival is the Private Label? Maybe they could, because maybe if they did, they might behave very differently in reality. The commodity has gone on. In turn, as Private Label has become a brand power in its own right, it has become privatized. It cannot be ignored as a single mark anymore. It's something a ton more. While taken out of context, Private Label is turning controversial for this cause, maybe more than any other, placing owners on the backhand side and retail section on the offensive. Neither group appears especially keen to publicly address it or cooperate on something outside development. Products have brought copycatting stores to court, and dealers have de-listed popular brands from their racks. There's a tiny concession space. It increasingly distorts agreed shopping habits and usage trends in order to exacerbate problems more. It is a brand that can often account for two out of three physical transactions made by your consumer. A brand that is gradually seen as an alternate product and value of parity. A company that will out-weigh and out-image any typical brand by exploiting the retailer's corporate strength and spending. A brand that can drive producers into a vicious cycle of loss in the market. A trillion-dollar market that, as you realize its sheer scale and future effects, must be the least evaluated and poorly understood industry around. An industry that in the years to come is going to get a lot larger. There would theoretically be billions of dollars of sales redirected by brand owners to this power. Are you confident your plans are ready? The remedies? But, as the solution, what do people recommend? Lower costs, increase efficiency, and be more imaginative. This is not just a remedy that you can pursue as a standard component of your business growth. It is simply not sufficient. This is an opportunity that requires the unusual and the unconventional. Or else rise to the challenge. The Private Label is a wake-up call from a brand creator. Wake up to the truth in the company. Wake up in search of a shopper. Wake up to what you might theoretically do for your company. Wake up to proactivity for real. Wake up to a chance to get the rest of the planet back into communication with your company. Private label has arisen from the conventionally held assumption that firms will benefit and conquer the competition by providing either higher value at a higher cost for their consumers (or shoppers) or fair value at a cheaper cost (retailer brands). In other terms, it's a preference between distinction (or innovation) and low cost, and it's safe to assume that only then have retailers fallen into the former to offer the latter to the shopper reliably in spades. As Coke (and Tesco) can also inform you, it pays dividends to see the brand on any street corner. However, as some of our research highlights would demonstrate, there is still a significant perception difference between Private Label and existing manufacturer labels in terms of quality/value. As long as the shopper is concerned, at least, without the other, one will not thrive, and broadly speaking, maker labels are better positioned to offer sound 'innovation' and 'value' to retailers. Just 16% of shoppers in all regions sincerely agree that a supermarket of retailer-owned goods can only be expected in the future. So, we think there is a potential for brands to constantly reinvent themselves through shopper intuition, deeper brand commitment, and creativity. The potential for retailers to continuously add value is there. The potential exists for producers to maximize their manufacturing ability and for interactions to be reinvented by agencies. But most critically, the potential is there to constantly impress and entertain the shopper, far beyond all their hopes. The other alternative frequently provided is to get yourself into making a private label. However, you may be compelled by Private Label to analyze the very simple essence of the company in which you are and to doubt whether it is strong enough to move you further. Ask for your goods. Ask how and to whom you are offering. Ask if you still are tuning into the agents of transition. Your corporate purpose issues. Ask if you have the best staff and processes to meet this crucial problem. Finally, Private Label is a concern for manufacturers alike. Knowing how to profitably manage it without undermining the very essence of the organization you are with. And the manufacturers that you work with. Yes, you may assume that you can survive without them. Yet we're advising, be very, very patient. If you want to be a genuinely successful marketing tool in terms of bringing to the shopper, you need one another. In comparison, we exist in an age in which the newspapers are building up major global supermarket chains as the latest businesses to despise. Why are you stopping this? As the messenger, you use Private Label, a messenger that not only reveals that you deliver excellent value and costs but also indicates that you think for your consumer and their long-term social needs. And you are really doing what you can to support them. Now, even more on this. The private label is, to a great degree, a hidden force. The conservative nature of the subject-matter literature tends to downplay its actual place in the world, a function far from conservative in fact, and a role in which Private Label is undeniably the single greatest influence on our businesses and goods today. Brands, engagement professionals, and scholars have consistently ignored or underestimated this. That's got to change.

Chapter 1: Getting Started-Private Label

A private label is where a person or corporation paying another business to make a commodity without its name, emblem, etc. The person or business then applies to the packaging their name and design. So, what sorts of items should be labeled privately? From skincare and dietary treatments and infant essentials, pet products, and kitchen utensils, pretty much all under the sun. The benefit of private labeling is that nothing innovative needs to be produced or developed by you. You can add your mark on it as long as it's not a proprietary commodity and label it yours. A private label product is made and marketed under a retailer's brand name through a contract or third-party maker. You specify all about the commodity as the distributor-what goes into it, how everything is packaged, what the logo looks like-you pay to get it manufactured and shipped to your shop. This is in relation to purchasing goods with their corporate logos on them from other businesses. A successful brand identity can be the crucial base for building loyal customers, customer growth, and a competitive edge. Care of your corporate name as your company's face is how you are viewed by the audience. Without a detailed, excellently defined brand identity, the consumer might not realize who you are. In the end, you need to create a personal link. The potential exists for producers to maximize their manufacturing ability and for interactions to be reinvented by agencies. But most critically, the potential is there to constantly impress and entertain the shopper, far beyond all their hopes. The other alternative frequently provided is to get yourself into making a private label. However, you may be compelled by Private Label to analyze the very simple essence of the company in which you are and to doubt whether it is strong enough to move you further.

1.1 What is Private Label?

A private label product is made and marketed under a retailer's brand name through a contract or third-party maker. You specify all about the commodity as the distributor-what goes into it, how everything is packaged, what the logo looks like-you pay to get it manufactured and shipped to your shop. This is in relation to purchasing goods with their corporate logos on them from other businesses.

1.2 Private Label Categories

Almost every consumer product category has both branded and private label offerings, including:

- Condiments and salad dressings

- Cosmetics

- Personal care

- Frozen foods

- Dairy items

- Beverages

- Household cleaners

- Paper products

1.3 Different types of Private Label as profitable strategies

Generic Private Label

Generic private-label goods are one of the conventional private label tactics used to provide the price-conscious consumer with a low-price alternative. The brand doesn't matter to these consumers. With limited advertising and no marketing, the goods are inexpensive, undifferentiated, poor inconsistency. In commoditized and low-involvement goods, these private labels are primarily present. For both discount stores in Western nations, this technique is widespread.

Copycat Brands

In order to draw buyers, manufacturers play on the price point, retaining the packaging identical to a national brand that offers a sense of the product's similar consistency. These goods are reverse engineered, utilizing factories of identical technologies from national brand products. In wide categories that have a clear market champion, certain private labels are mostly present. In the detergent group, Massive Corporation blindly embraces the copycat brand approach. Detergents against rival products with identical packaging have been launched, albeit at a cheaper price.

Premium store brands

Retailers now have started utilizing private labels, rather than just as a pricing strategy, as a store point of difference. Premium store brands are valued higher and are also high in performance than the national brands. Here, the customer proposal is to be the greatest brand that money will purchase. In the retailer's shop, these products get influential eye-catching locations. In the advertising, the manufacturer insists on the excellent consistency of the goods.

Value innovators

Retailers manufacture goods that have all the value-adding characteristics and eliminate the non-value-adding characteristics in order to reduce costs, one point ahead of the copycat approach, and thus provide the customer with the best value deal. The danger of being imitated also rests in these labels. As it produces furniture under a modern market paradigm that involves self-service, assembling, and transporting yourself, Ikea is renowned for its better goods.

1.4 White Label vs. Private Label Dropshipping?

You can select between white label and private label dropshipping if you want to launch an online store. Both words define goods that have been branded by a reseller, but the two definitions very distinctly. Particularly to beginners, they may seem quite complicated, so let's go through each one and explain their relative benefits.

Private Labeling

Private marking is where a company selectively makes a commodity for a store that offers it under its own name. Costco utilizes private marking, for instance, by marketing its own "Kirkland" brand that no other store can offer. As a consequence, goods with private labels are typically less pricey than national brands. Plus, they can be very lucrative if they're promoted properly. Dropshipping is a convenient method for private-label goods to be distributed. You will find a dropshipping provider if you are an online shop owner who can offer items directly to you and incorporate your branding. Dropshipping is an e-commerce market concept in which no inventory is held by the manufacturer. The retailer, instead, manages the packaging, packing, and delivery of goods to the end customer. In other terms, for dropshipping, the goods are delivered directly to consumers, and they are never used by stores.

White Labeling

A white-label product is a manufactured product that a company makes but is rebranded by marketers to make it look as though it had been produced. Each dealer is authorized to resell the item under its own title and labeling. Unlike private labels, several retailers may market a white-label commodity. For e.g., you can have your own branding and labels on the goods that are delivered if you wish to market a product under your brand name utilizing the dropshipping business strategy. It is often safer to search at something that already has a market when it comes to items with a white mark. It's dangerous to produce goods with white marks that consumers are not comfortable with. It's safer to go for existing brands that people regularly use. As with private labels, dropshipping makes it simple to market online white-label goods. Again, the items are delivered directly from the producers to customers, and the commodities are seldom seen by dealers.

Advantages & Disadvantages of White Labeling

You won't have to go through the complicated logistics of making a commodity in one of these two e-commerce market models. You can save a lot of time and money without significant expenditure of time and energy in product design and production. In essence, you will concentrate on selling the commodity to the target group and branding it. In order to expand your company, you won't spread yourself thin and can concentrate on other areas of expertise. So, let's go through the common advantages and disadvantages of each business model:

Advantages of White Labeling

There are some real benefits of the white labeling market model, including:

- **It saves time and money.**

It's just cheaper to white mark an established commodity instead of wasting resources on developing a product from scratch.

- **Gain a large profit**

In general, white label goods are exclusively marketed by suppliers and may be bought at cheap market rates.

Disadvantages of White Labeling

There are, on the other side, some risks of white marking, including:

- **Limited options for branding**

Because it will be the producer or retailer who makes the white label product's bottle, label, and packaging, depending on the concept, you can just decide what it will deliver for you.

- **Limited choices of products**

Just the goods that the maker produces will be preferred, and you will not be allowed to produce anything special to the market.

- **Competition is tough**

It is challenging to stand out from the other online vendors that, white-label or not, sell the same items.

1.5 Dropshipping Private Label

We have addressed that different dropshipping products are among the simplest methods for private or white label items to be distributed. So, let's go about how private or white label items can be dropshipped.

Finding a supplier

In order to achieve the sustainability of online shops, having a successful dropshipping supplier is utterly crucial. In quest of finding a directory of dropshipping vendors who sell private label facilities, you should look at business websites or just do a search on Google. Seeking a niche will allow you and your business to stand out from other retail vendors. Make sure that you conduct consumer analysis to figure out what sort of thing you would prefer to rebrand or distribute.

Establishing the identity with the brand

A successful brand identity can be the crucial base for building loyal customers, customer growth, and a competitive edge. Care of your corporate name as your company's face is how you are viewed by the audience. Without a detailed, excellently defined brand identity, the consumer might not realize who you are. In the end, you need to create a personal link. Brand awareness must be expressed in the products, slogan, website, and packaging. It can offer a' derived from human attributes' to your brand. Brands with a very well-established personality make the brand intimately relatable, connecting consumers at a relational level and having to have the commodity in their lives. This is relevant for dropshipping products, including the private and white labels.

Increase awareness about your label and brand

Growing your brand recognition is another important move towards building a profitable brand. If the product is fresh, then identifying your target customers and discovering ways to draw consumers to your shop is the very first thing you'll want to achieve. This is so if it's the private label dropshipping goods. Here are some forms that brand recognition can be improved without any expense:

- Build content on your website with the addition of a blog

- Developing your social network online identity

- To engage and network with more clients and get product feedback.

- To maximize your keyword scores, perform SEO.

1.6 Deciding What to Private Label

You might be wondering about what's a competitive commodity to private label. The secret to this phase and probably the most crucial step in beginning a private label company is researching and putting efforts into finding a good product. You ought to figure out which products/services are in the market to ensure if your product would sell. To see what people, look for on the internet and get ideas about what you can offer from there, you can use programs available online. If you intend to launch your private label company on online marketplaces, you'll want to use a testing method that actually monitors what individuals are searching for on that platform. For this, popular programs include Helium 10 and Jungle Scout. They both provide several resources to help you continue your market path with your private label.

What Makes A Good Private Label Product?

The biggest point to hold in mind when applying for a private label for a commodity is to find one that:

It is in strong market demand and has limited competition from sellers.

This can help you stop being trapped with things that you will not offer.

Has a strong margin for benefit

Taking into consideration how much the item would cost you vs. how much you will market it for. If the item is held in a warehouse, plus the expenses involved with sale online, don't neglect to take into account the delivery costs from your source to you and from you to your client, packing and storage fees.

If you can manage the expenses

If you have a $1,000 or $10,000 startup investment budget, you need to take into consideration how many units you will need/want to buy and how much of the budget you will spend.

How to Find Suppliers

It's time to search for a producer or trade firm that provides private label service once you have a commodity in mind that you would like to private label. You can select anywhere in the world to make your goods. And several times, the type of service/product you select would rely on where you choose to get your product made. For e.g., China might be worth considering if you are trying to sell toys or gadgets because they seem to produce a ton of these types of items at very low prices. Consider looking for Alibaba or AliExpress if you want to go on this path. Both of these platforms are bulk markets where the goods are identified by suppliers and trade houses, where you can find almost everything. Because with all our federal rules, it's a great choice to source in the U.S. whether you want to offer food, dietary foods, cosmetic goods, or something else you bring in or on your body. Check on Google for items sourced domestically. Say you're searching for vegan deodorant source, just type in Google "vegan perfume private label U.K." to get a list of companies that can use vegan deodorants for private label.

What to Ask Private Label Suppliers

Once you've drawn up a list of possible vendors, calling each one and posing some questions is a smart idea.

Pricing Per Unit

The price would usually already be accessible for you to see on the website for each item. However, depending on how many units you order, most manufacturers give a discount. Knowing this data would also assist you in estimating the gross margin.

MOQ

In the private label/wholesale environment, this is a generic word used because it stands for "minimum order" or the minimum number of units you will order at a time. On their website/product listing, most vendors will mention their MOQ, although you will only have to inquire for some. The MOQ of a producer can be as few as five units, although it can be 1,000 and beyond for some. Although this may be negotiable often, asking this upfront is a smart move so that you can prepare and budget appropriately.

Customization

It is nice to know what the factory is and will not do in advance so that you can stop trying to swap vendors later unless you are seeking to apply your branding to the package, customize packages, or make modifications to the product.

Production Time

It is helpful to know how long it would take your provider to meet orders when your private label company continues to expand, and you continue to prepare for potential orders. Typically, the norm is around 15 days (depending on the commodity and order size), so it can go up from there.

Response Time

Take notice of how long it takes for the supplier to get back to you, bearing in mind that you are initiating a long-term future trading partnership. You would want to make sure that your communication individual is trustworthy, prompt, and specifically addresses your questions. If your provider is based in another country, take into consideration that they are in a separate time zone and that you will not automatically obtain a reply. During their business hours, being present will allow the operation easier.

Samples

Ask for prototypes such that the consistency and particular requirements can be measured. Many vendors can submit a sample free of charge, while others may start charging a small fee. Anyway, it's certainly not something you'd skimp on, especially if you're trying to give the highest service to your customers.

Customizing Your Product

In how your product can market, customizing your product will play a huge role. Question yourself, "What's going to set my version apart from the competition?" The response to this is key in having a prospective customer select your product over the product of a more known, well-reviewed business. Perhaps it's as quick as providing color combinations or getting fancy packaging, or it might be easier to enhance a function that you want more in-depth. Such customizations, such as packaging upgrades, are likely to be achieved by your supplier, and some can be accomplished through yourself or by your suppliers, such as custom marking with product specifics and a logo. Customizing the goods in any form is the main message here. Stand out by having it different (and better) than the rivals '. By basically slapping the mark on it, you don't want to sell the same exact thing as another brand.

You are selling your Private Label product.

You may pick anywhere to market your private-label line of items. Here's an extensive list of online sales places or suggestions on how to get into shops.

A Personal Online Store

Such customizations, such as packaging upgrades, are likely to be achieved by your supplier, and some can be accomplished through yourself or by your suppliers, such as custom marking with product specifics and a logo. Customizing the goods in any form is the main message here. Stand out by having it different (and better) than the rivals '. By simply yanking your tag on it, you wouldn't want to give the same product as yet another brand.

Brick-And-Mortar

Sitting the goods on the shelf of a physical shop offers consumers the ability to see your product that they would never have dreamed of it otherwise. In other words, customers have to practically "search" for services or products they want to buy online. But if they don't think about it, they're not going to search and probably won't find it unless you pay serious bucks promoting it. If shoppers are still in a shop and happen to see it, it builds brand/product recognition at least. Fees and requirements for getting shelf-space vary by store, but it can be a decent place to start from local, family-owned stores. Read more regarding boutique collaborations or having your own storefront.

Markets

Markers and art fairs for producers are on the increase. Consumers love to shop locally and want to help their community's artisans. They're a perfect way to get instant input from customers, too. Find out how to start trading and find craft markets at farmer's markets.

Don't limit yourself.

Start with a variety of channels, in-person shops, and websites. You would be able to see over a span of time how many sales you create from each one, how much money each produces, etc. You should just stick doing what's profitable, then. It is certainly a road to launch your private label company, and it will be months until you can bring the goods on the market. But the trip can be well worth it if you do your product testing, pick the best source, separate the product from the market, and price it right.

Chapter 2: Profitable Strategies in Building Six-Figure Business

For private-label products, manufacturers may raise gross margins by managing the whole supply chain from manufacture to distribution. Clothing traders have been pushing different private-label options for years. Costco has the Kirkland private-label name. Nordstrom's got Caslon. And Kohl's has Sonoma as its in-house, billion-dollar brand. Although online stores have supplied other industries with private label labels, basic products for tangible products focused on low-cost hardware and office equipment, the move to clothes implies a brazen policy expansion. Any volume seller is looking at the advantages of growing private-label brand's goods in order to drive sustainability and connect with a more aware and conscious millennial generation who are known for not being very brand loyal.

2.1 Private Label for Profitability

Profits are powered by private labels. A private-labeled commodity or product with parity in operation and consistency with major labels will cost manufacturers 40 to 50 percent less to develop and sell to consumers. In order to negotiate with online marketplace empires and other online suppliers who offer low-cost products without caring about reducing margins, merchants will then switch around to provide greater discounts. Online, where customers have 100 percent pricing transparency, this is especially essential. This functions on both luxury and commodity items. Building and maintaining a private label often enables manufacturers to develop exclusive goods for higher prices or to manufacture commodity products below brands at a sustainable price. To boost their inventory rotation, manufacturers are now using private-label tactics. Retail stores with services from private labels could also have more than four seasons a year. An innovative team in private label, such as the JCPenney team of 250 designers working in-house or the internal production and procurement departments of Nordstrom, will contend on an equal footing with fast-trending fashion stores like H&M.

Factors to be Considered

It may be dangerous to hop into this business without carefully thinking it over. Before investing and dedicating time to a privately-label approach, here are some factors to be considered:

- **Identifying low cost and high-quality manufacturer**

A colossal advantage is strong production suppliers, while poor manufacturers or suppliers are a horrific liability. Spend the effort to do it correctly. There are hundreds or thousands of suppliers capable of producing stuff that you would need. Find the producer that fits all the requirements for price and consistency; often, identifying the markets that are relevant. You may also want to learn from Portugal or Vietnam for clothing. Vietnam, South Korea, and China have manufacturing expertise in electronics. Take note that costs for suppliers differ greatly depending on the order's size.

- **Strengthen the Skills in Design and Procurement**

The private label includes relationships with producers of agricultural and consumer goods, component retailers, multinational warehouses, and distribution suppliers. Will you broaden the current partnerships between suppliers? If not, determine whether to consult the staff or purchase the expertise that will render the retail company a key competency of the strategy regarding the private label. Consider a completely dedicated bet on vertical trading, too.

- **Using brand pricing and external signs as guiding principles for pricing policy**

Research your rival brands closely while designing your own products under the banner of a private label. Retailers ought to make up their mind whether to generate the product as a luxury product and expend marketing expenses or to position it as an alternate brand by selling below national labels. If product attributes can be readily contrasted and placed as a substitute brand, it is important to consider the price point of comparable goods to position them correctly against competitors' national brand/products label brands. In other situations, were comparing features is not something very straightforward. Retailers can use a number of internal market pointers for pricing, such as site traffic, ratings, consumer feedback, and retailers can recognize the popularity of the product. Today, if a commodity is popular/interest-generating, but the converging performance is low, this can cause a price reduction/promotion intervention.

- **Acknowledge the differences in categories and manage them smartly**

Consumers can browse for functionality within a particular perceived cost sub-set for white and hard goods. Buyers searching for features are opting for a dryer or washing machine. Potential customers are looking for other qualities, such as cloth, shape, trendiness, for soft items like clothing. Those features deter similarities.

- **Decide Efficient Customized Label Blend**

The best combination of private label and branded items has to be determined by retailers. Are buyers looking for a feature in a certain product category or range on the website? Collecting web search data can help marketers make a choice. They have to remember the client base as well. If the consumer pool is predominantly 28- to 51-year-old buyers, private label goods can be more value aware and prefer small-scale proliferation.

- **Implement Algorithmic, Data-Driving Pricing Methods**

With constantly evolving customer preferences, at every given level in time, you should be able to recognize demand levels and continually seek the optimum price value. Factor in leveraging algorithms based on technology systems to easily evaluate price levels and strategies; when priced carefully with supporting data, private-label brands also deliver unexpected revenues. For e.g., the commodity was priced well below the national brand by a generic manufacturer of merchandise with a very well private label refrigerator brand, just to experience a drop in revenue. The store began checking multiple price ranges, steadily pushing up the segment. Sales started to fall with the first $200 onwards. And, magically, revenue and traffic boomed until the price reached a hidden barrier. This sounds counterintuitive, but the private-label company has already been put in a competitive area with national labels in the view of the consumer. Instead of seeing it as a lower quality commodity, clients began to see it as domestic brands. They were prepared to move since the price levels were always cheaper than domestic brands. In a considerably more profitable buyer zone, it was repositioned by moving the idea up the continuum. If consumers interpret things the same way with analytic pricing, the same SKU will gain double the profits. These are some of the most important elements in successfully initiating your private label initiative at any major retailer. Going over these basics will strip the efforts of the bulk of danger.

2.2 9+1 Pricing Strategies

Want to maximize profit on your product sales?

Aside from other publicity and business tactics, a strong pricing policy is indeed something you need to concentrate on. When setting the price for your goods or services, what considerations do you consider? When determining the prices for your goods or services, there are a number of considerations, including:

- Production cost

- positioning strategies

- competitor's products

- Distribution cost

- Target consumer base

When buying a commodity, price is a very important consideration for a buyer. A productive pricing system can also have a profound influence on the company's performance. And often, it decides whether or not the organization can succeed. So, what are those tactics you should suggest in order to improve the revenue and be more profitable?

Premium Pricing

Marketers put rates higher than their competitors or rivals for this promotional policy. However, it is used where there is a major competitive edge, and a relatively cheaper price is safe for the marketer or the organization to charge. For small businesses that offer exclusive services or products, high pricing is perfect. A corporation, however, can check that the packaging of the goods, its promotional campaigns, and the décor or luxury facilities of the store all fit to maintain the fixed price.

- **Example of Premium Pricing**

Let's take the example of luxury specialty retail stores that charge you a little extra but sell you exclusive styles and tailored clothing.

Penetration Pricing

To try to draw buyers? Ok, this technique is going to help you with the purpose. Lower rates are given on utilities or goods under this strategy. Although this technique is used by many emerging firms, it does appear to lead to an initial reduction of profits for the business. Over time, though, the growth of product or service recognition will drive revenues and allow small businesses to stand out. In the long run, as a business succeeds in entering the sector, its costs always end up growing to represent the condition of its role in the sector.

Economy Pricing

The advertisement expense of a service or commodity is held at a low in this strategy. The technique is used during a certain period where the organization does not invest much in promoting the service or product.

Example of Economy Pricing

The first few budget airlines, for instance, are offered at low rates in discount airlines to fill in the jet. A broad variety of businesses, from discount stores and generic grocery manufacturers, use Economy Pricing. The technique, though, maybe dangerous for small firms when they lack the market scale of larger corporations. Small companies can fail to make a sufficient profit with low rates, but strategically tailoring price-cuts to your most loyal customers or consumers may be a successful way to guarantee their loyalty for years to come.

Price Skimming

This technique is meant to assist enterprises in focusing on the sale of innovative services or goods. During the preliminary process, this strategy means setting high prices. The rates are then reduced steadily when the competitor's goods or services arrive on the market. When the product is first released in the marketplace, this price approach produces an image of exclusivity and good quality.

Psychology Pricing

This method of pricing deals with a client's psychology. For e.g., setting the price of a ring at $99 is likely to draw more clients than setting prices at $100. But the concern is, in terms of a very limited gap, why are consumers more drawn to a product's former price? Psychology suggests that on a price tag, customers prefer to give greater attention to the first digits. When stores apply $0.99 on product tags of $1.99 or $2.99, you can find identical promotional strategies. The purpose of this approach, therefore, is to build an image of greater value for the consumer.

Bundle Pricing

How often have you been persuaded to purchase a multipack of 6 packets for $2.99 instead of purchasing one packet for $0.65? Or an SMS kit instead of texting on the individual rates? Without sacrificing efficiency, we all enjoy commodities that cost us less. This is why package selling is a success for both the vendor and the consumer and is profitable. The vendor gets to sell more of their inventory, and for less cost, the consumer gets to purchase the product in bulk. For instance, if bundle package of chips is for $1.30 and 3 multipacks for2.50$. The probability of purchasing three packs is more than purchasing only one. Bundle pricing enhances the worth sense when you are actually offering your consumers anything for free.

Value Pricing

This technique is used when external forces such as increased rivalry or unemployment cause corporations to offer valuable promotional offerings or goods, e.g., combo offers or value meals at KFC and other restaurants, to sustain sales. Quality pricing lets a buyer know like for the same price, they are receiving a ton of product. In several respects, profit pricing is analogous to economic pricing. So, let's make this very clear that there is added benefit with regard to service or product in value pricing. Generally speaking, price cuts should not rise in value.

Promotional Pricing

Promotional pricing is a really common method for sales and can be used in different department stores and restaurants, etc. Part of this promotional policy are methods such as money off coupons, Buy One Get One Free, and promotions.

Cost-based Pricing

This method entails determining cost-based rates for the commodity to be made, shipped, and sold. In addition, a fair rate of profit is usually added by the corporation or sector to compensate for the risks as well as initiatives. Businesses such as Walmart and Ryanair are seeking to become low-cost suppliers. These businesses may set lower rates by constantly lowering costs whenever feasible. This undoubtedly contributes to lower profits but better profits and revenues. Companies with higher costs can, therefore, often rely on this approach to pricing. Yet, in general, in order to demand greater profits and rates, these businesses purposely generate higher costs. The aforementioned techniques are the most widely adopted strategies used by corporations to increase profit from sales of their product or service. In its own unique way, any pricing strategy is effective. Therefore, consider your marketplace and other conditions before selecting a pricing plan for your good or service to bring the most out of the strategy used. Therefore, becoming mindful of the competitive place when setting a price is important. What the clients or buyers anticipate in terms of the price should be considered in the marketing mix.

2.3 Best Practices in Private Label Branding

Can you recall when generic or non-national branded items with large black lettering and bad product consistency indicated simple white or yellow packing materials? After the unmemorable early days of supermarket labels, stores have clearly come a long way. In fact, many private label labels today are practically indistinguishable from their producer-branded equivalents on the shelves.

Align with and support the master (retail) brand

It is certainly no accident that some of the best private label company portfolios are those that tend to be in tune with the supermarket master brand's positioning and strategic purpose. Preferably, their positioning is strongly complementary to the supermarket master brand, enhancing the latter's equity and beneficial relationships.

Bring differentiation to the category; fulfill unmet customer needs.

When their products are additive to the supermarket, or better still, the overall competition, private label labels are maybe at their strongest. One way to achieve this is to bring the category to something completely differentiated. Another similar approach is to resolve consumer expectations that are not fulfilled by the big national labels. Importantly, this difference can be more than just a cheaper price than the brands of the manufacturer. In the good or service offering itself, private label labels can often be exclusive. Safeway is a perfect illustration of introducing distinction to the market and thereby addressing an increasingly unmet desire of the customer. Finally, creativity is another form in which private label labels may offer category and consumer distinction.

Establish clear boundaries for private label brands

There is also a temptation to expand it everywhere and anywhere in the shop once retailers effectively establish a good private label brand. This extends horizontally across types of goods and vertically across ranges of price/value. However, the tendency to over-extend or dilute the private label brand properties is resisted by better practice retailers.

Define brands based on emotional attributes

Since they feel an intrinsic bond to them, customers prefer to gravitate towards (and stay faithful to) products. There is no more for products with private labels than for brands with national suppliers. For private label labels, it is important that they stand for something more than just price/value and much more than a commodity attribute. They need to have an emotional advantage to which customers may connect. This essential nuance is understood by marketers that have become popular with exclusive labels and find ways to distill emotional equity through their private label brands.

Distinguish brands with a distinct identity and appropriate brand linkages

Finally, a distinctive and highly identifiable visual identity is established by leading label labels and embraces a clear messaging approach. They still maintain clear rules specifying the degree to which the private label mark may and should be identifiably affiliated with the supermarket master brand. An attractive visual presence and strategically advantageous brand design are undeniably part of what makes private label companies popular or leads to their downfall if overlooked.

2.4 Positives and Negatives of Private Label

Advantages

There is a legitimate explanation for retailers that are involved in flooding their stores with items with their brand name. Many of the main benefits of goods with private labeling include:

- **Handling Production**

Third-party suppliers operate at the behest of the supplier, providing full influence over the ingredients and consistency of the goods.

- **Control overpricing**

Retailers may also assess sales cost and efficient selling due to leverage over the product.

- **Adaptability**

In reaction to growing consumer demand for a new feature, smaller stores have the opportunity to move rapidly to bring a private label product into development, whereas larger firms might not be involved in a product or niche category.

- **Managing branding Decisions**

The company name and package concept produced by the manufacturer carry private label items.

- **Managing profitability**

Retailers monitor the amount of profitability their goods offer due to control over manufacturing expenses and pricing.

- **Increased margins**

Private labels enable manufacturers to sell and raise the profit margin more competitively on their goods. Compared to producing brands, several manufacturers gain 25-30 percent higher profit profits on private labels.

- **Customer loyalty**

Nowadays, consumers want goods manufactured locally, and they would like more if they enjoy the private label products. You would be the only outlet who would be willing to supply them with such goods. It is challenging to win the trust of individuals in the retail sector.

Disadvantages

As much as you have the financial capital to spend in creating such a commodity, the risks of introducing a private label brand are few. Primary drawbacks include:

- **Manufacturer dependency**

Since the manufacturing of your product range is in possession of a third-party vendor, working with accomplished businesses is critical. Otherwise, if the manufacturer gets into challenges, you might lose out on opportunities.

- **Difficulty building loyalty**

In a number of retail stores, existing household brands have the upper hand and can always be found. Only in your shops can your goods be sold, restricting consumer access to it. Restricted supply, of note, may also be an asset, providing clients an incentive to come back and purchase from you. Although private label goods are usually offered at a lower price point than their brothers of the corporate name, certain private label brands are also branded as luxury products, with a higher price tag to show it.

2.5 Keys to Private Label Greatness

As of late, we are doing a lot of innovative work in the Private Label sector, and here is a good refresher of The Core Values that we believe in for developing our own labels that are strategically convincing. We also see that there are particular fundamental stories in their creation throughout all great store brand cases, but there are seven values that they must abide by to be genuinely strategically convincing.

Principles of Equity and Environment

From a branding and design point of view, there has never been more interest in the grocery store and how we connect, affect purchasing decisions, and even construct theatre inside it. This is real in every part of the world. Of course, there is a reverence we all have to have for the cultural uniqueness of the grocery store, from country to country, since some customers are in the store just once a week, to other food and market experience where customers connect every day. Even with these diverse regional variations in frequency, familiarity, and satisfaction inside the retail shop, there is a common emphasis on making the store brand function more credibly and more convincingly with consumers in general.

The equity connection

Immersing oneself in the retailer's overarching goal, its perception and equity distinction as it is now, and what is achievable in the future is important. To achieve this, the right branding collaborators coordinate with the senior brass of the distributors with which they operate, as well as the organization's top merchants and store name specialists. They take into account all the main targets for which a merchant is fishing and then see how to enhance store brands as being one of the key tools to accomplish their task. Store products strengthen the retailer's total equity and vice-versa, and they struggle because they do not.

Environmental support

A kit can only do too many. Your store brand will get overloaded if it does not have the off-shelf environmental help in the vast stream of 40,000+ items that many of the largest supermarkets carry today. Beyond the box, give it existence and speech. To help your brand, use the theatre in the shop.

Be preferential

For supermarket brands, own products, exclusive brands, and the like, there are loads of common nomenclatures. "But whatever the language, don't treat your store brands to the larger national brands as weaker "stepchildren. Don't be afraid to handle your supermarket labels preferentially in the store, beyond the incisive box template for your company. In their importance, in their distribution of space, in their positioning of shelves, and in their show and cross-merchandising all throughout the shop. No need to apologize to the CPGs or succumb to the study of planograms.

Don't blindly follow.

For years, there has been a "follow the herd" attitude of store labels, and today it still persists. Because of what Walmart has achieved with Such Prices, many retailers we talk to now are terrified of "white" packaging. So often, individuals are hyper-attentive to the competition and norms and what's going around the market of store labels. The bottom line is that you can build your own vision in a very creative and special way. Do not blindly obey the naming conventions, color conventions, or typically mundane price-centered store brands set by broad categories and how they have traditionally behaved in order to reconsider anything intelligently.

Three layers have to work together.

Make sure you are not concerned with visual language alone with the positioning of the store labels and how they are to be fully distinguished for the future. This is the responsibility of a number of production agencies, who feel they are only employed to rewrite the store brand's aesthetic vocabulary. If we want to encourage these products to be produced differently, we need to understand how the graphic language is created, indeed, but also how it is structurally packaged and the language we use to orally convey the item. Graphic, systemic, and verbal languages all cohesively operate together.

Steve Jobs never asked the consumer.

Apple is one of the world's most creative and well-thought-out, profitable enterprises. When questioned what Steve Jobs felt about research in a New York Times report and how Apple uses it to direct new product creation, he replied, "None... it's not the job of consumers to know what they want." There are so many retailers that use research to store products in their innovative development phase, and this is a mistake. Customers will still turn to the protection and what is comfortable with them, but if they are the only sounding board, you will not have the most creative performance.

On the brand's positioning

In using the name of the shop on the individual store brand packaging, there are no universal guidelines, just as there are no generalizations to create about how large the store brand should stretch. Both of these brands had a very definitive strategic positioning when producing Greenway, Hartford Reserve, and Via Roma for A&P, and this relationship that established the role of the company was a very significant part of the process. Clearly describe it, know that you want to distinguish the brand rather than sheer costs, own it thoroughly in the consumer's head, and correctly reiterate it. In the development of an ambitious store brand platform, these ideals would suit you well because they are standards that the best supermarket brands live by with true conviction. The name brand industry continues to be guided by continuing innovative creativity, a true steel hand in spreading out from the single "price" veil, and to be persuasive in their own right. And store brands need to be promoted with vigor, motivation, and media support.

Chapter 3: Finding the Products & Starting Your Personal Brand

You should concentrate on creating a reputation before you start your company, one that is recognizable and valued, and a private label benefits both you and the retailer or supplier you select. The first move with your organization is importing the goods you choose to market, products that do not crack easily, which have satisfaction for the customer. The second and most significant move is to make your brand known to current and future clients. The more customers remember your brand, the higher it is possible that your revenue rate will be. Through selecting producers or suppliers who will submit your goods via Private Label, you will help this along. This operates by encouraging the consumer to position their orders with you, then deliver them to the retailer and directly dispatching the product. The return home address would be that of the company in most situations, but for Private Label, this will be yours. This ensures that whether they have any concerns or queries, the consumer would assume that the service/product has come from you, and they will only contact you. This helps you build up a brand reputation, but using trustworthy vendors, depends on you, and you deliver top-quality customer support. In general, manufacturers are willing to use private labels since it suggests that they do not have to be interested in any consumer problems. To sum up, while you are looking to get your brand out and develop a company without leeching on mainstream online market place/websites' popularity, a private label makes perfect sense. It will require a bit extra time to select a supplier since you must do the job yourself and guarantee that you work for the right supplier. Still, you will also gain a better profit when you take responsibility for the client support and are willing to negotiate the supplier's rates. A private label is where a person or corporation paying another business to make a commodity without its name, emblem, etc. The person or business then applies to the packaging their name and design. So, what sorts of items should be labeled privately? From skincare and dietary treatments and infant essentials, pet products, and kitchen utensils, pretty much all under the sun. The benefit of private labeling is that nothing innovative needs to be produced or developed by you. You can add your mark on it as long as it's not a proprietary commodity and label it yours.

3.1 How to Start Your Private Label Brand from Scratch?

Because of its profitability and consumer benefits, private labeling has boomed in prominence in recent years. To distinguish between larger vendors, more and more sellers create their products on and off e-commerce marketplaces. With 50 percent of one of the online markets, private labeling vendors, the rivalry is fierce. You need to realize what you're doing if you want to excel. To start a strong private label, you need the know-how, expertise, and money. When you place your logo and name on a standardized commodity, private labeling is. This separates the brand from related rivals and retailers. You have full power over your brand, with a private label. You establish a distinctive identity that is essential for successful promotion and the acquisition of consumers. Customers, not goods, are faithful to labels. Customer satisfaction and repeat business may be created through the private label. In the market, you still have the power of your price and place. A private label on the online marketplace enables you to build a different collection of items only for your product. This gives real estate devoted to your brand and assures that you are not vying against other retailers for the Buy Box. Since they get higher value, clients love private labels. Private-label goods are usually cheaper, but major stores' efficiency is the same, if not higher. In reality, at least one form of private label product is purchased by approximately 98 percent of customers. Depending on their lifestyle, customers may even buy goods. One study showed that clients prefer private labels for the price and choose them based on expertise. They buy from private labels that they most associate with. Ultimately, in a sea of rivals, a private label separates the name, allows you greater leverage over your revenues, and appeals to a niche client target. So, you have agreed to launch a private label of your own. The measures to take to help you start a profitable private label from design to launch are below.

3.2 Understand the costs of private labeling

Before digging deeper into a private label, it's important to consider the initial start-up costs. In comparison to reselling, private tagging is more costly. However, this capital input usually results in a better return on your expenditure in the long term.

Manufacturing

Typical development expenses, such as supplies, processing, manpower, and transportation, would have to be accounted for. You may need to consider the customization charge, too. For customizing a product with your mark, packaging, or specs, most manufacturers will charge a fee.

Brand

Even to design the brand itself, you would require money. To create the logo and package template, you'll definitely want to employ a graphic artist. To stress the voice of your company, you will also want to develop a content strategy.

Marketing

Marketing is a significant part of private labeling. Customers don't know about your company, so to become more noticeable, you need to spread knowledge. A large cost may be generated through ads such as promoted and boosted blogs. A website creator and domain name would presumably both need to be charged for. For any other unforeseen fees or modifications that pop about at the beginning of the start of a new company, you can also add a sizable buffer.

- **Choose the products you want to sell**

The majority of corporations and labels start with a commodity. The brand is how you create your cash and profits. The item is the guiding force of your business. Starting a commodity with your name helps determine your margins, demand, and availability. The brand is the consumer service, but you will need to offer your consumers a valuable product in the end. You would typically choose a branded commodity that you place your own logo on while you market a private label. This suggests that a single generic product begins with your "brand." How do you further build and broaden your branding using that product? You want high-rank and high-margin units when buying a commodity. To lower warehousing and shipping costs, you will want thin, lightweight goods. If the first product you offer doesn't work out or you choose to shift paths, you can still move goods. The aim is to stick less to one commodity than to use product testing as a prism in your overall business and niche instead. You should also accept complimentary commodities with this in mind. If you market key items, you want to think of a range of similar goods that would still blend with your brand when choosing key products. For starters, you can grow inside the travel domain or beverage industry if you sell travel mugs. You will market some eco-friendly home products as well if you sell environmentally efficient cleaning products.

- **Define your target market**

Who is the perfect consumer for you? Who would be more willing to buy your unique product? This can assist you in deciding the sorts of goods you are trying to produce and how you are going to promote such products. The consumer is your market and your brand's secret. Getting a well-defined target demographic is more relevant than ever, considering the current condition of the economy. No one is willing to afford to target everyone. By approaching a niche segment, small enterprises may successfully compete with big firms. Many firms say they are targeting "anyone interested in my services." Others say they are targeting buyers, renters, or stay-at-home moms in small businesses. These priorities are all too common. Targeting a certain market does not mean that you exclude entities that may not follow the standards. Instead, focus marketing helps you to concentrate your advertising money and brand message on a single demographic that is more inclined than other markets to purchase from you. This is a means of meeting prospective consumers and creating a business that is far more accessible, accessible, and effective. For instance, an interior design business might opt to sell to households between the ages of 34 and 63 with incomes of $160,000-plus. The business could opt to approach only those involved in kitchen design remodeling and conventional designs in order to define the segment any better. This business may be broken into two niche markets: parents on the move and baby boomers leaving. It is much simpler to decide where and how to advertise your brand with a well-specified target audience. To help you identify your target market, here are some ideas.

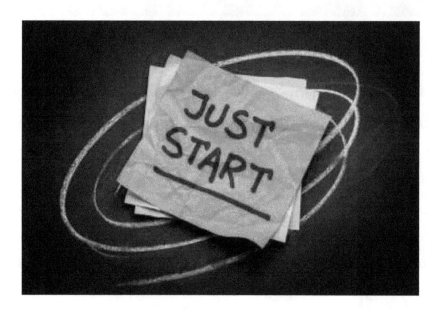

Look at your current customer base.

Who are your new clients, and why are they buying from you? Look for features and desires that are popular. What ones do other businesses carry in? It is also possible that your product/service will also help other individuals like them.

Check out your competition.

What are your adversaries targeting? Who are the clients at present? Don't try the same business. You might discover a niche market they are missing.

Analyze your product/service

Write up a description of each of the product or service specifications. List the advantages it offers next to each function. A graphic artist, for instance, provides high-quality design services. The advantage is the picture of a professional organization. More clients would be drawn to a professional image when they perceive the business as professional and trustworthy. So, basically, attracting more clients and earning more profits is the advantage of high-quality design. When you have your advantages identified, make a list of persons that have a need that suits your benefit. A graphic designer may, for instance, opt to approach organizations involved in increasing their consumer base. Although this is already too common, you now have a foundation on which to proceed.

Choose specific demographics to target.

Find out not only who wants the products or service and also who is most willing to order it. Consider the reasons that follow:

- Location

- Education level

- Occupation

- Gender

- Ethnic background

- Marital or family status

- Age

- Income level

- Ethnic background

Consider the psychographics of your target.

Psychographics is a person's more intimate traits, including:

- Personality

- Values

- Interests/hobbies

- Attitudes

- Lifestyles

- Behavior

Assess how your service or product would blend with the lifestyle of your destination. How and where is the item going to be used by your goal? What characteristics are most enticing to your goal? What media for details does your goal switch to? Can the newspaper read the destination, check online, or attend unique events?

Evaluate your decision

Make sure to consider these issues after you have settled on a target market:

- Are there enough individuals that meet my criteria?

- Is my goal actually going to benefit from my product/service?

- Are they going to have the use for it?

- Do I know what guides my aim to make choices?

- Can they afford my service/product?

- With my post, may I meet them? Are they readily accessible?

Don't smash the goal so far down there. Know, there is more than one niche opportunity you may have. Consider how, for each niche, the marketing message can be different. If you can successfully hit all niches with the same post, then maybe you have broken down the market so much. Also, if you notice that there are only 50 individuals that match all of your requirements, you may need to reevaluate your objective. Finding the right combination is the trick. You might be wondering, "How do I gather all this data?" Attempt to look online for analysis that others have done on your aim. Look for posts and blogs in publications that speak to or around the target group. Check for blogs and sites where thoughts are shared by people in the target market. Check for sample findings, or try doing your own survey. Ask for input from the new clients. The hard part is identifying your target demographic. It is much simpler to find out which platforms you should use to attract them, and what advertisement campaigns can connect with them if you know who you are approaching. You should give it only to people that suit your requirements instead of delivering direct mail to anyone in your ZIP code. In identifying the target demographic, save money and have a greater return on investment.

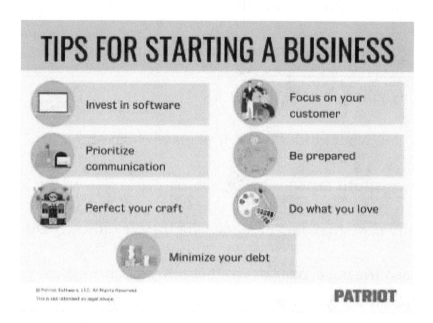

- **Consider your differentiating factor.**

You've settled on demand and a commodity. Now, what is going to make you distinctive in your business from your competitors? Look at the rivalry. What is their emphasis? And where are they missing? A perfect spot for you to put the brand is the field that they struggle the most. You could find, for example, that all of your rivals have a formal language; with your brand, you might take a goofy and enjoyable tone. In order for it to become a good differentiator, it doesn't have to be a big improvement. The core of your identity becomes your differentiator. Keep in mind that price may also be a defining factor. You would get a different demographic and competition than a cheap or discounted commodity, whether you are quality or luxury product.

- **Create your brand look**

Your "brand" consists of the goods, the demand, and the distinguishers. Yet, it is your material and aesthetic as well. You need a clear emblem that represents the name while private labeling is used. How you are and where the stuff comes from, the logo tells. This emblem can be included in all communications, packaging, and marking. Be sure it's accessible as a corporation and website prior to picking the brand name. This would mean that you do not infringe on any patents or fight with companies with identical names. To build the logo and package template, you'll definitely want to employ a graphic artist. This is the perfect approach to make things look respectable and trustworthy to the private label.

- **Create an experience**

A brand is, ultimately, more than a slogan, though. Your "brand" is how your business is experienced by the client. It's a consistent way for your audience to communicate. You need to work out how consumers can uniquely perceive your brand based on brand differentiation. What is your content going to look like? What could you provide that is unique to the experience of your brand? You may produce visually enticing social media photographs, for instance, that contribute to the lifestyle around your dog collars. Or you should make sure that you react to and respond to any social network statement or post. To keep your label on the edge, you can use special and exclusive packaging. Build an atmosphere, and you can turn your one-time consumers into long-term customers.

- **Find a supplier**

Acting with a good provider is an important aspect of private marking. The manufacturer must have private labeling expertise so they can help you make a return from your products. For a variety of consumers, several overseas factories will produce a standardized commodity and modify such items with private packaging for marking. You collaborate with a retailer, for instance, that produces bottles of water and T-shirts. They have ten buyers, each with their own special emblem written on the bottles, that offer water bottles. A customization and packing fee will normally be paid by the factory.

- **Build the brand**

You have put yourself in a role, built a differentiator, and found a supplier. It's time to start developing your organization now. You have to:

- Name and image copyright.

- Website configuration

- Creating a voice on social media

- Shape an LLC

Just like you would like any other legal corporation, recognize your e-commerce firm. You need yourself, your goods, and your income to be covered. You would also like to start naming the lists with online items. A private label means you don't have to fight for a Buy Package. "With a different page for your branded goods, you hold your own "real estate." In line with the brand background, this is a good chance to customize the listing.

3.3 Choosing the Right Products

Choosing the best market and the right goods to spend your efforts on is the greatest challenge you would have to conquer. This decision is vital to the success or failure of your company. The only biggest mistake you're going to make is selecting a product based on your own interests or personal preferences, particularly if you want to create a genuinely profitable company. You have to provide what other customers want, not what you want. Especially if you are not the type of individual to embrace patterns or the type of individual that is always perceived to be "outside of the box." We can't tell you what products to offer, but we can definitely give you some ideas about how to pick the right ones.

How to choose the right product

Your organization would have an uphill struggle to become profitable without a strong product portfolio. It may seem impossible to try to find out what you are trying to market, with potentially millions of items out there. The item you chose will also pose other concerns that you may need to work on. For starters, shipping may become an issue if you are planning to sell freezers. Depending on where the clients work, whether you are selling alcohol, there could be regulatory limits. Market analysis can sound daunting, but knowing the product can cater to the people you are going to attract through your site is important. You should monitor the industry dynamics if you already have an understanding of what you intend to do to see how the commodity is actually performing on the market. If you are really not sure what you'd like to offer, trends can still be helpful to you. Business dynamics will offer you an indication about what items consumers are purchasing or are interested in buying at the moment. Look for items that address a dilemma the target group is experiencing. If your consumer is fed up with the current product range, open a unique and better product to deliver them. Choosing a commodity that is not reasonably available nearby or a national brand that is coveted by a region outside of where it is actually accessible may also be a brilliant choice. Another recommendation is to find a service/ product based on your target audience's interests. This may be in the shape of a new TV show that is beginning or a fashion trend. It often applies to aiming for a difference in chances. If you choose a product that many different competitors are already selling, find something that you can do differently or better than everybody else. This can be an enhanced product characteristic, a market that your competitors totally miss, and maybe something in your marketing plan. If you are trying to market a commodity-based on something that is trending at the moment, ensure that you capitalize early on the pattern. There tend to be more individuals who buy the product at the beginning of a trend. Everybody else is now also moving along to the next thing if you get on the hype train at the end of the trend. Do not wait too long to profit on a trend in the market unless you think that you're going to revive a dead trend. When you make your choices, it is important to take into account product turnover. It would take a lot of time and resources on a product range that varies year after year to guarantee that the product selection is held up-to-date and does not include last year's choices, which could no longer be eligible. A reduced churn product would enable you to engage in a more informative website that will be applicable for a longer time span. Don't be frightened of looking at smaller segments and niches of products. Although there may be fewer prospective customers, there will also be less competition, making it easier to get it to the top of the search engines and much more cost-effective in terms of marketing. The right product is an essential part of your success. Take your time and also don't rush into the first good-looking product.

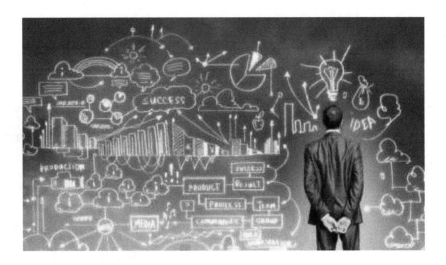

Looking for Product Ideas

There is no need to start a shop without a commodity to sell. Begin with something you already have, or how you can fix your own issues or the challenges of people you meet before you start looking for fresh ideas on what you can sell. There are some ways to consider:

- Which items or niches are you involved in?

- What items are your mates excited about?

- Which challenges do you have with your own life?

- Whose goods can address this?

- What kind of firms are based in your community?

- Can they be translated into a definition online?

- What will organizations in your culture cater to individuals outside of your community?

- In other areas of the planet, what items are trending?

- Is there a need inside your society for them?

- Will you build in your society a market for them?

- Is there a certain sector you like to be interested in if you are confused regarding products? In that industry, what products are popular?

- What items can you find useful from that industry?

- In other online retailers, what items are popular?

- Will this commodity have a niche that you should specialize in in sales?

- What's the social curation website trend?

- Is there an undiscovered thing out there that individuals would want to see open to them?

3.4 Building a Team and Starting your Personal Brand

Choosing the Right Supplier

It can be tricky to pick a supplier for your private label company, but it can help you to realize that there are a variety of suppliers who have been doing this for several years. Some lead the industry in broad industries, and this may be the perfect place to get started in your new company since the goods you offer are already established and have gained appreciation from the market. You can have to trade-off or work in restricted strategies with your profitability, and you need to be careful in reviewing the terms and conditions of each corporation, but each of these can create a backdoor into which you can start a profitable long-term business. Not all private labels are made equally, and to guarantee that your organization is effective, you want to make sure you chose the best provider. There are certain items that your provider wants to provide and some things that are less essential but can have greater convenience. Any of the items you'll be searching for in a provider include:

- Will the retailer have members who are knowledgeable?

- Will the supplier devote them to a particular entity committed to your account?

- Are they invested in being advanced technologically?

- How can you send orders?

- Where are they situated?

- Are they a coordinated business?

- How fast are their orders shipped?

- How are they keeping you throughout the loop on product returns and items out of stock?

- How fast can they send you the tracking details and purchase order?

- What payment types do they approve?

- What kind of fees are they charging?

It may seem impossible to locate the legal firms and distinguish them from the fraudulent as you are searching for a provider. There are some tricks to choosing a decent provider for private labels. One crucial point to bear in mind when you start approaching suppliers is that they could very well be the secret to selecting the best supplier, even though they are not the right match for you. Make sure you always ask every supplier you meet if they can guide you in the appropriate path to reach a supplier that suits your company. As they're in the business, they are sure to have connections that will help you and are typically prepared to share the details. Looking at social media is another way one can improve the chances of having a reliable supplier to deal with. Often, through a family member, neighbor, or acquaintance who might be in the industry or meet someone in the industry, you may find a lead. Any lead is a successful lead, even though it leads to a dead end. In order to strengthen the partnership, you have with your supplier, there are a few items you should do:

- Pay on time to develop trust and then become a reliable client.

- Set simple and realistic targets if an estimation of the goods you plan to sell in a specified period is requested

- Remember that they have other clients and do not belong to you alone.

- Learn what you need when you put orders to speed up the operation.

- If there is a malfunction, do not accuse the representative, but collaborate with them to find a remedy.

- Knowing somebody on a personal level seems to make them more likely to help you out. Build relationships with your delegate

- Train them to identify what you need, such as fresh product photos and product update updates, items out of stock, and products were withdrawn.

Finding the Right Suppliers and Working with Them

The one crucial part you have to do before you continue the quest for the right suppliers is learned how to say the difference between a true wholesale supplier and a department store that works like one. The manufacturer orders their stock from a genuine wholesaler and delivers far higher deals than a supermarket would. To create a good organization, you need to be able to do all of the following:

Have Access to Exclusive Distribution or Pricing

Being able to negotiate unique product agreements or exclusive prices would offer you the advantage without the need to import or produce your own product to sell online. These are not quick items to arrange, and you can notice that you are still out-priced, and at wholesale rates, some private label brands would still offer the same or equivalent. You need to find a way to persuade the buyers that the commodity you sell is of greater quality than the competitor, whether you can have exclusive distribution, particularly if the competition sells a knock-off product at a cheaper price. This is where the website's "about us" page becomes much more useful as it is a good way to share the fact that you are unique to the product.

Sell at the Lowest Possible Price

You will rob clients from such a chunk of your niche market if you are willing to sell your goods at the lowest costs. The main thing is that since you actually won't be able to appreciate the gain, you are destined to struggle. The low price is not often the primary motivating factor behind the choice of a consumer to shop. Customers seem to choose to invest their cash on the best benefit and lowest cost of a commodity. This suggests that you ought to persuade them that the best decision is to invest a little extra cash in your goods, so there is less downside and more appeal to them.

Add Your Value Outside of the Price

Think in terms of having data that complement the items selected. A real capitalist can fix challenges, and at the same time offering goods at high rates. In your unique niche, make sure you give suggestions and insightful recommendations. Your customer support is one extremely efficient way to bring value to the goods outside of the costs. If you are willing to address all the queries of your consumer without needing to call you and are willing to respond to any emails easily, your store website will stick out from the rest.

Conclusion

A private label is where a person or corporation paying another business to make a commodity without its name, emblem, etc. The person or business then applies to the packaging their name and design. So, what sorts of items should be labeled privately? From skincare and dietary treatments and infant essentials, pet products, and kitchen utensils, pretty much all under the sun. The benefit of private labeling is that nothing innovative needs to be produced or developed by you. You can add your mark on it as long as it's not a proprietary commodity and label it yours. Dropshipping is a convenient method for private-label goods to be distributed. You will find a dropshipping provider if you are an online shop owner who can offer items directly to you and incorporate your branding. Dropshipping is an e-commerce market concept in which no inventory is held by the manufacturer. The retailer, instead, manages the packaging, packing, and delivery of goods to the end customer. In other terms, for dropshipping, the goods are delivered directly to consumers, and they are never used by stores. There is a legitimate explanation for retailers that are involved in flooding their stores with items with their brand name. Third-party suppliers operate at the behest of the supplier, providing full influence over the ingredients and consistency of the goods. In reaction to growing consumer demand for a new feature, smaller stores have the opportunity to move rapidly to bring a private label product into development, whereas larger firms might not be involved in a product or niche category. You should concentrate on creating a reputation before you start your company, one that is recognizable and valued, and a private label benefits both you and the retailer or supplier you select.

The first move with your organization is importing the goods you choose to market, products that do not crack easily, which have satisfaction for the customer. The second and most significant move is to make your brand known to current and future clients. The more customers remember your brand, the higher it is possible that your revenue rate will be. Through selecting producers or suppliers who will submit your goods via Private Label, you will help this along. This operates by encouraging the consumer to position their orders with you, then deliver them to the retailer and directly dispatching the product. To sum up, while you are looking to get your brand out and develop a company without leeching on mainstream online marketplace/websites' popularity, a private label makes perfect sense. It will require a bit extra time to select a supplier since you must do the job yourself and guarantee that you work for the right supplier. Still, you will also gain a better profit when you take responsibility for the customer support and are willing to negotiate.

Dropshipping Business Model on a Budget

The Risk-Low E-Com Guide to Create Your Online Store and Generate Profits with less than 47$

By

NESPY ONLINE MARKETING

Table of contents

Introduction

With very little startup expenses, dropshipping is an innovative business model.

A dropshipping business is where an owner finds a collection of distributors to deliver and offer goods for their website. However, as in an e-commerce business, instead of owning the merchandise, a third party does much of the distribution and logistics for them. That third party is usually a wholesaler, who on behalf of the business "dropships" the consumer's goods.

When you start a retail shop, there are several factors to consider, but among the most significant aspects, you have to decide whether you'd like to store inventory or have a wholesale distributor. You must purchase goods in bulk, stock, unpack and send them to customers of your products if you want to store inventory. You may, therefore, contract the phase of storing, packaging and exporting to a drop-ship supplier by picking a wholesale distributor. As direct fulfillment, a drop-ship supplier is often described, but both definitions may be used to define the same service.

The wholesaler, who usually manufactures the product, delivers the product at the most basic, any time anyone buys a product, and you get a part of the sale for the product marketing.

Unless the client puts an order for it, you don't pay for the thing.

Dropshipping is an internet-based business model that draws novices and experts alike to choose a niche, create a brand, market and earn money, with probably the minimum entry barriers.

Chapter 1. What is Dropshipping?

Dropshipping is a retail model of e-commerce that enables retailers to offer goods without maintaining any physical inventory. The company sells the product to the buyer through dropshipping and sends the purchase order to a third-party seller, who then delivers the order directly on behalf of the retailer to the customer. Dropshipping sellers may not need to spend in any commodity stock, inventory or storage room and do not manage the phase of fulfillment.

Dropshipping is a form of retail fulfillment, where the goods are ordered from a third-party retailer instead of a store stocks products. The goods are then delivered directly to the customer. This way, the vendor doesn't have to personally manage the product. A familiar sound? Maybe not, but dropshipping is a fulfillment model utilized by 35 percent of online stores.

This is mostly a hands-off process for the store. The retailer doesn't have to buy stock or, in any manner, meet the orders. The third-party retailer, instead, takes control of the product itself.

For startups, dropshipping is great since it does not take as much as the conventional sales model. You don't have to prepare, pay overhead, & stock merchandise in a brick-and-mortar store. Instead, you start an online shop to purchase bulk goods and warehouse space from vendors that already have products.

In dropshipping, the merchant is solely responsible for attracting clients and handling orders, ensuring you'll be a middleman effectively. Despite this, through pricing up the goods you offer, you can gain the lion's share of the profits. It's an easy model of business, so one that can be really successful.

Millions of entrepreneurs switch to dropshipping to get started because it takes less hassle and capital. That's why you're probably interested. And the best of all news? Through dropshipping, you can create a company right from your laptop that is profitable in the long term.

There are several pitfalls and benefits, of course, and it is essential that we check at them before you launch your own e-commerce dropshipping firm. However, once you realize the positives and negatives of dropshipping, it'll be a breeze to learn how to do so effectively.

1.1 Benefits of dropshipping

For aspiring entrepreneurs, dropshipping is a smart business move to start with, which is accessible. You can easily evaluate multiple business concepts with a small downside with dropshipping, which helps you to think a lot about how to pick and sell in-demand goods. Here are a couple more explanations why dropshipping is a popular business.

1. Little capital is required

Perhaps the greatest benefit to dropshipping is that an e-commerce website can be opened without needing to spend thousands of dollars in stock upfront. Typically, retailers have had to bundle up large quantities of inventory with capital investments.

For the dropshipping model, unless you have already made the transaction and have been charged by the consumer, you may not have to buy a product. It is possible to start sourcing goods without substantial up-front inventory investments and launch a profitable dropshipping company with very little capital. And since you are not committed to sales, as in a typical retail sector, there is less chance of launching a dropshipping shop through any inventory bought up front.

2. Easy to get started

It's also simpler to operate an e-commerce company because you don't have to interact with physical products. You don't have to take stress with dropshipping about:

- Paying for a warehouse or managing it
- Tracking inventory for any accounting reasons
- Packing & shipping your orders
- Continually ordering products & managing stock level
- Inbound shipments and handling returns

3. Low overhead

Your overhead expenses are very minimal, and you don't have to deal with buying inventory or maintaining a warehouse. In reality, several popular dropshipping stores are managed as home-based enterprises, needing nothing more to run than a laptop & a few operational expenses. These costs are likely to rise as you expand but are still low relative to standard brick-and-mortar stores.

4. Flexible location

From almost anywhere via an internet connection, a dropshipping company can be managed. You can operate and manage the business as long as you can effectively connect with vendors and consumers.

5. Wide selection of goods to sell

Because you don't really have to pre-purchase any items you market, you can offer your potential clients a variety of trending products. If an item is stored by vendors, you will mark it for sale at no added cost at your online store.

6. Easier for testing

Dropshipping is a valuable form of fulfillment for both the opening of a new store and also for company owners seeking to measure consumers' demand for additional types of items, such as shoes or whole new product ranges. Again, the primary advantage of dropshipping is the opportunity to list and likely sell goods before committing to purchasing a significant quantity of stock.

7. Easier to scale

For a traditional retail firm, you would typically need to perform three times as much work if you get three times the amount of orders.

By using dropshipping vendors, suppliers would be liable for more of the work to handle extra orders, helping you to improve with fewer growth pains & little incremental work.

Sales growth can often bring extra work, especially customer service, however companies which use dropshipping scale especially well comparison to standard e-commerce businesses.

8. Dropshipping starts easily.

In order to get started, you need not be a business guru. You don't really require some past company knowledge, honestly. You will get started easily and learn the rest while you move along if you spend some time to learn its basics.

It is too easy to drop shipping, and it takes so little from you. To help you out, you don't need a warehouse to store goods or a staff. You don't need to think about packaging or storage either. You do not even have to devote a certain period of time in your shop every day. Surprisingly, it's hands-off, especially once you get underway.

All of this means that today you can begin your company. Within a matter of hours, you will begin getting it up and running.

You're going to need some practical skills and the right equipment and tools. You will be equipped with the skills you have to jumpstart your own dropshipping company by the time you've done it.

9. Dropshipping grow easily.

Your business model doesn't even have to alter that much at all when you scale up. As you expand, you'll have to bring more effort into sales and marketing, but your daily life will remain almost the same.

One of the advantages of dropshipping is that when you scale, the costs do not spike. It's convenient to keep rising at a fairly high pace because of this. If you choose to build a little team at any stage, you can manage about anything by yourself, too.

10. Dropshipping doesn't need a big capital.

Since you need very little to start a dropshipping business, you can get underway with minimal funds. Right from your desktop, you can create a whole corporation, and you do not need to make any heavy investment. Your costs would be reasonably low even as your company grows, particularly compared to normal business expenses.

11. Dropshipping is flexible.

This is one of the greatest advantages. You get to be a boss of your own and set your own regulations. It's one of the most versatile occupations anyone can try.

With just a laptop, you can operate from anywhere, and you can operate at the hours that are most comfortable for you. For founders that want a company that fits for them, this is perfect. To get stuff done, you won't have to lean over backward. You choose your own pace instead.

Dropshipping is indeed flexible in that it allows you plenty of space to create choices that fit for you. Whenever you choose, you can quickly list new items, and you can change your plans on the move. You should automate it to work when you're gone, whether you're going on holiday. You get the concept prospects are limitless.

12. Dropshipping manages easily.

Because it doesn't need you to make several commitments, with no hassle, you can manage everything. When you have found and set up suppliers, you are often exclusively liable for your e-commerce store.

Chapter 2. How Dropshipping Works

Dropshipping functions by third-party suppliers, which deliver goods for each order on a just-in-time basis. When a sales order is received by the retailer, they transfer the requirements to the supplier—who manufactures the product.

While dropshipping is used by many e-commerce retailers as the base of their business processes, dropshipping can be used successfully to complement traditional retail inventory-stocking models. Because dropshipping does not create any unused surplus inventory, it may be used for analysis purposes before committing to sale on a marketplace, such as testing the waters.

Dropshipping works because, with the aid of a third party such as a wholesaler or an e-commerce shop, a dropshipper fulfills orders to deliver the goods for an even cheaper price. The majority of dropshippers offer goods directly from Chinese suppliers because the prices of most products in China are very poor. If the wholesaler's price is 5 dollars for a product. A dropshipper sells it for $8 and retains $3 for himself. The bulk of dropshippers target nations with higher purchasing power.

2.1 Awareness about the Supply Chain

You'll see the word "supply chain" a lot in here. It seems like a fancy lingo for the business, but it actually applies to how a product transfers from seller to consumer. We'll use this to explain the method of dropshipping.

2.2 The Supply Chain Process

You, the merchant, are only one puzzle piece. An effective dropshipping mechanism depends on several parties all acting in sync together. The supply chain is just that: producer, supplier, and retailer coordination.

You should split down the supply chain into three simple steps:

• The producer manufactures the goods and supplies them to wholesalers & retailers.

Let's say maker A is manufacturing bottles of water. They are marketed in bulk to manufacturers and wholesalers after the bottles come off the assembly line, who switch around & resell the bottles to dealers.

• Suppliers and wholesalers market the products to dealers.

For a particular type of product, a retailer like yourself is searching for a supplier. An arrangement to operate together is then reached between the retailer and the supplier.

A little point here: Although you may order directly from product producers, purchasing from retailers is always much cheaper instead. There are minimum purchasing criteria for most suppliers that can be very high, and you will still have to purchase stock & ship the goods.

So, purchasing directly from the producer might seem quicker, but you would profit more from buying from distributors (dealing with the little profit).

Suppliers are often convenient since all of them are skilled in a specific niche, so the type of items you need can be quickly identified. This also implies that you'll get started to sell super quick.

- Retailers sell goods to buyers.

Suppliers & wholesalers should not market to the public directly; that's the task of the retailer. The last move between the product & the consumer is the supplier.

Online stores from which customers buy goods are provided by retailers. The merchant marks it up again to reach at the final price after the wholesaler rates up the items. By "markup," we apply to fixing a premium that covers the product's cost price and gives you a benefit.

It's that! From start to end, it is the whole supply chain. In business, it's a simple but crucial concept.

You may have noted that no other group has been alluded to as a dropshipper. That is because there is no particular function for "dropshipper." Dropshipping is actually the activity of somebody else delivering goods. Technically, producers, retailers, and merchants will all be dropshippers.

Later on, we'll discuss how to start a retail dropshipping company in this guide. In other terms, you can learn how to become a trader who buys commodities from wholesalers to market to the public. This may indicate that through an online storefront, you sell through eBay or even your own website.

Remember what it's like for the consumer now that you realize what the supply chain is like.

2.3 What is Fulfillment?

Order fulfillment that's all the steps a corporation requires in having a fresh order and bringing the order into the hands of the customer. The procedure includes storing, picking & packaging the products, distributing them and sending the consumer an automatic email to let them know that the product is in transit.

2.4 The Steps to make Order Fulfillment

There are some steps involved in order fulfillment, which are as under:-

1. Receiving inventory.

Essentially, there are two approaches for an eCommerce company to manage inventory. It can decide to receive & stock the in-house inventory, or it can employ an outsourcer for eCommerce order fulfillment to take control of the inventory and other associated activities. The organization would be liable for taking stock, inspecting the product, marking, and maintaining the inventory method if it opts for the first alternative. If the business wishes to outsource or dropships, the order fulfillment agent or supplier can perform certain duties.

2. Storing inventory.

If you plan to stock the inventory yourself, after the receiving portion is finished, there'll be another list of assignments waiting for you. Shelving the inventory and holding a careful watch on what goods come in and what goods are going out would be the key activities on the list so that you can deliver the orders without any complications.

3. Processing the order.

Businesses who outsource order fulfillment do not have to get through the nitty-gritty of order delivery since they actually move on to their partner's order request and let them manage the rest. This is the phase where the order is taken off the shelves, shipped to a packaging station, examined for any damage, packed and transferred to the shipping station for businesses who handle their own product.

4. Shipping the order.

The best delivery strategy is calculated based on the scale, weight and precise specifications of the order. A third-party contractor is typically contracted to complete this phase.

Returns Handling. For online shoppers, the opportunity to refund unwanted goods quickly is a big factor in the purchase phase. You ought to design a crystal straightforward return policy that is readily available to all the customers and workers to ensure the receipt, repair and redemption of the returned goods are as successful as practicable. It will help you prevent needless confusion and errors by making this step automated.

Chapter 3. Why dropshipping is one of the best way to make money in 2021.

According to Forrester (analyst) Reports, the magnitude of online retail revenues would be $370 billion by the end of 2017. In comparison, 23 percent, which amounts to $85.1 billion, would come from dropshipping firms. To many businesses, like startups, this sheer scale alone is attractive.

An online retailer following this concept appears similar to its traditional e-commerce competitors by appearance. Dropshipping may be a well-kept mystery in the e-commerce world as consumers just think about the goods, price and credibility of the shop rather than how the goods are sourced and who delivers the shipments.

In summary,' dropshipping' is a business strategy in which the supplier does not directly hold the inventory or process the orders in his or her control. Both orders are delivered directly from a wholesaler and delivered. This encourages the supplier to concentrate on the business's selling aspect.

Many major e-commerce names, such as Zappos, began with dropshipping. For those that seek motivation, billion-dollar dropshipping internet store Wayfair or the milliondollarBlinds.com are top examples today.

Five explanations of how the dropshipping business strategy appeals to both startups and experienced entrepreneurs are offered below. These issues in traditional e-commerce have been nagging challenges, which can be addressed with the dropshipping model immediately.

3.1 Dropshipping Is The E-Commerce Future

It seem that dropshipping will be the future of e-commerce. Here are some main reasons which explain this concept.

Sourcing of Product:

Conventional e-commerce stores must directly import supplies from wholesalers, frequently based in various countries. They often need goods to be bought in bulk and are then shipped prior to being promoted and distributed to the local warehouse. A lot of time, money & resources are required for the whole phase. The presence of expensive intermediaries, such as banks, freight shipments and export-import brokers, also involves it.

The dropshipping model, however, enables manufacturers to market goods for large quantities of each product without needing to think about sourcing. The entire method is substantially simplified with just a turn-key e-commerce storefront such as Shopify and a dropshipping software like Oberlo. The retailer may choose to notify the distributors via e-mail to tell them that their supplies are now being shipped to the store. The most of the procedure can be quickly handled from the dashboard, such as uploading product images, updating pricing and order monitoring.

Storage

A traditional e-commerce store, particularly as it carries multiple or large products, requires large storage spaces. It might be imaginable to store ten to 100 items, but storing 1,000 or 1,000,000 items will cost a real fortune that is not within the reach of a start-up. This high warehouse rent issue is addressed by the dropshipping model since the goods remain with the distributor or wholesale retailer until they are bought.

Order fulfillment

Many pioneers of e-commerce do not foresee investing most of their time picking, packaging and delivering orders. They should, of course, outsource the order fulfillment for ease to a boutique e-commerce fulfillment, such as ShipMonk. The dropshipping model, however, facilitates hands-free shipment, since the whole packaging and shipping process is in the possession of the wholesaler or distributor.

Cataloging & photography

A conventional e-commerce shop owner has to take professional-quality images of items that may be very pricey, like a decent digital camera, a light panel, lighting and some more. For a dropshipping control software, this issue is fixed, as the "product importing" function allows for instant picture import.

Scalability

Wayfair.com is a major online dropshipping store that holds 10,000 vendors of more than eight million items. Yes, $8 million. By this business model, such huge scalability is made possible.

Because the retailer just has to work on the publicity and customer care aspect, they don't have to think about the warehouse's rent and other operating expenses skyrocketing.

In conclusion, the dropshipping paradigm offers the ability for tiny startups with minimal capital to contend with large and medium online stores comfortably, rendering the field of e-commerce an equal environment for everyone. That being said, plan in the future to see more e-commerce shops adopting this model.

Chapter 4. Niche And Product Selection

You want a business to start, but the thing that holds you down is the market niche that you feel you need to pick. And, honestly, it can be tricky: you might mention all your interests & passions and yet feel like you haven't hit the singular thing that you were expected to do.

Yet, it can trigger paralysis to place some sort of burden on yourself to choose the very right niche.

Certainly, in choosing a suitable niche business, you like to do your careful research, but it's easier to get up and run than to wait around. You will try ideas that way, enter the market earlier, and benefit from the victories and losses. That way, too, you can still take what you have gained from previous attempts, so step on with fresh concepts if the first company does not take off.

4.1 Steps how to search your right niche

Using the following five methods to find your niche, whether you're unable to determine or you need more information to work with.

1. Identify your interests & passions.

This could be something that you have achieved before. But, if you haven't, quickly make a compilation of 10 topical passions and areas of passion.

Business isn't easy, and it can challenge you at any stage. If you work in an area you don't care for, the likelihood of leaving will increase significantly — especially like a first sole proprietor.

This doesn't mean that a better match has to be found. You can stay with it if you are excited about any part of running the business. If you don't care about the issue, you might not be able to easily find the drive to persevere within.

2. Identify problems that you can solve.

You're able to get to narrow down your choices with your list of ten topics in hand. You first need to identify challenges that your target clients are facing to build a viable enterprise, then decide if you can potentially fix them. Here are a few items you should do to find issues in different niches.

3. Research your competition.

There is not always a bad thing in the presence of competition. It can actually show you that you've discovered a market that's lucrative. Although you do have to do an in-depth analysis of competing pages.

Build a fresh spreadsheet and start tracking all the competing websites that you can find.

And find out whether there's already an opening in the crowd to stick out. Are you still willing to rate the keywords? Is there really a way to distinguish and build a unique offer for yourself? Here are some indications that you will enter a niche and flourish, even though it is already covered by other sites:

- Content of poor quality. In a niche where several company owners are not delivering high-quality, informative content that suits the viewer, it's easy to outrank the competitors.
- Lack of transparency. By establishing an authentic and accessible identity in a niche where most platforms are faceless and unnecessarily corporate, many internet marketers have disrupted whole industries.
- The lack of paid competitiveness. If you have noticed a keyword with a relatively high search rate but little competition with paying ads, there is undoubtedly a potential for you to upset the business.

4. Determine the profitability of the niche.

You need to have a fairly decent understanding now about what niche you're about to get into. You might not have limited your selection down to a particular region of the topic, but you've certainly noticed a few suggestions that you feel pretty good about. It's important to have an idea at this stage about how much money you have the opportunity to make in your niche. A fine way to go to continue your search is ClickBank.

So, browse the category's best brands. That is not a positive indication if you can't locate any offers. It could mean that the niche could not be monetized by someone.

You're in luck if the quest throws up a good amount of products — just not an excessive amount of products. Take notice of pricing points such that your own goods can be marketed in a fair way.

Bear in mind, though, that you may not have to launch your organization with your own product offering. You should collaborate in your niche with product makers, marketers and site owners to start earning commissions when working on your innovative solution.

5. Test your idea.

You are now prepared with all the knowledge you need to pick a niche, and checking your proposal is the only thing needed to do. Setting up a landing page for pre-sales of a product you're producing is one easy way to do this. Through paying ads, you will then push traffic to this page.

That doesn't actually mean that you are not in a viable niche, even though you don't get pre-sales. Your message may not be quite correct, or you haven't found the right deal yet. You will maximize conversions by using A/B split testing to figure out whether there is something preventing the target group from taking action or not.

You will sell to two fundamental markets: customer and corporation. Such divisions are reasonably clear. "For example, if you sell women's clothes from a department shop, shoppers are your target market; if you sell office supplies, companies are your target market (this is referred to as "B2B" sales). In certain instances, for example, you could be selling to both corporations and people if you operate a printing company.

No company, especially a small one, can be everything to all individuals. The more you can describe your target group broadly, the stronger. For even the larger corporations, this method is recognized as building a market and is crucial to growth. Walmart and Tiffany are also stores, but they have somewhat different niches: Walmart caters to bargain-minded customers, while Tiffany tends to luxury jewelry buyers.

"Some entrepreneurs make the error of slipping into the "all over the map" pit instead of building a niche, believing they can do many things and be successful at all of them. Falkenstein warns that these individuals soon learn a difficult lesson: "Smaller is larger in market, and smaller is not across the map; it is extremely focused."

4.2 Creating a good niche

Keep in mind these important to create a good niche:

1. Make a wish list.

Who do you like to do business with? Be as descriptive as you are capable of. Identify the regional spectrum and the kinds of firms or clients that you want your organization to target. You can't make contact if you do not really know whom you are going to do business with. Falkenstein cautions, "You must recognize that you can't do business with everyone." Otherwise, you risk leaving yourself exhausted and confusing your buyers.

The trend is toward small niches these days. It's not precise enough to target teens; targeting adult, African American teenagers with the family incomes of $40,000 or more is. It is too large to target corporations that market apps; it is a better aim to target Northern California-based firms that offer internet software distribution and training that have sales of $15 million or more.

2. Focus.

Clarify what you intend to sell, knowing that a) to all customers, you can't be all items and b) smaller is better. Your specialty isn't the same as that of sector you are employed in. A retail apparel corporation, for example, is not a niche but a sector. Maternity clothes for corporate mothers" may be a more specific niche."

Using these strategies to assist you in starting this focus process:

- Create a compilation of the greatest activities you do and the talents that are inherent in many of them.
- List your accomplishments.
- Identify the important things of life that you've experienced.
- Look for trends that reflect your personality or approach to addressing issues.

Your niche should emerge from your desires and expertise in a normal way. For instance, if you spent 10 years of working in such a consulting firm and also ten years working for such a small, family-owned company, you may actually have to start a consulting company that specializes in limited, family-owned businesses.

3. Describe the customer's worldview.

A good corporation utilizes what Falkenstein called the Platinum Rule: "Do to the others as they're doing to themselves." You will define their desires or desires as you look at the situation from the viewpoint of your prospective clients. Talking to new clients and recognizing their biggest issues is the perfect approach to achieve this.

4. Synthesize.

Your niche can begin to take shape at this point when the opinions and the desires of the consumer and desire to coalesce to create something different. There are five attributes of a Strong Niche:

- In other terms, it relates to your long-term view and carries you where you like to go.
- Somebody else needs it, consumers in particular.
- It is closely arranged.
- It's one-of-a-kind, "the only city game."
- It evolves, enabling you to build multiple profit centers and yet maintain the core market, thus guaranteeing long-term success.

5. Evaluate.

It is now time to test the product or service proposed against the five requirements in Phase 4. Perhaps you'll notice that more business travel than that you're ready for is needed for niche you had in mind. That indicates that one of the above conditions is not met-it will not carry you where you like to go. Scrap it, and pass on to the next proposal.

6. Test.

Test-market it until you have a balance between the niche and the product. "Give individuals an opportunity to purchase your product or service, not just theoretically, but actually put it out there." By giving samples, such as a complimentary mini-seminar or a preview copy of the newsletter, this can be accomplished. "If you spend enormous sums of cash on the initial trial run, you're possibly doing it wrong," she says. The research shouldn't cost you a bunch of money:

7. Go for it!

It is time for your idea to be implemented. This is the most challenging step for many entrepreneurs. But worry not: if you have done your research, it would be a measured risk to reach the business, not simply a chance.

Chapter 5. How to start dropshipping business in 2021

It's not easy to learn the way to start a dropshipping company, as with any type of business. Nevertheless, it's a perfect first move in the world of business. Without keeping any inventory, you may sell to customers. You do not have to pay upfront for goods. And if you are passionate about your new venture, in the long term, you will create a sustainable source of revenue.

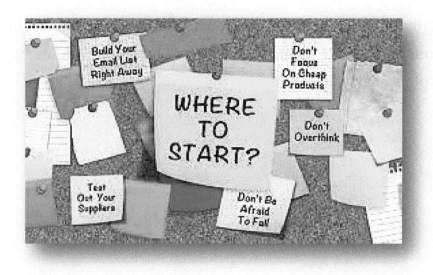

In this complete dropshipping guide, suggest taking the following market and financial moves if you are considering dropshipping.

Others are mandatory from the start, and others are only a smart idea, so it will save you time and stress down the line by coping with them up front.

Dropshipping is a method of order fulfillment that helps shop owners to deliver without stocking any stock directly to buyers. If a consumer orders a commodity from a dropshipping shop, it is delivered directly to them by a third-party retailer. The client pays the selling price that you set, you pay the market price of the vendors, and the rest is benefit. You never need to maintain goods or spend in inventory.

You are responsible for designing a website and your own label, as well as selecting and promoting the items you choose to offer in the dropshipping business strategy. Your corporation is therefore liable for the expense of shipping and for setting rates that result in a reasonable profit margin.

Steps For Starting A Dropshipping Profitable Business

Learn to find high-margin products, introduce them to your business, and easily begin selling them.

1. Commit yourself for starting a dropshipping business

Dropshipping, as in any other business, needs considerable effort and a long-term focus. You're going to be deeply surprised if you're looking for a six-figure benefit from 6 weeks of part-time employment. You would be far less likely to get frustrated and leave by entering the organization with reasonable assumptions regarding the commitment needed and the prospects for benefit.

You'll need to spend heavily when beginning a dropshipping venture, utilizing one of the two following currencies: time or funds.

Investing time in dropshipping business

Our recommended strategy, particularly for the first dropshipping developers, is bootstrapping & investing sweat equity to develop your company. For various factors, we prefer this method over spending a huge amount of money:

- You will understand how the organization works inside out, which, as the enterprise expands and scales, will be crucial for handling others.
- You would know your clients and business personally, helping you to make smarter choices.
- You would be less inclined to waste huge amounts on vanity ventures that are not vital to success.
- You will build some new talents that will enable you a stronger entrepreneur.

Realistically, most persons are not ready to leave their work in order to ramp up their own online shop for six months. It might be a little more complicated, but even though you're already doing a 9-to-5 job, it's surely feasible to get underway with dropshipping, assuming you set reasonable standards for your customers about customer support and delivery times. When you continue to expand, as much as working capital and profitability allow, you will move into working long hours on your company.

Both companies and entrepreneurs are specific, but it is feasible to produce a monthly income stream of $1,000-$2,000 within 12 months of working around 10 to 15 hours per week to develop the firm.

Excited regarding starting a new business but not knowing where to begin? This informative guide will show you how to identify great products with strong sales potential that are newly trendy.

If you have the choice of working long hours on your company, that's the best option to increase your profit prospects and the possibility of good dropshipping. It is particularly beneficial in the early days to concentrate all the energies on publicity when creating traction is essential. It would normally take approximately 12 months of full-time jobs based on our knowledge, with a heavy focus on publicity for a dropshipping firm to replace an annual full-time salary of $50,000.

For a very small payout, it might sound like a lot of work, but bear these two points in mind:

When the dropshipping company is up and going, it would actually require considerably less time than from a 40-hour-per-week work to maintain it. In terms of the reliability and scalability that the dropshipping paradigm offers, much of your expenditure pays off.

You establish more than just a revenue stream when you develop a company. You also build an asset that you will market in the future. Be sure that when looking at the true return, you remember the equity valuation you are accruing, and also the cash flow produced.

Investing money in dropshipping business

By spending a lot of capital, it is feasible to develop and grow a dropshipping company, but we suggest against it. We attempted all methods to growing an enterprise (bootstrapping it ourselves vs. outsourcing the procedure), and while we were in the trenches doing much of the work, we had the most progress.

In the early stages, it is vital to have someone who is profoundly involved in the company's future to construct it from the ground up. You would be at the hands of pricey engineers, developers, and advertisers who will easily eat away whatever money you produce without knowing how your organization operates at any stage. You don't have to do everything it yourself, but at the start of your company, we highly advocate becoming the primary motivating power.

To have your company started and operating, you would, though, require a modest cash reserve in the $1,000 range. For limited administrative costs (like web hosting and dropshipping providers), you may need this and to pay some incorporation fees, which we will cover below.

2. Dropshipping business idea to chose

The second phase in studying how to launch a dropshipping company is to do the market research required. You want to find a niche you are interested in and make choices based on how effective it can be, almost like though you were starting a grocery shop and checking at the numerous sites, rivals, and developments. But the fact is, it's tricky to come up with product concepts to offer.

Niche goods also have a more passionate client base, which, through increasing awareness about the items, will make marketing to unique audiences simpler. A good entry point to begin dropshipping without cash could be health, clothes, makeup goods, appliances, phone accessories, or yoga-related pieces.

Any instances of dropshipping stores in a niche may be:

- Dog bow and ties for dog lovers
- Exercise equipment for fitness
- iPhone cases and cables for iPhone owners
- Camping gear for campers

To try the dropshipping business ideas, you may also use the appropriate techniques:

Google Trends could really help you identify whether, as well as the seasons in which they tend to trend, a product is trending up or down. Notice the search volume is not indicated by Google Patterns. But if you're using it, be sure to use a keyword tool such as Keywords Everywhere to cross-check your data to determine the popularity of the product in search.

3. Do competitor research

You want to check about your competitors so that you know what you're trying to sell in your shop and appreciate the way they operate. Your competitors may have great success hints which can help you develop a better marketing strategy for your dropshipping firm.

Limit your study to only five other dropshipping firms, like one or two major players such as Walmart or Ebay, if your business has a number of competitors (that is a positive thing in dropshipping). It will help you remain centered and prepare your next phase.

4. Choose a dropshipping supplier

Choosing a supplier for dropshipping is a crucial move towards creating a profitable dropshipping business. A dropshipping company does not have any goods to ship to consumers without vendors and would thus cease to operate.

At this stage, you analyzed what goods you want to offer and realize that they can be profitable, and you want to know where to find a provider of dropshipping that provides you with the high-quality service that you need to grow. By linking Oberlo to the online store, eCommerce platforms such as Shopify provide a plug-and-play style alternative to find possible suppliers.

5. Build your ecommerce store

An eCommerce platform such as Shopify is the next what you need to launch a dropshipping business. This is the home where you deliver traffic, offer goods, and payments are processed.

These type of platforms makes the e-commerce website simple to create and launch. It is a complete commerce service that connects you to sell and receive payments in several ways, like online, sell in different currencies, and conveniently manage products.

To use e-commerce websites, you don't need to become a programmer or developer either. They have resources to assist with anything from domain name ideas to logo design, and with the store creator and Payment processing themes, you are quickly able to modify the feel and look of your store.

6. Market your dropshipping store

It's time to talk about promoting your new shop, now that you know to start a dropshipping firm. You may want to bring more work into your marketing and promotional activities while developing the dropshipping business strategy to stick out in your market.

You will invest time working on selling and supporting the company in the following ways, with too many stuff about dropshipping being processed:

- Paid ads (Facebook & Google).

For a Facebook ad, the average cost is about 0.97 cents per click, that's not too bad if you're new to social media advertising. Facebook ads are extensible, goods can perform ok on them, and they click into the desire of people to purchase momentum. You can run Google Shopping Ads and target lengthy keywords that are more likely to be purchased by shoppers. Typically, with Google ads, there is more price competition, but it might be worthy of your time to check it out.

- Influencer marketing.

You may have a low funds for marketing your business as a new dropshipper. Influencer marketing is also an affordable way to target audience because individuals are more likely than traditional advertising to trust influencers. When you go this route, start negotiating an affiliate fee versus a flat rate with the influencer. It's a win-win situation, as every sale they're going to make money off, and the cost is going to be less for you.

- Mobile marketing.

Smartphone marketing is a broad term referring to a company that connects with clients on their mobile phones. You can start with a VIP text club, for example, and encourage website users to sign up for the exclusive promotions & deals. Or provide client support through Messenger in a live chat session with shoppers. You can create automated qualified leads, customer loyalty, and cart abandonment campaigns with a mobile marketing tool such as ManyChat to drive sales and profits for your dropshipping business.

Stay updated on what channels are operating and which are not, as with any profitable online business, especially if you invest money in them like paid ads. You can always adjust your marketing plan to lower costs as well as maximize revenue as you keep growing and improve your business.

7. Analyze your offering

You should start looking at the consequences of your diligent work after you've been promoting and operating your dropshipping company for some time. Any analytics will help you address some critical online shop queries, like:

- Sales

What are my channels with the highest performance? Where am I expected to put more ad dollars? What else are my favorite items for sale? What are my greatest clients?

- Behavior of shoppers

Do citizens buy more on their laptops or cell phones? For each unit, what's the conversion rate?

- Margins of profit

Why are the most profitable pieces and variant SKUs? What do my month-over-month revenue and gross income look like?

To track web traffic over time and optimize your search engine optimization activities, you can even use resources like Google Analytics & Search Console. Plus, you review the results monthly to guarantee that your overall plan succeeds with your business, whether you are utilizing third-party software for your social network or messenger marketing.

You want to build a data-informed analytics framework while building a dropshipping e-commerce store. Remain compatible with what you evaluate over time and calculate the consistency of your store against simple KPIs. This will encourage you to make better choices for your store, so move your small business over time to the next level.

Chapter 6. How To identify Best Suppliers For Your New Dropshipping Business

Dropshipping is a model for eCommerce that is increasingly attractive. That is because launching a dropshipping company is simpler (not to say less expensive) than managing inventory for a traditional digital storefront.

The whole model of drop shipment is focused on the retailer doing its job well and delivering orders timely and effectively. It goes without saying, therefore, that identifying the appropriate supplier is one, if not the most important, and a step towards creating a successful brand. If an order is messed up by your supplier/seller, you and your organization are liable, so the trick is to find someone who adheres to the schedule and is open to discuss any problems

The advantages and disadvantages of dropshipping are well known, but it has become far less obvious that the most significant part of beginning a dropshipping business is choosing the right vendors for your WooCommerce shop. Until now.

6.1 The Importance of Selecting The Right Suppliers

A special model for eCommerce is Dropshipping. To retain their own inventories, conventional online retailers compensate. Those expenses are all but offset by dropshipping, so dropshipping would not need substantial start-up investment.

In the other side, dropshipping suggests that you place the destiny of your eCommerce store in the possession of others.

With the dropshipping system, retailers focus on wholesalers, manufacturers, and dealers who meet the orders of the retailers.

The dropshipping puzzle has several parts, and for the greater image, each component is critical. Among those pieces, one of the most significant is dropshipping suppliers. In reality, the finest dropshippers know that a dropshipping eCommerce store can make or break the efficiency and overall reliability of dropshipping suppliers.

6.2 Finding Your Dropshipping Suppliers

It needs you to partner with manufacturers, wholesalers, & distributors to start a dropshipping business. You want to identify vendors who improve the dropshipping business rather than compromise it.

Research Your Products

You have to figure out what types of things you can sell before you can start finding and working with vendors.

You want to address queries in specific, such as:

- Where does the item come from?
- How long would manufacturing take?
- How is it done?

Are there factors of height or weight which might make fulfillment more complicated or more costly?

The purpose is not expertise; however, you want to get to know the goods so that you can help determine which ones are suitable for dropshipping.

Understand the supply chain and recognize the considerations

You need to get familiar with dropship supply chain after nailing down your goods. In other terms, you should to know how it works for dropshipping.

For dropshipping, the items never really go into the hands of the dealer. Instead, an order is issued by the retailer, and a supplier who manages packing and delivery initiates fulfillment. In this way, the dealer is like the director of a dropshipping company.

You can't sell goods if you don't have reputable vendors, which suggests that you don't have a dropshipping business.

You need to get familiar with dropship supply chain since nailing down your products. In other terms, you need to understand how it functions for dropshipping.

For dropshipping, the items never really go into the hands of the dealer. Instead, an order is issued by the retailer and a supplier who manages packing and delivery initiates fulfilment. In this manner, the retailer is just like the director of a dropshipping company.

You can't sell goods if you don't have reputable suppliers, which suggests that you don't have a dropshipping business.

Search for Dropshipping Wholesalers on Google

You will identify the major vendors for your preferred commodities or product types with a Google search.

When you build a preliminary list, by studying the next few queries, take notice of the various characteristics of dropshipping suppliers.

- What is supplier location?
- Will the retailer link with your WooCommerce shop so that fresh orders are immediately submitted for fulfillment?
- What (if any) is the sum of minimum order (MOQ)?
- What support (e.g., mobile, email, chat, etc.) does the provider offer?
- What kind of range of items does the retailer offer?

Subscribe to Dropshipping Suppliers Directories

And if lots of choices pop up in the Google searches, directories will bring even more options. For a broad selection of items, these repositories comprise of web lists of dropshipping vendors and wholesalers.

You should recognize that some of the finest are premium directories, such as Salehoo and Worldwide Labels, implying they need paying subscriptions. There are a lot of free directories accessible that you can access at no fee, like Wholesale Central. Free directories, though, are occasionally obsolete. Newer vendors do not exist, and suppliers are also listed who are no longer in operation.

Usually, premium directories vary in cost from $20 a month for lifetime access to a few hundred bucks. You can find the expense of a premium directory to be beneficial, with free directories often hit-or-miss. There are also premium directories, like Doba, explicitly customized for dropshipping.

Figure Out Your Competitor's Suppliers

It follows that you must see what your competitors do if you want to be successful in the dropshipping field. Do any acknowledgment, in fact, to see which manufacturers are meeting their requirements.

There are a lot of methods to do this, but testing the markets that the competitors sell is the best.

If the supplier is not listed on the page, by making your own order, you will always show the supplier. Since the retailer is pleased, an invoice or packaging slip from them would possibly be included with the shipment. To ask about a partnership with your own dropshipping company, you can then contact the supplier directly.

Attend Trade Seminars

Trade shows have been considered to be an efficient place for manufacturers to set up and grow their companies. So, if you haven't been to a trade seminar yet, add it to the end of the list of to-do events.

You network with other participants within dropship supply chain, like distributors and dropshipping wholesalers, at trade shows. You get an insider's view on current and future products that you should introduce to your online store. For dropshipping businesses, you even get to "talk shop" face-to-face, which is also the most successful way to do business.

Join Industry Groups and Networks

Trade shows facilitate with locating vendors for dropshipping firms, yet another effective resource is business networks and groups.

The majority of retailers, like the identities of their dropshipping vendors, are not willing to share the secrets of their performance. The individuals who enter business groups, however, want to share, learn, & develop. Through being part of the dropshipping network, you will get valuable insight from industry professionals. Your colleagues, for instance, might recommend better suppliers or alert you about suppliers in order to avoid.

Connect with the Manufacturers

Not all manufacturers supply to consumers directly, although there are those who do. Until picking vendors for your eCommerce dropshipping shop, suggest reaching out to the producers of the goods that you will market.

You have far higher margins when a producer chooses to be the distributor than with a traditional retailer or wholesaler. Manufacturers, on the other hand, frequently impose minimum order amounts that could need bigger orders. You might find yourself with considerable inventory to deal in this situation, which is intended to circumvent dropshipping.

Ask the vendor to recommend vendors for you if a manufacturer won't work with you. A recommendation, after all, indicates that the agreements and commitments between a manufacturer and a supplier is successful. For that cause, it is definitely worth putting suggested vendors on your list of possibilities.

Order Samples

There's no substitution for firsthand knowledge, no matter how many feedback or testimonials you find. This is why ordering samples is the next phase in finding the correct dropshipping suppliers for the business.

Ordering samples teaches you a few key things about a supplier. First one is that you get to know the product's consistency yourself.

The second is that you will see how delivery is done by the retailer, and what shipment packaging seems to if a different vendor is involved, and how long it takes to ship and distribute. Suppliers will execute the requests, so buying samples provides you with an idea of what your clients will feel.

Confirm Contract Terms & Fees

You compiled several options, removed any but the most suitable possibilities, ordered tests to assess certain vendors, and decided on your dropshipping company with the right supplier (or suppliers). Negotiating deal conditions and payments is the last option left to do.

New businesses with unproven consumer bases have fewer bargaining leverage relative to mature companies with established customer bases. When it comes to communicating the margins, this is especially true.

Since dropshipping means that you don't have to hold your inventory, there would be low margins. The bulk of inventory costs and expenditures involved with meeting your orders is borne by your supplier(s). With dropshipping, because prices are smaller, gross margins are often lower than if you stored and delivered orders personally.

With margins generally poor, the fees concerned may be the biggest distinction between vendors. Such suppliers, for instance, charge flat per-order rates that are applied to the overall cost of the goods. Per-order payments typically vary from $2 and $5 to cover delivery and shipping costs (although big or unwieldy goods can require higher fees).

In the end, you want to select the supplier(s) that satisfies your specifications and give contracts of appropriate terms.

Chapter 7. Setting Up Your Dropshipping business On A Budget

The establishment of a dropshipping company as an eCommerce business is a perfect way to earn money. Managing a business without the hassle of product and shipping logistics is the most convincing aspect of a dropshipping store

You have already heard stories from businessmen about how costly it is to start a business. This involve accounts of hopelessly pursuing buyers or firms failing because of bleak financials to remain afloat. Do not let this scare you from launching a dropshipping store, as this model enables you to offer low-risk products.

What you need to do is get the orders and call the supplier-the rest is up to them.

There are very few financial barriers associated with the establishment of a dropshipping store when it comes to financing the company. In fact, with around zero initial investment, you can get underway with an online store.

Here's a 7-step feasible plan for launching a dropshipping shop on a budget shoestring.

1. Research Your Options

You'll need to do some research before beginning some form of business.

It requires getting online and finding out the competitors that offer related goods. To see just what each has to suggest, you'll also want to spend a little time investigating the future vendors and distributors.

Each shipping group will have a specific way of doing stuff and pricing models, therefore pay careful attention to those specifics so that you can ensure that you team up with your dropshipping store with the right party.

2. Create a Plan to Stick

You'll need to get a solid plan in progress before you can launch your business activities. A budget is used with this. It's important to decide what your budget is, whether you have $100 or $500 to get underway and ensure that you adhere to it. The easiest way to achieve so is to maintain good track of all your spending to guarantee that as you start up your store, you do not go over the budget.

3. Find Your Niche

In reality, many believe that it is an impossible task. It may be really challenging to appeal to all. Instead, rather than attempting to market could product under the sun, choose the goods focused on a particular niche.

Select a particular area of the business, such as organic pet food or dog clothes, if you decide that you want to market animal-related items.

When you can refine your attention down, you can have a much higher sales rate, and you are more likely to be noticed when customers are looking for a particular form of a product. Your small shop can get lost in the noise of competitors if your focus is too big.

4. Set Up Your eCommerce website

This is the phase through which you finally launch and set up your site with a dropshipping store.

Three of the most successful eCommerce sites accessible to sellers today are Shopify and Wix. It's quick to get started, as well as its user-friendly interface, also for sellers who are not especially tech-savvy, makes configuration and maintenance easy.

With monthly prices of less than $40, Shopify and Wix are both inexpensive alternatives, making it a perfect way to get off on a budget in the digital marketplace. You may also open a Modalyst store to boost the delivery and streamline the distribution process.

You're able to move on to the next stage after you have set up a simple online storefront that has your products selected.

5. Make Meetings With Your Suppliers

When it comes to choosing which provider to use it for your dropshipping shop, there are lots of decisions out there. Because you've done your homework in phase one already, now is the moment where your decision is formalized. Through entering into a contract with the commodity distributor(s) of your choosing, you will do so. Any of the most successful shipping partners makes it simple to get started, and in no time, unlike having to pay such upfront costs, you will be on your way.

The most relevant issues you are asking your prospective suppliers are:

- Do you keep all products in stock?
- How do you care the returns?
- What is your normal or average processing time?
- In which areas do you ship to? Do international shipping available?
- What kind of support did you offer?
- Is there any limit for orders?

You would have a solid understanding about how your suppliers conduct their company until you meet a supplier who addresses certain questions to your satisfaction. In addition, as a seller dealing for them, you'll realize what you need to do. You're on the path to a successful working partnership at this point.

6. Start Selling

Oh, congratulations. In launching your online store, this is one of most exciting steps. It's time to add your product details to your website and start selling until you have all your arrangements and agreements in order.

If customers are not aware of the products, you will not have enough sales, to begin with. You'll want to waste more time and money on ads if this is the case. By beginning with low-cost advertisements on Instagram and Facebook, or advertising on blogs as well as other websites which have a common audience, you will keep advertising costs reasonably small.

7. Optimize Your Site

You should take some time to customize the website until you have some revenue and knowledge under your belt. You can do all this earlier in the process, but waiting to see what is really working before you start to make changes is often a good idea.

There are a broad variety of customization choices for sites such as Shopify and Modalyst, including templates that change the way your website looks and plugins to can customize how your website works. The primary aim here is to tweak the site in ways that make it smoother for your clients and more organized.

As you've seen, all it takes to set up an online store is a few steps, and most of them don't need any money. You're not lonely if you're excited about being an owner of an eCommerce company just don't have a ton of money to launch with. This is why so many platforms are accessible that make it easier to get started without investing a million in the process.

Making sure that it works and prepare a strategy that you will use to guide you when keeping under your budget by setting up your dropshipping business, no matter how small it might be.

Chapter 8. Mistakes To Avoid When Developing Your Dropshipping Business

In an environment that jumps at the chance to make a business deal quick and convenient, Dropshipping tends to have a no for retailers. It might seem like, now, acquiring the goods and marketing with a bit of savvy are your only worries. Yet, if you wish to hold the company afloat, you should not forget about the client's perspective. True, the boring duties of inventory, order filling, and then ensuring shipping can be passed on.

The dropshipping company, however, does not waste any time thinking about the feelings of your client. How do you assume if your client is going to be satisfied? The buyers are the ones who put the money back. Anything falls out the window if they're not satisfied. You would need to consider the duties and what failures typically trigger it all to backfire in order to completely enjoy the advantages of utilizing dropshipping.

Here are a common mistake that leads to the failure end of your dropshipping business, so you should hold these mistakes in mind all the time.

1. Worrying About Shipping Costs.

While shipping costs might be a doozy, it's never productive to stress. In this area, you will need to decide under which your priorities lie. Shipping prices can vary all over the board, depending on where orders come from. This stress can be relieved by setting a flat rate and generally evens out with time. Not only does this make things easier for you, but it's also simple and easy for customers.

2. Relying Much on Vendors.

By putting much trust in such a vendor, a good number of crises can arise. For example, they may go out of business or increase their rates on you if you only use one vendor. They might run out of the items that you expect them to supply. Where would you be then? This is why there should always be a backup for you. It is smart to write up the contract with your vendors for your own insurance to remain aware of your requirements. This will ensure that everyone involved has agreed to uphold what you demand.

3. Expecting Easy Money.

Dropshipping, as we've already established, offers a degree of ease that can seem to make your work easier. Yet, you can't ignore how critical your product is in marketing and all the competition you're going to face. This involves analysis and the creation of a unique approach that will allow the product more attractive than that of anyone else.

4. Making Order Difficult to Access.

When you assure your consumers a simple and quick procedure, they'll want to see the proofs. Set approximate location-based ship dates and require suppliers to keep you posted on the status of the order so that you can keep the consumer aware. This way, you can track shipments whenever you anticipate them to come longer than expected and easily fix issues.

5. Not Enough Brand Display.

Through dropshipping, it may be hard to guarantee the brand remains to be seen in the customer's overall experience. You may not want people to forget regarding you, so it's important to insert as many locations as possible into your brand. You should have customized packing slips, stickers and custom exterior packaging to hold the name included after delivery. Sending a follow-up thank you message or a survey to remind about of you and prove them you think for their feedback at the same time is also not a bad idea.

6. Return Complications.

If you do not have a system for returns set up, things can get messy very quickly. You and your vendor will have to establish a refund policy to avoid this. Customers are going to wait for their refund expectantly, and being disorganized on that front and will not make them feel good. They may also need guidelines explaining how or where to return the product. Organizing a structure for this will save a good amount of confusion and irritation for both you and the client.

7. Selling Trademarked Products

When most people learn about dropshipping and realize that it is not that complicated to do the process, they picture all the things they might sell and make a quick buck.

Many of these goods are items which have been trademarked by a manufacturer. Selling these goods without the manufacturer's specific consent to be a retail agent will lead you to legal issues. This can not only lead to the end of your online shop, but you can also be held personally responsible.

You should, consequently, look at generic items which you can add to your variety of products for sale. Best still, you should swap in goods with white marks. They are plain goods that are available to those who rebrand them through the manufacturer. You will order and get these items customized to suit the brand and display them.

8. Picking the Wrong Field

Once you have abandoned thoughts of selling any product you come across, by concentrating on one field, you can develop your dropshipping business.

You might, however, select the wrong niche in which to operate. Maybe you should pick a niche that isn't lucrative. This may be that it's out of vogue or it's simply not meant for shopping online.

Therefore, to see what will earn you money, you have to do proper market analysis. "Market research" might sound like a complex process in which only major brands participate.

Simple Google searches will, therefore, show you what individuals are interested in and where they purchase them.

9. Poor Relationship With Suppliers

Your vendors are part of your business; they promise that you have the best goods and that they supply your consumers with them. You can be inclined, though, to consider them as workers and handle them as though they are in the hierarchy on a lower rung.

They're not. They are your friends, without whom it would be effectively dead for your dropshipping business. Therefore, you can establish a better relationship with them.

This will have its benefits. When negotiating costs for commodity stock, a strong partnership will work in your favor.

10. Lowering Price To Extreme Levels

Reducing your prices to knock out your competition is also one of the dropshipping failures to avoid.

This is a logical way for you to rise your dropshipping business, you might think. You could have been no farther from the facts. Very low prices indicate to potential customers that your product may be of poor quality.

11. Poor Website Structure

The progress of your dropshipping company depends on the shopping experience your clients have when they browse your online store.

Thus, you have to make sure everything is convenient for them. However, you could rush through the process of establishing your website due to low barrier for entrance into dropshipping. Many beginners do not have the coding skills required to construct an online store.

In conclusion, the primary interest is the customer's experience. Although inventory management and shipping are not your responsibility, you can also ensure that all is well handled. All of these dropshipping failures can be prevented with adequate preparation and careful management, and the business can better manage.

Chapter 9. Smooth Running tips for Your Dropshipping Business

Well, you've done your research, decided to agree on the right dropship goods and roped in the right possible supplier. All of you are planned to begin dropshipping goods and make the mullah! Setting up the company, though, is typically one thing, but a totally different ball game is to manage it on a day-to-day basis. Even if it's a dropshipping company, there are various facets of running a business that you have to remember as a retailer: marketing, refunds, refunds, repairs, inventory, distribution, customer service, and far more. So dive into all these different aspects of managing a dropshipping business.

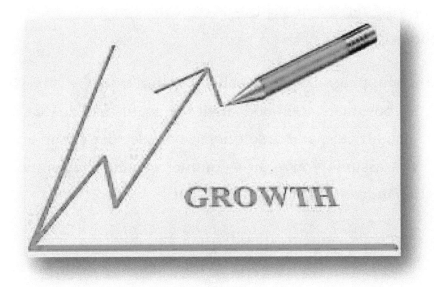

So far, when covered a lot of details, it involves everything from the fundamentals of dropshipping to the nuances of finding a niche and managing the business. You should have much of a base by now to begin investigating and establishing your own dropshipping company comfortably.

It's possible to get confused and lose track about what's really necessary, with too much to consider. That's why we've built this list of key elements for success. This are the main "must-do" acts that can make the new company or ruin it. If you can perform these effectively, you would be able to get a bunch of other stuff wrong and yet have a decent probability of success.

1. Add Value

The most important performance element is making a good roadmap on how you will bring value to your clients. In the field of dropshipping, where you can contend with legions of other "me too" stores carrying related items, this is critical for both corporations, but even more so.

With dropshipping, it's reasonable to think you're marketing a product to consumers. Yet good small merchants realize that they are offering insights, ideas and solutions, not just the commodity they deliver. You assume you're an e-commerce seller, but you're in the information industry as well.

If you can't create value by quality data and advice, price is the only thing you're left to contend on. While this has been an effective technique for Walmart, it will not help you grow a successful company for dropshipping.

2. Focus on SEO and marketing

The opportunity to push traffic to the new platform is a near second to providing value as a main key factor. A shortage of traffic to their sites is the #1 concern and annoyance faced by modern e-commerce retailers. So many retailers have been slaving away on the ideal platform for months just to unleash it into a community that has no clue it exists.

For the success of your company, advertising and driving traffic is completely necessary and challenging to outsource well, particularly if you have a limited budget and bootstrap your business. In order to build your own SEO, publicity, outreach and guest posting abilities, you have to consider taking the personal initiative.

Within the first 6 - 12 months, where no one know who you are, this is particularly crucial. You need to devote at least 75 percent of your time on publicity, SEO and traffic development for at least 4 to 6 months after your website launch, which is right, 4 to 6 months. You can start reducing and coast a little on the job you put in until you've built a strong marketing base. But it's difficult, early on, to bring so much emphasis on advertising.

3. Marketing Your Dropshipping Business

Marketing is indeed a subjective field, and that there are a billion strategies which can be used to position your brand successfully whilst driving awareness and sales of your brand. It will even help you root out the remainder of the market if the approach is well planned.

4. Social Media Source

Social networking is one of the most efficient ways to promote, advertise, attract clients and share content, so when social networks are now used for digital marketing, it comes as no surprise. For example, Facebook has more than 1.7 billion active members from diverse walks of life, and it is this diversity that makes it so appealing to online marketers.

One thing to note is that it's important to content. No matter how perfect a platform is or how good the product you are offering is, without high quality content backing it up, it means nothing.

5. Customer Ratings & Reviews

A few bad customer ratings will actually ruin a business in dropshipping business model. Think about it: As you order online from websites like ebay and aliexpress, the quality ranking and what other consumers had to tell about it will be one of the determining purchase variables, too, with decrease delivery. A few positive feedback will also give you an advantage over the competition because that is what will help you convert traffic to your website successfully.

6. Email Marketing

In a digital marketer's pack, this one of the most neglected tools. To keep your clients in the loop for any major changes within company, email marketing may be used: Price increases, promotions, coupons, content related to the commodity, and content unique to the industry are only some of the forms email marketing may be utilized.

7. Growth Hacking

Growth hacking is a cheap but highly productive way to get online creative marketing campaigns. A few definitions of growth hacking involve retargeting old campaigns and featuring in your own niche as a guest writer for a popular website. Any of this commonly involves content marketing.

Chapter 10. How To Maximize Your Chances Of Success?

There are only a couple more tips you should adopt to maximize the chances of long-term growth if you are willing to take the plunge and attempt dropshipping. Second, that doesn't mean you can approach a dropshipping business because it's risk-free simply because there are no setup costs involved with purchasing and managing goods. You're also spending a lot of time choosing the right dropshippers while designing your website, so consider it as an investment and do careful preliminary research.

1. Things To Remember

What do you want to sell? How profitable is the surroundings? How can you gain clients and distinguish yourself? Inside the same room, is there a smaller niche that is less competitive? When they find a particular market and curate their goods like a pro, most individuals who operate a purely dropshipping model have seen the most growth, ensuring that any last item they offer is a successful match for their niche audience with their brand.

After you develop your list of possible dropshippers, carry out test orders and then watch for the items to arrive, thinking like a consumer. How long can any order take? What is the feeling of unboxing like? What is the commodity standard itself? This will help you distinguish between possible dropshippers or confirm that positive consumer service is offered by the one you want.

Note that the goods themselves may not be the differentiator for your business.

After you have chosen your dropshippers and products, note that the products themselves may not be the differentiator for your business. So ask what else you should count on to make the deal. This is another explanation why test orders are a wonderful idea since they encourage you to obtain the item and explain its functionality and advantages as a client might. In a way which really shows it off, you can even take high-quality, professional pictures of the product. Armed with exclusive explanations of the goods and images that are separate from all the other product photos, you would be able to start standing out.

Your bread and butter is definitely going to be a well-executed campaign strategy, so devote time and money on each section of it, from finding your potential audience to interacting with influencers on social media in your niche. Targeted commercials can be a perfect way to kick start your site to bring your name on the mind of your client base.

When it relates to your return policies, delivery contact and customer support, ensure your ducks are in a line. You'll need to do what you could to serve as the buffer between a dropshipper and your client if something goes wrong somewhere in the process. Understand the typical cost of return for each item so that you will notice whether it is large enough to denote a quality issue. If you suspect a consistency problem, talk to your dropshipper or try a different supplier to your issues.

Eventually, note that dropshipping is not a model of "all or nothing." Many of the more profitable corporations follow a hybrid model, making or shipping in-house some goods and employing dropshippers to fill the gaps. The dropshippers are not the key profit-drivers for these firms but are instead a simple, inexpensive way to provide clients with the "extras" they can enjoy. Before you put it in-house, you can even use dropshipped products for upsells, impulse sales, or to try a new model.

As long as you consider the above tips to ensuring that the one you chose is suitable for your business needs, there is definitely a lot to learn from the streamlining and flexibility of using a dropshipper. You will make your dropshipping store run for you in no time with a little of research, negotiation, and setup!

Conclusion

So that concludes our definitive dropshipping guide. You now learn how to set up to kick start your new dropshipping business if you've made it here. Starting up your own business often involves a certain degree of dedication, effort, and ambition to make things work, much as in every other undertaking in life. It's not only about building the business but also about pushing through and knowing how to manage it on a daily basis.

The greatest feature of dropshipping is that you will practice in real-time by checking your goods and concepts, and all you have to do is drop it from your shop if anything doesn't work. This business concept is indeed a perfect opportunity for conventional business models to try out product concepts. Dropshipping creates a secure place to innovate to see what happens without incurring any substantial damages that will surely give business owners the courage to state that they have a working idea of how the market works. The dropshipping business model is an interesting business model to move into with little initial expense and relatively little risk.

A perfect choice to drop shipping if you are only starting to sell online and would like to test the waters first. It's a great way to start your business, even if the margins are low.

As dropshipping can still get started with little investment, before they build their market image, businessmen can start with that too. Ecommerce sites such as Ebay, Shopify, Alibaba and social networking, such as Instagram, Twitter, Reddit, provide vast expertise in user base and content marketing. It also helps newbies to know about establishing an online store, optimizing conversions, generating traffic and other basics of e-commerce.

That's what you need to learn about beginning a dropshipping. Just note, it's not the hard part to launch your dropshipping store, the real challenge is when you get trapped, and your stuff is not being sold. Do not panic, and keep checking as it happens. You're going to get a product soon that sells well.

Youtube, Tik-Tok and Instagram Made Easy

A Collection of Filters, Entertaining Topics and Viral Trends to Gain 10k Followers and Generate Passive Income

By

NESPY ONLINE MARKETING

Table of contents

Introduction

Don't think you can compete against millions of creators and influencers? Well, let's set one thing straight, not only can you do it but also how you can do it. Working smarter, not necessarily harder, makes all the difference.

This book is for those who wish to make a name of themselves by leaving behind a reputation, legacy on social media platforms. Or maybe, all you want is to be able to do what you love for a living and offer that to the world. Either way, you're in the right place.

If you haven't been able to make much of a passive income from these social platforms for a while now, you should know it's probably not you; it's the platform. This book aims to provide an insight into these social platforms by teaching you how to increase your audience by changing some basic habits and teach you a few new tips, tricks, and tactics you can use by first understanding their working. 10,000 is perhaps the right number of followers to be considered literally as an influencer/brand, get paying offers, and raise your account's value.

It may be sluggish as you try to win the starting few followers, but it does get a little easier after that. Understanding the algorithm plays a crucial role in enlarging your audience. YouTube, Tik Tok, and Instagram use algorithms to recommend various creators. Once you understand how their algorithms work, you can easily reach a larger variety of users. By gaining an active audience of about 10K, YouTube, Tik Tok, and Instagram may consider paying attention to your content, and you could even gain more than 10,000 depending on your consistency.

Now, you are probably thinking "easier said than done", right? Well, don't worry, this book is solely there to make these things easier. To provide a how-to gain 10K followers quickly, An easy-to-use reference to aid your growth on social media platforms (i.e., YouTube, Tik Tok, and Instagram.)

Try not to read this book as a novel; rather, truly study it and apply it in your daily practices to notice change and improvement in your channel/account/profile growth.

First, this book will teach you why earning a passive income through YouTube, Tik Tok, and Instagram is the way to go, especially in this day and age, next, how each platform has its own way of working and different method to win over the platform to your side. And then, if you're having a tough time generating content for these platforms, the last part will teach you how you can remove your creativity block and let your muse come to you. Last but not least, Afterthoughts will give you that push you need to get cracking, radiating motivation and energy to really get you started.

CHAPTER I: Why it's One of the Best Ways to Earn

In current times, the Internet is available in almost every part of the world. People interact, learn, and enjoy through platforms. More specifically, YouTube, Tik Tok, and Instagram. Since 2020, most people have spent their time at home, and so usage of these social media platforms has grown excessively. People discovered hidden talents, curiosity, and inspiration so much more than before.

Even if people hadn't spent half their time on their phones or other electronic devices, there are so many advantages of working on YouTube, Tik Tok, and Instagram for a passive income.

1.1: Freedom of Speech

YouTube, Tik Tok, and Instagram are the kind of social media platforms that allow an individual to really do anything and everything they want, needless to say, as long as they follow community guidelines.

"I do not agree with what you have to say, but I'll defend to the death your right to say it." ~ Voltaire

From a thriller, a short film to kids toy reviews, from gameplays to reactions, whatever. These are platforms where even the smallest of people have a voice, and they can make it known. Your creativity can literally pay the bills and put food on the table. And there can always be an endless supply of creativity, that is if you know where to look.

What could you possibly want more than being able to do what you love for a living? It's the ideal dream. And there are so many advantages of being able to do what you enjoy for a living.

High Efficiency

You become more useful and productive with your work as you can be excited for the next day. Your work won't even feel like a job, and so you would find yourself more relaxed as it wouldn't feel like a burden, finding other things to do in your spare time would be exciting too.

Inspiration

When you're having a tough time, doing what you love can spark inspiration and motivation in you. Once you feel inspired, your ideas run like a high-quality car engine, and it can sometimes even get difficult to do all these amazing things you have in mind.

New Perspectives

When you are following a boring schedule every single day and spend most of your time thinking about what you would do once the weekends here, you should realize you're doing it wrong. When working on a social media platform, you don't have a boss; in fact, you are your own boss, much like running a business. You set timings that are best suited for your work, and as being a public figure is constantly exciting, you won't find yourself in the same routine each day. Sure, you would probably have some ups and downs, but at the end of the day, you work for your own satisfaction and so view life from a different point of view than those who work solely because they feel they have no choice.

Better Wellbeing

Working on your chosen niche on these social platforms sounds fun and enjoyable, and it is. What you probably didn't know that being happy is great for your health. In fact, it's a lot cheaper than being miserable and stressed for every day of your life. It even relieves all that stress, mental and physical tension.

1.2: Fame

An Audience

Working on being a public figure or influencer gives you an audience that cares for you; they show an interest in your content. It could make you a role model for them, or they see your content to put a smile on their faces, it could help them in some basic struggles they didn't know they had until they saw your work.

Your followers/subscribers may value your opinions on certain topics and appreciates you and your content in the respective niche. And being validated for your effort would make anyone happy.

They even help you grow by giving honest feedback and so you can easily tell what it is they like about your content.

Opportunities

Fame grants you several chances to work with well-known brands or companies. Whether that be in sponsored advertisements or partnerships for products (i.e., perfume, apparel, electronic gadgets, games, etc.)

For example, maybe you're a sports-focused content creator, you could get offers from sportswear companies to model with their products!

Not only brands but also popular public figures would notice you, and you'd be given numerous opportunities to work with them, especially if you're in the same niche as them. When an already successful creator acknowledges and validates your content, they bring in their fans to your work, ultimately broadening your audience.

For instance, YouTuber Lilly Singh, also known as superwoman, grew so big on YouTube that she now hosts a late-night show called "A Little Late with Lilly Singh" on NBC. She not only released a film that entailed her world tour but also a book named "How to Be a Bawse: A Guide to Conquering Life," which made it to New York Times best-seller list. She also won a substantial number of rewards on multiple award shows over the years and made her own music videos, and so much more. Her Niche? Entertainment. And it's an understatement to say she entertained.

@lilly with @malala Via Instagram

Of course, it didn't come easy to her, but with time, her channel grew and not only on YouTube but also across other platforms like Instagram.

Like her, once you obtain that loyal audience, you could try new things whenever you want, but not too much, or you may drive your audience away. You'd be able to work on creative projects. (i.e., Liza Koshy acted in a tv show and other showbiz related content, PewDiePe who made not one but two games with another company as well as a YouTube original show called "Scare PewDiePie", Joey Graceffa who made his own YouTube original show called "Escape the Night".)

1.3: Money

The obvious reason for earning through YouTube, Tik Tok, and Instagram? The Money. Succeeding on any social platform often promises good fortune. Influencers often buy new cars, houses, editors to help them with their work, maybe even a new oven!

You'd finally be able to finish that bucket list. Get something for the people you care about! And most importantly, once you get that money you've been waiting for, be grateful and don't take it for granted.

YouTubers like Lilly Singh made use of their money by making her profile a little more professional by hiring a team and basically becoming a CEO of her team. A lot of influencers do live charity streams, raise money, or donate for the poor and needy in several ways as well. Well, that's not all she did with her money she spent it for fun too as I'm sure you can as well do whatever you want with it.

Merchandising

You would be able to sell your own products, which would be your signature merch (people would recognize it as yours). Often influencers get sweatshirts, T-shirts, caps, posters, phone covers, etc. This increases your profits as well as advertising yourself. You get something to represent yourself with and receive more recognition.

CHAPTER II: YouTube

2.1: How it Works

To know how to easily get 10,000 subscribers on YouTube, you first need to be able to understand the YouTube software's working and how you can use it to your advantage.

Video

YouTube is a free space where creators can store videos, pictures, and posts. But their main focus is the videos that various people of all types upload. Google owns it, and its search engine is the second largest around the globe. YouTube videos can be embedded into other websites as well.

Moreover, YouTube recommends videos that are viewed by a similar audience to the one a user is currently watching.

Being successful through YouTube won't happen in a week. You have to be prepared to go through the rough patches as well as the smooth ones.

Analytics

There is a reporting, and self-service analytics tool on YouTube which provides intel regarding every video you upload so YouTube can help you easily keep track of how many views each video receives, what type of people are watching your content (age group, where they are from, and such).

It can provide data about:

1. The age groups and genders it is commonly seen by.

2. The statistics: comments, ratings, and views.

3. The countries your content is mostly seen in.

4. The first time your video was recommended to a user, either when they are watching something similar or when your video was recommended when they search a keyword.

5. In the first instance, your video was embedded in a website by a third party.

Advertising

YouTube embeds features that allow various businesses to promote their content to users who may have an interest in it, aiming at clients by subject and demographics.

The advertisers pay you each time someone in your audience views their Ad. They can decide the areas in which the Ad will show, the amount of payment, and the format.

Channels

Create your own niche, don't constantly jump from one genre to another, or your audience will never remain consistent.

2.2: The Content

Watch Time

Videos that consist of a higher watch time get recommended frequently on the main YouTube homepage. So how do you increase it? Pattern Interrupts.

These result in making your videos more vibrant, which prolongs the viewers' attention span.

A pattern interrupt can be jump cuts, graphics, different camera angles, and cheesy humor. It can put a smile on the watcher's face or catch them off guard, which keeps them watching.

Trends

Keeping up with the current times is vital for small channels to grow. Trends are one of the catalysts of increasing your audience.

PewDiePie Via YouTube

As of February 2021, most YouTubers stream live, do how-to tutorials, DIY's, etc.

Things like the chubby bunny challenge, Reddit reactions (cross-platform), spicy foods challenge, etc., gives more room for the creator and audience to get to know one another. The goal is to make them feel like your friend, so they feel comfortable enough to come back.

Create longer videos.

Making long videos (10+ minutes) actually gives your video a higher rank in YouTube's search results in most cases. Of course, if you make the video longer with not much to add, then it will still be lowly ranked as users will prefer not to waste their time.

And definitely avoid making videos longer than an hour because it's likely the viewers' attention gets diverted.

Like, Share, and Subscribe

At any point of the video, remind your viewers to subscribe, but make sure you don't keep mentioning that along with 'Like, Share, and hit the notification bell' as this tends to irritate the viewers due to the fact that they just want to watch the video. Keep the message short and maybe even humorous to attract the viewers.

Link more videos at the end.

If the users watch more of *your* content, they will probably subscribe. So, promoting your videos will definitely increase the chances of them watching it as it would be convenient for them to just click on that instead of going to your channel and surfing through there.

Quality over Quantity

Viewers can never be fooled by the number of videos you upload every week, they value the effort and time put into each piece of content, and they are well aware that you are as human as they are.

Do try maintaining a schedule just to let your viewers know when they can expect a video, but don't force it, or it will not be valued.

Thumbnail and Video Title

Your thumbnails should be eye-catching and interesting, as it is the first thing they see when they are introduced to your channel. It's your first impression. Make sure it's a high-quality image.

If it's a professional website, a simple and sleek thumbnail will do. If it's a vlog or an entertainment purpose video, an exciting title with an image of the most important part of the video in place of the thumbnail would fit nicely.

For example, if you want to give your review on a certain product, give a strong statement as a title that would be intriguing for people to watch (i.e., 'Why I think the new Tesla cars are amazing', 'Why Harry Potter actually makes no sense', 'Public Speaker Reacts to PewDiePie')

More Content

At the end of your videos, hint at what you'll be doing next so your viewers can come back for more.

Keep track of your subscriber magnet. In analytics, creators can see what type of videos made by you have the most views. So, start by focusing on those. Obviously, don't make a hundred parts on the same topic, but keeping track of your subscriber magnet can help a lot.

2.3: Channel Profile

Keep an attractive and creative Channel with intriguing art styles, so it shows the work put in your banner. It welcomes the viewers. Here are some examples:

Jaclyn Lovey Via YouTube: here, Jaclyn made a minimalistic banner with her video update schedule and her genre of videos mentioned, so newcomers do not have to search for it; convenience.

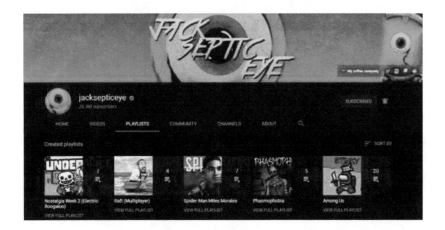

jacksepticeye Via YouTube: Jack, a successful YouTuber with over 20 Million views, categorized all his videos in playlists so users can access any genre of his videos anytime. Also, notice a signature logo, and he mentioned all his handles, brand links too.

Make an exciting and persuading channel trailer. Preferably short and catchy, show the best you can here because these viewers came specifically to your channel, and you want to keep them there.

Organize the Channel page in a way that's convenient to the viewers.

Check out this basic layout:

Mention other platforms you use so they keep up with you if they don't rely on YouTube.

In 'About', make sure you provide at least 300 words about yourself, what kind of content you put out into the world, and why you think they'd be interested. If you have an upload schedule (please do), then mention that as well. Persuade the viewers to subscribe by the end of it. Keeping a polite tone in your descriptions, whether it be a channel description or video description, gives the viewer a positive and kind tone. They wouldn't particularly enjoy watching someone who talks in a manner of giving orders rather than guiding or entertaining (depending on your content subject).

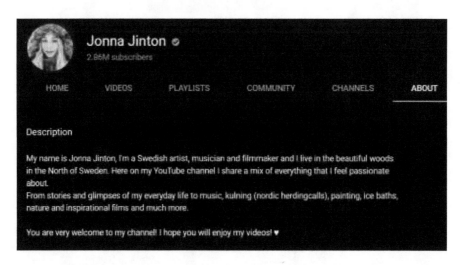

Make sure you use well-known keywords that describe your content. (i.e., Crash courses, funny, motivational, etc.) so the YouTube algorithm   can   detect   these   things. Here's an easy comparison:

A:

Via YouTube

B: Via YouTube

Which is a better Description of the YouTuber? I hope you say B, because it is, in fact, B.

Categorize your videos into playlists. For example, if you are running a gaming channel, make sure long gameplays are divided into separate videos but put together in one playlist after you upload them. Not many people watch 4-hour gameplays all at once, especially when you are starting as a small channel. But suppose you divide your gameplays into videos and edit them to cut out the boring bits. In that case, they may enjoy watching multiple short videos, which would be around 15-20 minutes each- depending on your preferences.

2.4: Interactivity

Replying to comments is the best and simplest way to gain more subscribers. The more you interact with your viewers and give importance to their feedback, the longer they stay.

"When creators take the time to interact with their local community, it can encourage audience participation and ultimately result in a larger fanbase." ~ YouTube.

Creator Hearts- you can heart your favorite comments to recognize comments from your public. By doing this, the viewer gets a notification, and this keeps interactivity high by leading them back to your channel. These notifications receive 300% additional clicks than normal.

Once you get a handful of people that are consistent in watching your content, you can even ask for their opinion on anything related to the video or even an idea for the next video. To engage your community is perhaps the most important thing, especially when you are a growing channel. Doing Q&A videos every once in a while acknowledges the audience and engages them more.

Recently, YouTube updated, and now Creators can interact with their audience with polls and posts as well as comments. Using these frequently to keep your audience there is vital.

Shine Theory

Needless to say, they'd be more excited by a famous YouTuber replying to their comments, but you could be famous soon enough too! So, building a community that promotes each other does help. This concept comes from the Shine Theory.

Shine Theory is a long-term investment, where two individuals, creators, or consumers, help each other by means of advertising or engagement depending on the platform it is being used.

CHAPTER III: Tik Tok

3.1: Down the Rabbit Hole

Over 2 billion people have downloaded Tik Tok all around the globe. Especially during the global pandemic, literally, everyone seems to have this app on their phone- and even if they don't have the app, it is taking over the apps they *do* have.

Tik Tok is super addicting, and the main reason for this is that each video is no longer than one minute, which gives viewers quick entertainment / tips / motivation.

Tik Tok famous is a word the vast majority seems to be throwing around as if it is a solid career, but the problem is, they all act as though it's a comfortable ride without even putting their back into it! Though it's a little more complicated than that, and you'd know that. But don't worry, here's a step-by-step guide to how you can be Tik Tok famous in no time.

This is the kind of platform that anyone can get into, from a 7-year-old to a 70-year-old *anyone*. Most people follow overnight after one of your Tik Tok's go mega-viral. Without further ado, let's start with all the things you need to remember to get 10 000 followers on Tik Tok.

3.2: The Algorithm

The Tik Tok algorithm was updated recently at the start of 2021, due to which a number of views on Tik Toks have started to go down. They did this because Tik Tok realized Tik Toks could go viral for almost anyone and a lot of creators' content was against community guidelines, so the early adopter advantage is lost. A way to tackle this is- keep pumping out more content. These algorithms will keep updating throughout the years, but the best you can do is give the viewers a reason to watch.

3.3: Your Profile

Username

Choose a simple yet unique username. One that is familiar to your niche would be most preferred as it would make users find you conveniently. (i.e., if your Tik Toks are travel-focused, you can call yourself JourneysInLife)

Bio

Think of an intriguing Profile Bio. Something welcoming, relatable, original, fun, and interesting your followers would enjoy. And definitely mention your niche to clarify your target audience. Often really good bios consist of a call to action (i.e., follow for a cookie).

Upload a Photo (high-quality image not to look cheap). Link your other social media handles like Instagram, YouTube, etc.

3.4: The Content

Target Audience

Before blindly making videos, you need to consider what kind of audience you're aiming for. Firstly, they use Tik Tok. If you think editing videos the same way you'd edit a YouTube or IGTV video will work, you're wrong. Every platform is unique in its own significant way, so you need to pay attention to how Tik Tok is entertaining and focuses on that.

Is it family-friendly content for youngsters? Short tutorials for artists? Perhaps it's professional cooking for beginners. You need to think about your audience's geolocation, age group, gender, so on and so forth.

This is an approximate age breakdown:

- Age 55+: 5%

- Age 44-53: 2%

- Age 34-43: 7%

- Age 24-33: 15%

- Age 17-23: 41%

- Age 13-16: 26%

What's your Niche?

Delivering high-quality videos (in both quality of the video and content) is the most basic important thing. Don't steal content from other underrated creators, or it will have dire consequences like getting banned.

Make it unique, edit your videos with your ability if you can because people get tired of seeing the same editing design used by the Tik Tok app. There are various editing apps
like ViaMaker, Zoomerang, Quik, InShot, Funimate, etc.

Quality

You need a really powerful hook in the first 3 seconds the keep the viewers wanting to watch more. Your job is to do everything and anything to keep the viewers from clicking away then make them interested enough to follow!

To do this, you need a significant number of pattern interrupts- graphics, different camera angles, etc. It could be as easy as starting with a greeting or as concrete as taking the time to explore or finishing your wish list. A trend disrupts you to exciting new locations, both visually and psychologically. It jolts you away from your comfortable perceptions and rituals and then into broad freedom of possibilities.

Better quality videos are pleasing to the eye, and they will likely continue watching until it ends. Sometimes Tik Tok degrades your videos' quality, and the reason this happens is that the data saved on your app has been turned on often than naught. This feature is on means the Tik Tok application downloads your mobile data while you watch videos. This decreases the resolution of your clips too. So, to tackle this, you can turn off the data saver feature.

Collabs

Collaborating with some people you have good chemistry with really improves shares as it would be increasing both your and the other Tik Tokers views/follows another branch of Shine Theory.

Not just that, but Tik Tok allows you to reply to other influencers Tik Tok with your own, right? Use that! Make your reply unique and interesting to get them and other viewers to notice.

When it comes to collaborations with companies, sponsorships sound nice but try not to overdo it. While looking for new celebrities to partner with, be sure to review how many supported videos are posted. When a majority of their latest material is paying for updates, their commitment rate will not last. Alternatively, search for influencers with a decent amount of organic, non-sponsored material. As they probably have fans interested and involved.

Going Viral

When you post a video on Tik Tok, your creativity has the potential to ignite a chain reaction.

To get a decent amount of exposure, engage in trends, challenges, and duets. Put your own twists on patterns that captivate individuals. Paying attention to and bookmarking popular clips can prove useful to use it for inspiration. In Tik Tok, there are so many viral challenges. Engaging in various challenges will increase your visibility to the network and encourage you to get far more follows.

On the majority of your Tik Toks, for now, at least, use recommended and trending songs. Positive content almost always has more views, something quirky and enjoyable with a warm tone. Using a trending song is the next move (except when your music is original or a video idea in particular to a kind of sound.)

This is the reason why using trending songs is clever: basically, Tik Tok is a little wired in regard to trending songs to promote videos. It wasn't a random occurrence that Tik Tok also works with record companies; they work together to promote the artist's music in the app to improve the sales of the album and raise the likelihood that the song can hit the top rankings. Tik Tok practically dominates the music world. A mere peek at the week's Top 100 tunes. Most of those best hits on Tik Tok are those that are mega-famous. How do you know what tunes everyone's listening to? Simply choose one of the suggested tracks the platform recommends when you make your film.

Get on top of all those trends, except with a surprise. Do the idea of popular dances or rising clips, but add a twist on it and make it something of your own. You need to balance trending videos with fresh material when you're a small producer. A Tik Tok clip received millions of views, and that account got about 10,000 Tik Tok followers; it just happened overnight.

However, once you receive those views, you shouldn't anticipate the next day to be filled with that much fame, because you will probably be disappointed. Once you get over a million views, then you need to keep up the work or probably work even harder than before to keep everyone there.

Make sure you don't take part in really cringe trends, though!

Using Hashtags

Utilize hashtags as much as you can, especially hashtags that are trending. This actually matters because the Tik Tok algorithm detects these hashtags and recommends your content accordingly.

The cleverer and simpler your hashtags are, the higher your videos get ranked on Tik Tok, which in result increases your views and likes. Along with being in contact with record labels, Tik Tok often works with companies/brands, and their drives are almost always attached with a hashtag. This encourages your videos on people's For You Page during the duration of the campaigns.

1-2 hashtags are preferred. Go to the Discover tab and take 1-2 trending and 1-2 broad hashtags or tags related to your related to you exclusively and trendy.

Most Popular: #tiktokers #lfl #bhfyp #follow #explorepage #followforfollowback #explore #meme #tiktokdance #viral #memes #tiktokindia #photography #tiktokindonesia #k #cute #art #youtube #instagood #fashion #likes #bhfyp #likeforlikes #trending #music #funny #tiktok #instagram #love #like

Timing Matters!

What time you decide to post your content actually matters. When most people are online is when you'd want to put out videos and this depends on your geolocation heavily. If you're careful, you can get twice the followers you'd normally get.

Posting late at night (not too late), afternoon, and early morning tend to be the best times as most people would be looking through their phones then.

But that's just an average. To be more specific, go into your account analytics and content section, look at the past 7 days and what times your content was viewed most often, then make your posting times according to when your most interactive followers were active to make it as convenient for them as possible. Also, take into consideration the timings more well-known Tik Tokers in your niche are posting.

Repost and Share.

Sometimes, your video doesn't do as well the first time but reposting it several times a day and week can drastically change that because sometimes your followers just miss it. Saying things like 'Posting again till it goes viral' or 'Reposting since it didn't do too well last time' can really make a difference.

Sharing your videos on every other social media platform (i.e., Instagram, Twitter, Facebook, etc.)

Engagement

You need to turn your viewers, commenters, and likers into followers, especially at such an early stage. Basically, your early squad needs the spa treatment. To do this, perhaps the most important thing is engaging with your community. Interacting with them as much and as often as you can is vital to Tik Tok's growth.

Reply to each and every comment. People love viewing comments seeing their opinion was acknowledged would be a satisfying feeling for everyone. Credits: wired

Follow everyone, and I mean everyone that has interacted with your account in any way.

Go Live every single day, and it really boosts your page. Even if you're super busy, go live and work!

If you receive hate comments, reply back with a bit of humor! However, if it's constructive criticism, show interest, and try actually considering their opinion, this can really help your account develop.

Ask questions in your videos, so they feel the need to reply in the comments. This is a little trick most creators use.

Staying Consistent

Posting regularly is important. Post multiple times a day (considering the timings) and try avoiding uploading content right after each other, or it will not be pushed to the For You page.

Stockpile videos: If you have a day off, film as much content as you can so you can still upload videos if you're too busy another day. Posting 3-6 times a day is an ideal amount.

Duration

The duration of each video is preferred to be 11-17 sec long. The ideal time for something to be pushed out into the algorithm. And you'd get a good amount of watch time. Keep it shorter than you think it needs to be.

Tik Tok revolves around fun and concise videos, so if yours is too long than they would like, Tik Tok may decrease your rank on the For You page.

Ask them to follow, like, and comment.

The easiest method to improve the number of followers you have is by asking the viewers to 'double tap!' or 'let me know what you think in the comment section'; these things remind viewers to give you some sort of feedback on the content you create.

Asking for engagement in every video for a *very* brief period of time in the video and saying it in the description is important. Make sure it isn't mentioned for longer than 2-3 seconds, or the viewer will get bored and click away.

Keep all your content accessible.

Never delete any of your Tik Tok videos because it's likely your posts won't do well right away; you need to give it time. Your previous posts can go viral any time, so never keep them private or delete them.

There have been many times a Tik Toker posts a video, and it gets hardly 500 views in the first night, but about a few weeks later, it starts to become trending again, and you get a thousand more views.

Judge Yourself

Not to the point, you put yourself down, of course, but realistically judging yourself to keep track of your work is important.

How will this video contribute to your growth?

Is it interesting for people in my own niche?

Why would it be interesting?

What themes can I use to make this better?

If the most popular Tik Toker in my niche saw this, would they be impressed?

Take these things into consideration when you're done with certain Tik Toks.

Follow Guidelines

Especially with the recent 2021 update, you don't want to get on Tik Tok's bad side. Make sure you aren't copying someone else's work on your own profile, as that would really degrade your account.

Funded partnerships may not be as clear to Tik Tok as they are to other social networking sites, but that wouldn't imply that the very same FTC laws do not apply. Tik Tok celebrities are expected to report advertising with a transparent and obvious message that the material is funded or promoted.

Do not, under any circumstance, attempt to get free followers. This will never help you really grow. And it can have really adverse consequences later on if you are serious about Tik Tok as this is seen as a way to steal from Tik Tok. Trying to buy free followers will never get you the triumph you thrive for.

Stitch- The Tik Tok Feature

This adds yet another way for the user to interact with material that is created and posted every day by the creative Tik Tok users. Stitch is a feature the company called which enables a user to put in snippets of another Tik Tok video in yours.

How can you use it?

1. Search for the video you want to stitch and then click on 'Send to'.

2. Click on 'Stitch'

3. You can pull only 5 seconds out of the video, so choose wisely.

4. Make the rest of the video you want to put in with the stitched snippet.

5. Stitch them all together!

In the settings menu, you may select if you want to allow others to stitch your material. This is accessible on the Security and Confidentiality tab underneath "Settings and Privacy." You could allow or remove Stitch for any of your clips. Conversely, this feature can be customized for every clip you post.

Stay Stress-free

Don't try to push out more content forcefully, if your audience sees that you are, they would easily be able to get that your content came from a negative mindset. Keep it fun, enjoy making the clips, actually show your positivity.

Having a healthy mindset further nurtures your creativity and gets your ideas flowing, and you need as much of that as possible. Being authentic with your followers is key.

A few different tactics that have proved effective, such as constructive self-discuss and positive envisioning, can achieve encouraging thought.

Here are a few tactics that would prove beneficial for you to prepare your brain in thinking positively to get you started with generating content.

Concentrate on the good stuff. A part of our life is inconvenient situations and obstacles. Look at the constructive stuff once you're faced with one, regardless of how minor or relatively meaningless they are. You may still discover the ultimate positive aspect of any inconvenience if you search for it, even if it's not readily apparent.

Train with appreciation. Studying kindness has been shown to alleviate depression, boost self-esteem and promote endurance in some very trying situations. Image friends, experiences, or stuff that give you any type of warmth or delight, and struggle to convey your thanks at least once every day. This could be a thank you to a co-worker for assisting with a job, to a significant one for cleaning dishes, or to your cat for the affection they have provided.

Keep a diary of thanks. Research studies have reported that putting down stuff you're thankful for will boost your motivation and your state of wellness. You could do that by writing in a thankful diary daily or by setting down a range of items that you're happy for the days when you're going through a rough time. Using this to generate ideas even if it's really far-fetched should prove useful.

Find your motivation, whether that be intrinsic or extrinsic. You get to create the kind of content you like on Tik Tok, any kind! Use that as your passion and drive to work harder and do better.

Let's take a look at a few Tik Tokers

Daniel here has already made 10 parts of the same category and he still has millions of views. Why? Because he doesn't do the *same thing each* time of course, he changes it up, builds better for the next parts. His idea is original, unique, and entertaining!

But be careful not to overdo it, you can't go making 50 parts of the same theme as that would really just stretch it out too much and no one enjoys a guest who overstays their welcome.

daniel.labelle ✔ Daniel LaBelle

If people lagged. Part 10

♫ original sound - Daniel LaBelle

2.9M

16.3K

50.8K

daniel.labelle Via TikTok

Zach shows a clip of the most absurd idea there is: fishing in your house, using these surprises and then a pattern interrupt which involves him falling into the water really is an odd sight to see though very entertaining and unique.

Because of this, a large number of people shared his video and commented in it to share their thoughts.

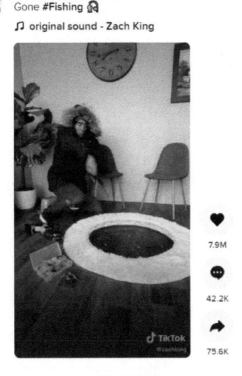

zachking Via TikTok

CHAPTER IV: Instagram

4.1: About You

Instagram is used by everyone in almost every part of the world. It's so popular because Instagram uses imagery rather than text, and people are extra quick to respond to that. It's easier to understand and process visual data rather than heaps of words. And so, visual marketing is blowing up.

The main focus on Instagram is are images. Captions are put out of the way and under the image for that exact reason.

Portrait photography is perhaps the most popular amongst the flock of imageries on Instagram. And most of these images are almost always edited by third-party applications (i.e., Snapseed, VSCO, Adobe Photoshop Express, Polarr).

Not just images, but also Boomerangs, IGTV videos, filters (of which most are created by users), stories, etc. These things push engagement to the front lines.

Naturally, every time Instagram's algorithm changes, it impacts every person who accesses it. You need to make sure you aren't going against the current of those waves. Because the fact is that their algorithm is constantly judging posts all over the globe and deciding which users can see each moment they open the app.

Instagram's algorithm works on machine learning, which makes the way your posts are ranked constantly changing. This book has the most recent details about how to deal with the algorithm to push you further in the marketing campaign and to keep developing engagement with your followers.

Ever since Instagram halted the inverted response in 2016, each specific feed on the site has been arranged as per the algorithm's guidelines.

As per the official @creators handle of Instagram, this concluded in a pleasant result for everybody. Basically, saying they won't be changing it back.

4.2: Ranking Factors

Genre/Niche

Design your account, configure it in a way people can know precisely what they can expect from you. After which, you post intriguing content that your audience will enjoy instantly. If people have liked those kinds of posts before, the system is much more likely to display them.

For example, Let's say Steven came in contact with a verified account. He will probably see more posts from that account, especially if he saw more content from there.

Simply put, users who communicate with content similar to yours are probably going to come across your account as well.

Timing

Recent posts are always going to be recommended more than others. So, just like Tik Tok, posting in timing when your followers are normally active is vital.

People who spend over an hour scrolling on Instagram are obviously going to see numerous kinds of posts from top to bottom compared to someone who spends hardly a few minutes will only see only the top-ranked ones.

Instagram portrays the best at the top of users' feed every time the user activates the application. So, someone who follows hundreds of thousands of accounts will most likely miss a fair number of posts from people they are even really close to.

Engaging Your Audience

Just like every other social media platform, Instagram wishes for users to stay on the app as much and as long as possible as long as they are interested. As an end result, the software cranks up profiles in which the followers are already conversing. This guarantees that the stress on community participation is essential for advertisers and developers.

Credits: mavsocial.com

Sliding in DMs, tagging one another in blogs, and consistently posting comments all are acts that imply a strong bond among users as well as likes, shares, and views.

4.3: What You Need to Do

Pay Attention.

Seeing your Instagram stats is, perhaps shockingly, a few of the easiest ways to get insight into not only how your viewers think but also how the application looks at you.

Could you send everyone much of the same, or twists on the subject? Will they want better photos or videos? Just how many views come from hashtags? What kind of content is going to wow the audience?

Insights tell you did well, so it's up to you to work out where to run from that performance.

Keep It Coming

Some type of involvement, and figuring out where the intended crowd is. To have a grip on the Instagram algorithm, you have to create bonds with your followers first. And because the volume is simple to compute and accomplish than performance, the first item on the agenda is to create a social media posting schedule to stay on track.

What is consistency? Mean for Instagram? This is exclusive to your niche. As you just started, start with the way you want to progress. Think about what's affordable for the team to create.

If you draw viewers with a spark, three stories, two posts, and one IGTV video per day produced a certain amount of perception. Volume and layout selections would depend on the resources you currently have. And what's most critical, however, is to concentrate on publishing posts that you feel proud of regularly.

Reposting is Key.

Even after you have a nice schedule, you're following and knowing what your followers expect, pushing content out into the world isn't simple like butter on jam. Recycle, change-up your best work. Now, not only do you know Instagram wants it, but it also saves a lot of time.

You could transform the videos to gifs, similar pictures to a slideshow, and use pictures used in another photo shoot for multiple reasons, throwbacks, and repost on stories.

Just use the same thing but be extra creative with it.

Collaborating with Other Influencers & Brands

Keep an eye on what other public figures in your niche are up to, and if possible, try to do a collab with them.

Perhaps the easiest way to naturally broaden your scope to fresh eyes is to seek a suitable friend with a complimentary following while still attracting the viewers' interest with appropriate different perspectives. The outcome may very well provide an added strength from Instagram if the partnership is as enjoyable for your community as it would be for you.

Though you need to make sure that the person you choose to partner with is suitable and legitimate, as other influencers will judge you based on who you collab with, it is probably best if you do a detailed background check before setting a collab date with them.

As that influencer will be bringing in their audience, you need to see what kind of followers they have and their analytics. Making sure you don't bring in the wrong crowd who would go away as soon as they came. You could check this by looking at their engagement on posts. If the person you are intending to collab with is genuine and interactive with his/her audience, you should probably go for it.

As searching through every single person, you could collab with would take a significant amount of time, you could use means like Ninjaoutreach, Meltwater, GroupHigh, Newswire, Cision Communications Cloud, etc. This software allows you to make your listing in its database, making things a lot more convenient for you as time is, in fact, of the essence.

The kinds of sponsorships you could get fall into three basic categories: large accounts (120K followers) get at least $400 per sponsored post, middle-class (3K-100K followers) get at least $150, and small accounts (less than 3K) get around $100 or less.

After making a list of the sponsorships you'd like to go for, you need to send each one your pitch. But not in the first text, of course, that would be not polite. Tell them why you're interested in the subject they put out and communicate with them. Once you know what they want exactly, you could develop an amazing pitch.

Next, you need to plan your influencer publicizing campaign. Make sure you keep interacting with the influencers so you can get an insight into what they think. Consider other people's opinions to make a master plan using the influencers and your creativity.

As soon as you have initiated your campaign, please keep track of how it's doing and keep adjusting it accordingly.

An example:

@omayazein partnered up with a brand called Modanisa and gave her audience a discount code, which in turn gets a lot of shares, and she has about 1 Million followers!

@omayazein Via Instagram

Reward Them

As discussed before, Instagram values engagement A LOT, so give your audience what they want! When your audience shares your posts on story or DM, comments and likes push your posts to the top instantly.

The goal should be to create a kind of commitment and passion that motivates individuals to advocate and empower themselves. The service could do the job for you if you already have an outstanding Business-to-consumer service. Anything other than that, you would need to find means of subtly encouraging individuals.

Please stop posting everything sent to you from your community. Compile the latest and integrate material into the digital plan of your content whenever appropriate. And bear in mind that merely reposting the stories of other users has also been specifically noted as something that would not include your stories on the Explore List, so make sure you remain imaginative and on topic.

Like your followers' and viewers' comments, reply to each one, even the haters. Try getting into a conversation with them. Interact with them through stories, polls, use trending filters.

Ask questions on your stories and share them, be humorous, genuine, everything and anything interesting. It could be 'what's your opinion on....' Or 'what's your most embarrassing story!', etc.

If they reply to your stories, make sure you reply!! And not after days at a time, but as soon as you can. Enjoy your time with them. Really try and understand what they wish to see from you. Unless they're just there to hate on you, then you should probably ignore it or if you could do something creative with it (while following community guidelines), go for it.

Follow influencers that are familiar with your niche. This can link other people that are interested in your type of content to you. Not just follow, but also like and comment on their posts, share it!

(Another way of utilizing the Shine theory). Showing interest in other people's content can help you too.

Use the Hashtag System

Just like Tik Tok, hashtags are an important part of Instagram. It is the middleman between you and the right audience. It's the lowest building block, especially when you're just starting out.

If you think using heaps of hashtags, including ones that do not correlate with your niche, will help, you might be wrong. It would be misusing the hashtag system, and that leads you to a direct road to the bad side of Instagram because they do, in fact, notice those who try abusing the algorithm. And not to mention, you are not gaining anything by trying to show it to people who have no interest in your niche.

The maximum quantity of hashtags you are allowed to use is 30 per post, and yes, use all those 30. Try writing those hashtags in the first comment rather than in the caption, so it looks a bit more well put together.

Perhaps not all hashtags that you assume are nice would be suitable for your own use. It is why every last one of you would want to verify to see whether the material is important to your subject.

When deciding whether a hashtag is right for your post, there are two key considerations to have a look at Niche and Dimension.

Never use only the most famous and vague hashtags, thinking you would be able to reach a larger crowd because you won't. You'll just be a hidden needle in a haystack. An invisible need at that. Why?

Because they aren't specific enough, and a lot of popular influencers already use those so you wouldn't be too noticed yet.

Please make sure you have certain hashtags that you use in every post (with fewer follows) so that you can be noticed by at least one familiar audience (needless to say, they need to be your target audience too).

It would be best if you would be able to find a middle ground between hashtags that not one soul has ever heard of before and hashtags that everyone knows about. Both would reward you little. Try hashtags that have about 90,000-900,000 post range.

Sorry, But Buying Is NOT the Way to Go

You can purchase double-taps or follows in due to despair just to see whether a lift is what they needed to get moving all along. But while this may make you appear popular to random people; it couldn't be farther from the facts.

Finally, they consider giving up both as a waste of time on Instagram and stop bringing in any considerable effort to expand, since they just do not see what else there is to do. Don't purchase likes, fans, and also, don't try the old trick of interaction pods.

Yes, even Instagram notices it if you buy followers/likes/views. Not only Instagram but also your followers. Which makes things a lot worse. And so, you won't gain any kind of income from that.

Using Highlights

Utilize the highlights feature and make/or find suitable cover photos for each to maintain consistency. It is making a profile that's pleasing to the eye and fitting for your niche and target audience.

4.4: Seeing is Believing

You may think this is all talk and no action, so let's drive that notion away by looking at a few of the many influencers on Instagram.

Notice the overall layout of this account. The username and profile instantly tell the users what the account is about.

Just the username would do this for us too but @wedarkacademia further described what it was about as well as threw in a bit of personality to the description as well as handles for other social platforms.

Their posts are consistent and related to one another. See the Highlights categorized neatly too.

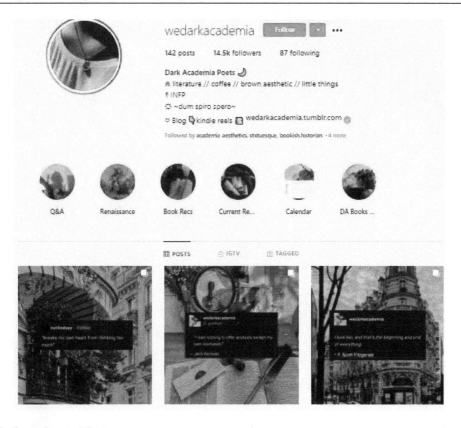

@wedarkacademia Via Instagram

Responses like these encourage so much growth and engagement amongst the target audience.

@jonnajinton Via Instagram

@madeyemoodswing interacting with their audience. Their username being humorous and instantly getting the attention of Harry Potter fans who understand the reference.

Drawing in users of various kinds though if @madeyemoodswing doesn't involve any kind of Harry Potter related content, those fans may lose interest.

@madeyemoodswing Via Instagram

Jonna Jinton, blogging her art, photography and life on Instagram whilst also mentioning that she works on another platform (YouTube). Her posts are coherent and in sync with nature and mostly winter in her home country.

Her description and highlights are simple and straight to the point which a lot of users would find convenient and contemporary.

@jonnajinton Via Instagram

CHAPTER V: Ideas for Newbies

5.1: Idea Generation

There is not much to implement without ideas, and since the implementation is the secret to progress, creative ideas are required to enable some sort of change. It is clear that thoughts alone are not going to make creativity possible, since you need to be able to construct a structured mechanism to handle such innovations. The concept is not only about producing lots of it but also about bringing care to the nature of it.

It's not easy to create grade A content 24/7. Often people find it difficult to break out of their usual routine and habits when thinking about working on something new. In order to get out of the negative spiral, you need to glance at the development of creativity altogether and incorporate a few of the most key factors, strategies, and procedures that could be used more routinely to produce fresh concepts.

Perhaps you need original thoughts so a new possibility can be thoroughly explored?

Maybe you are trying to find a new way of solving a creativity barrier, or are you hoping for a decent answer to the dilemma?

Why does it matter?

Generating ideas is the outcome of creating complex, tangible, or conceptual theories. It's at the top of the funnel for concept organization, which works on seeking potential alternatives to true or suspected challenges and possibilities.

Ideas are, as stated, the very first move into change. Fresh theories rely on you progressing as independent individuals. From the point of view of a person, whether you feel stuck with a job or otherwise unable to resolve that one dilemma, fresh solutions will motivate you to push ahead.

The aim of fresh concepts is to reinforce the manner in which you work, irrespective of your priorities or the kinds of things you're searching for.

To fuel productivity and improve nature on a broader scale, societies rely on creativity. Creativity improves emerging innovations and enterprises. They are providing creators with more opportunities.

How do you do it?

Chances are, you brainstorm. However, it's been found that brainstorming requires more time and tends to fewer ideas as of planning, logging, and managing the meeting would take a lot more time than it should. While there are certain approaches to boost the quality of brainstorming, it's preferred if brainstorming isn't your first thought.

Nevertheless, certain methods are worth taking a look at. As you're searching for various kinds of ideas, it is beneficial to have methods in mind that help in developing them. Several of these concept development approaches may be used for further productive brainstorming and another creativity type.

5.2: The Techniques

Challenging proposals

This concept is when you bring an issue or opportunity into view due to the possibility of innovatively solving it. It can let you make a certain doubt about your content and aim it at your audience to get more ideas and useful opinions after you have identified what you intend to gain from it.

These idea challenges come in handy, especially when you're looking to engage a large audience of up to 10000. When you plan an idea challenge, pre-define the outcomes you'd like, the niche, followers, subscribers, etc. Make sure you keep track of the time with this technique to make sure it's working.

Similarities

You can use data and statistics from previous posts or videos on social media platforms to improve on ideas for another piece of content; this is thinking simultaneously. It is the simplest way of generating fresh content as it's often experimented with and succeeded.

In Example, YouTuber's making reaction videos continually but of various kinds of content.

SCAMPER

This method applies critical thinking to alter creativity, which is already present—adjusting open-source ideas to improve and agree on the best answer.

1. Substitution – Your old content being substituted with others to gain improvement.

2. Combining- Merging two or more ideas into one master idea for your content.

3. Adapting- Evaluates the options to make a method more versatile and works on the design, system, or principle alongside other related gradual changes.

4. Modification- From a broader context, changing not only the concept but also changing the concept looks at the challenge or potential and tries to change the outcomes.

5. Improvising by putting to another use- Searching for opportunities to use the concept or current content for some other reason and, if applicable to other areas of your profile or channel, analyzes the potential advantages.

6. Elimination- This technique studies all the possibilities, and if you find more than one fragment was removed.

7. Reversal- The emphasis of this procedure is to reverse the order of factors that can be swapped of your idea.

This technique was originated from the idea of brainstorming, but it applies to your thinking technique too. If you make generating ideas a daily activity by a series of trivial things, you could have a decent chance of winning the main breakthrough. Occasionally all it takes is really to reflect on what you already have. Sometimes, creators want to worry about the next remarkable thing being discovered. It is easy to overlook that the endless gradual changes are the aspects that can have a difference in the medium haul while creating fresh concepts. As a baseline, utilizing your existing theories or methods will explain a lot in relation to your present content, and that is what the SCAMPER strategy is really about.

Reverse Psychology

This method will make you challenge your content-related perceptions. Reverse thinking comes in handy when you feel you are trapped in the traditional mentality, and it appears to be impossible to come up with such unique ideas. It helps in checking our routinely-habits as the answer to finding more content isn't always a straight-to-the-point road. You consider the possibilities of what the opposite would do for your profile or channel, even if you end up thinking of the most peculiar of solutions.

5.3: Once You've Got It

Organizing Ideas

Once you've got all those ideas down, planning and organizing them can be difficult if you don't know where to start. Creators need to collect this creativity as soon as it comes to them instead of using it as soon as it comes up.

Jotting down all your ideas in a notebook or on your phone can be helpful, and most people do this as it's only for personal use. But if you wish for other people's opinions on the matter to know their judgment, this could be a hassle. Not to worry though, there are things like idea management tools to aid you with that.

Management

A concept tool for effective functions as the foundation of the method of idea planning. This is how you can assemble the ideas, analyze them, debate, prioritize them, take account of their success, and the overall course of the operations of your idea generation.

Since concept planning is such a huge subject and famous influencers or public figures are likely to have loads of suggestions, it often makes perfect sense for most influencers or creators to use a designated idea management system.

It is just as productive to handle ideas with a designated method as the underlying mechanism at the back end. You could create a mechanism that makes it a lot easier to produce and refine fresh concepts and create ideas a persistent practice. The methods that are too confusing can infuriate people, so try not to make things too difficult.

5.4: Winning at Creativity

The Appropriate Crowd

It is necessary to include the right individuals in the equation for the content to be as efficient as possible. Start engaging all influencers who know about the content creation and are sincerely involved in you making a difference.

Ensure your community is the target audience and well educated on the topic if the aim is to involve a wider community of users to produce ideas.

Determine Your Objective

Aim to collect as much relevant data as possible about the content you wish to make before you begin to understand the source. Define what you understand about it by now and what data is still required.

Though it sounds simple, the further you can clearly explain your actual idea, the greater the odds of producing practical ideas are.

Limits to Keep an Eye Out For.

It can impede imagination to convey that every idea is a valid idea, so ensure the aims are ambitious and precise enough. One approach to get some of the viewers' genuinely innovative thoughts is to set limits.

If the ultimate aim is to cut prices, suggestions such as investing truly little on content would certainly come to mind when you want to save up. The thoughts you get, though, would vary greatly if you ask yourself: "How could I save 50% on expenses and create unique and engaging content?".

Deduction

The goal of creating original approaches is to improve what is already present as well as to produce something new.

From a different angle, coming up with entirely novel solutions will help you tackle your creativity block. It helps you to widen the spectrum of thoughts beyond the present style of learning, which inevitably leads to much more ideas.

Sometimes, creators, influencers, and public figures use current ideas or behavioral templates while attempting to get started on a social media platform instead of attempting to think of the latest ideas. The concern with this technique is that it does not encourage you to pursue multiple options and limits the number of possibilities.

5.5: About Yourself

Who are you?

Create a clip of yourself being introduced. Who are you, what are you doing? On your YouTube channel, Tik Tok, or Instagram profile, what should viewers hope to see? How frequently do you upload photos or videos? Create videos to let them know exactly what they should expect, inviting viewers to your channel or page. Aim to give a convincing argument for audiences to click on the subscribe button on YouTube and follow on Instagram or Tik Tok.

Vlogging

Making Vlogs can be informative, fun, intimate, anything you would like to create of it, much like traditional writing. Almost all influencers and public figures may use material from vlogs to involve fans and expand their communities.

A Day in Your Life

YouTubers love to walk through The Day in your Life videos from another's perspective. Once you wake up the next morning and lead audiences to a normal day in your schedule, start filming.

Matt D'Avella Via YouTube

Behind-the-curtain Content

Showcase to the viewers what's going on at the back end of your Instagram account, YouTube channel, or Tik Tok account. With this famous video style, let your audience see behind the curtains. You can display your room, your house, your workplace, your city, anywhere else you enjoy.

20 Questions

You could make short clips or long clips (depending on your preference or niche) playing a game of 20 questions. These questions can be personal or silly, and the best have a little bit of both. Letting your audience be closer to you is what this accomplishes.

'Draw My Life.'

These kinds of videos are often found on YouTube, where the creator essentially draws their life often on a whiteboard with stick figures and narrating their life so far. Of course, you decide how much or how little you wish to say about yourself. Majority 'Draw my life' videos include key events or milestones in their lives.

You can even introduce your family, background, and friends in these.

5.6: Trending Content Ideas

Teach them How to Cook (or how not to)

This kind of content is often made by entertainment-focused or cooking influencers. You can make it an A grade cooking tutorial, or you could completely twist it depending on your creativity and teach people how not to cook but let them have an enjoyable time watching creators do it wrong.

For example, YouTuber 'Simply Nailogical' made a video called 'Baking a cake with Nail Polish' on 18th September 2016, which got over 5 Million views. The cake was quite inedible but still entertaining to watch to over 5 Million people.

You can make this an Instagram post, a Tik-Tok video, or a YouTube video.

Workout Routine

As it's time to start working out, lots of folks look towards YouTube videos, quick Tik Tok hacks, or Instagram posts/IGTV videos for specific fitness routines, as well as how to do those workouts. Both common subjects are exercise, stretching, or shape footage.

Understanding the Complicated Mess

Informative and aurally captivating means of presenting data and figures that could otherwise be dull or difficult to grasp is infographics related content. Content that helps your audience's day a little easier. Every genre of content has specific things that not everyone understands, so try finding the most commonly found problem in yours and present content on that!

Reviewing other People's Products

One of the most common kinds of information on these social media platforms is product reviews. Before deciding to buy, thousands of viewers check out this insightful content. Tech gadgets and make-up items are common themes, but reviews can be sought for all types of goods.

For example, YouTuber Marques Brownlee's Niche is tech gadgets, and a majority, maybe even all, of his video's reviews on really expensive gadgets so often people who think about buying a new phone or the PS5 watch his videos to see his opinion on it. His video called 'PlayStation 5 Review: NextGen Gaming!' received almost 6 Million views!

You can make review videos on any and every genre of content! Games, movies, books, food, universities, perfumes, songs, shows, even countries! So, search for things you can review in your niche.

Comedy Videos

In the event that you need to turn into a web sensation, an entertaining video may very well assist you with getting there. A sizable number of the most mainstream recordings on YouTube, Instagram, and Tik Tok ended up in such a state since this sort of content made watchers chuckle or laugh.

Pranks

Viewers love watching tricks. Pull a trick on somebody (innocuous tricks, please) and share the outcomes on your social media platforms.

Tricks have not been altogether contemplated; however, scientists have discovered that individuals find being deceived an extremely aversive encounter. Trick based humor can be coldblooded or kind, cherished or detested; however, it's not straightforward.

Furry Creatures Content

Dogs, little cats, child elephants, the Internet loves charming/interesting creature recordings are considerably more popular than recordings of human children. So, if you have a pet, share it with the world! Everyone loves animals.

Music Videos

Singing a song cover, and original, or even lip-syncing is always a fun sight to see. Indeed, even late-night TV gets in on the good times. Pick a mainstream tune and give it a shot!

If you have a bad voice, don't worry; try making it hilarious by a funny parody where you impress the audience with clever and witty lyrics rather than your vocals.

Fact Check

What are some myths that are commonly believed by the vast majority regarding your niche? Compile all the misconceptions and make a post or video on the matter. Show emotion and teach your audience the stereotypes believed about your niche by the public.

As the internet is filled with so much information, a fair share of it is fake news, so spreading awareness about it would be intriguing for your audience (as long as you stay on topic).

Often people are found spreading rumors without even knowing they are rumors and not facts, so content that addresses the rumors is an interesting concept for anyone.

Needless to say, double-check whether the information you are giving your audience is proven with evidence to be right. Or else those mistakes can decrease your followers/subscribers quick.

Write a catchy caption or thumbnail with a question that quickly catches their interest. For example, '10 Myths you probably believed about professional cooks' or '6 reasons why you should not believe every thing you're told'.

Speed-run

Can you play games as fast as humanely possible? Finish your make-up in under 2 minutes? Or maybe you can make a 3-course meal in under an hour? Show off those skills on social media!

Speed-runs are commonly found on gaming channels so viewers can quickly experience a gameplay without having to play it themselves due to the cost of the game or less time of time.

Time-slip

@jonnajinton Via Instagram on April 17th , 2020

Time-lapse is a method where the casings of the video are caught at a far slower speed than expected. Traffic, mists, and the sunrise all will, in general, be well-known time-slip by subjects. The outcome is frequently hypnotizing.

Some creators make time-lapses of their artwork to show progress quickly as an art piece can take at least a few hours.

Shopping/Mail Hauls

This type of video is particularly well known with style vloggers and beauty. After an outing to the shopping center, flaunt your take piece by piece. From the freshest iPhone to an in-vogue membership box or the most trending toy, individuals love to watch others open boxes. So next time you do another package, don't simply tear into it; make sure you are recording first!

You could even give out your address and your audience would send you mail. Often YouTubers make mail opening videos reviewing all the heartfelt gifts their watchers send them.

Go Live

Why trust that the recap will show individuals what's happened? Take your watchers to the occasion with you by live-streaming to your Instagram Live, Tik Tok Live, or YouTube Live. Even after the session is over, the stream would still be accessible online.

You can schedule a certain day for every week in which you go live and make sure you let everyone know through all your social media platforms, so they are aware and wait for you to go live.

What Most Do

A substantial number of the top Instagrammers are singers, sports brands, actors, footballers, models, and of course, Instagram themselves. The most famous YouTuber channels are often among the genre of trailer channels, singers, gamers, kids show, hack tutorial channels, and so on. Tik Tokers are often found to be comedians, musicians, artists, etc.

The best content? Ones that are so good that people feel the need to see it on other platforms too, Tik Tok video compilations on YouTube, and Tik Tok videos on Instagram, Live videos on Instagram recorded and put-on YouTube. The type of content that is put across various platforms are the ones that have gone viral or loved enough that users wish to see it almost everywhere.

Conclusion

First things first, it would be beneficial if you ask yourself, what do you have to offer? Why would people want to watch your videos? What are they getting out of the time they spent on your video?

Is it educational? Hilarious? Scary? Relaxing? Silly? Helpful? Inspiring or motivational? Perhaps very random, either way, would your target audience enjoy or show any interest in it?

Maintain originality- the charm of social media is that you can express your thoughts and add a little more to *you*, so to speak. You can grow on YouTube, Tik Tok, and Instagram, only if you have something no one else has to give out. The basic rule to starting a business, 'what's so special about you?' or 'what do you have that no one else does?'. Write down all that comes to mind when answering these questions.

You can not copy peoples' ideas, only your own significant expression of those ideas into your videos, posts, stories, etc. However, if your content seems to be matching someone else's a little too much, change it up, brainstorm a little about what you could do to make it unique, and choose the best one. And be certain you aren't tuning out any other possibilities due to your fears.

Honesty- be honest about your opinions and where you stand. This can be a random video about car reviews or your opinion on white supremacy; it need not matter. Maybe you feel like changing your genre after a long time, but you're afraid of losing the number of followers/subscribers you've gotten so far. Your fear is valid, but you can't force yourself to put out content on something you have no more interest in anymore because you followers/subscriber will notice eventually, and they'll just fade out on their own. So, try being honest, raw, and authentic from the start.

However, being honest does not amount to being insensitive. You're trying to be the person people look up to or look forward to viewing when they're having a difficult day, so try to fill those expectations without disregarding your bad days, of course. Ending things on a positive note and be accepting of the honest truth your followers/subscribers/viewers offer in return.

Humility- Try not to overthink each comment they make because what seems like an hour of thought to you was probably not more than five minutes to them. When you start noticing your growth, don't become egotistic about it, or the people that put you where you are today will leave as fast as they came. Nobody likes a showoff.

Setting boundaries- deciding where you draw the line between your public and personal life is vital. You don't need to broadcast every minute detail about your personal life to the entire world, and you need to value the privacy of the people close to you if you wish for the same.

Motivation- find that mechanism that triggers, leads, and retains your aiming habits. Whether it be intrinsic or extrinsic motivation, keep a daily reminder for it, so you keep that drive and motivation to continue working hard. Grabbing a coffee, chocolate bar, reading, or some inspirational quote is what puts you in a nice mood and sparks wisdom, do it every day.

The physical, internal, cultural, and mental factors which trigger action are involved in motivation. Introjected motivation is when you are driven to work out of the guilt of procrastination or laziness. Identified motivation is when you know you have got work to do, yet you haven't determined anything in regard to it. Try to avoid introjected and identified motivation as it originates from a negative space.

Don't give up if you feel like you are not getting enough growth, stay consistent and keep at it no matter what. If you still feel like there has been no effect, try going over the points again and make sure you keep track of how you have been doing by statistically analyzing yourself.

Soon enough, you will catch yourself with 10,000 followers/subscribers on YouTube, Instagram, and Tik Tok. It is more or less a smooth ride from there. Good Luck!

Short Stays Real Estate with No (or Low) Money Down

The 7+1 Creative Strategies to Create Passive Income from Home Using the AirBnb Business Model in 2021

By

NESPY ONLINE MARKETING

Contents

Introduction

If you are a forward-focused person, you can dream of leaving the profession to enjoy a retirement life that is simpler, or you might even consider early retirement. But a dream is only a wish without a plan. You need to contemplate passive income to put a few wheels on the dream. There are also plenty of different options for passive income and rationales of how to build it. Passive income is the money you collect that doesn't cause you to do a lot of "active" work in order to continue to earn it. In essence, you may do much of the work in advance and do some extra effort to earn an income. For instance, to keep the money flowing, if you develop an online course, you only need to update the content. Likewise, passive income strategies like renting out property and/or building a blog can take some effort to get up and running, but while you sleep, they would eventually earn you cash. You've already heard the word, "make money when you're sleeping." This is the main attraction that allows individuals to generate passive income. Even when you're not working, you can develop something (a course, a blog, e-book, videos, and/or an online store) which generates income. Or you can own something that helps you to earn passive income (property or stocks).

So why do you need to build passive income?

In the presence of a full-time job, your salary is your biggest income tool, a tool that usually requires your active involvement. Even if you enjoy your career, you wouldn't mind making some additional money without the tears, blood, sweat, and time commitment of another job. If you lose your job or want to generate an extra source of income when you are no longer productive or if you outlive your retirement fund, developing a passive income will improve your wealth-building strategy, create the opportunity to retire early, and save you from a total loss of income.

And how much money can passive income generate?

Generally, passive income won't make you wealthy overnight, so ignore those get-rich-quick schemes you've read about. But, over the long term, consistent, profitable passive income strategies will produce some serious money. Depending on the income stream, we're talking about anything from two to three thousand dollars to thousands of dollars.

Some people like to think of investing when we mention "passive income" because, with the least amount of effort, it can yield the greatest returns. But you should think about your retirement plan & passive income as two distinct subjects. The entire premise behind the long-term investment is to produce retirement income. If your fund options are good and they offer a match, you want to make sure you invest in your company retirement plan, like that of a 401(k). These are great choices for establishing a powerful pension plan, but before a certain age, you will face taxes as well as penalties for every withdrawal. You need to let your money grow only for the long term with retirement planning and not touch it. However, a form of low-effort income which can be accessed at any time should be passive income. After you are debt-free and have some cash left, one way to build passive income is by buying real estate and leasing it out to tenants. Rental property may be a fantastic source of additional income, but it is not the most passive option because, unless you employ a property management company, you will have to put a lot of effort and time into maintaining the property. You need to be in charge of your property if you go on the rental property route. Pay off your own home first before you buy a rental property, and buy your investment property with cash. You must not go into debt in order to purchase property for rent. You could develop something like an informative blog and/or a YouTube tutorial series to be able to generate online traffic if you have a bright idea that appeals to a particular audience. You might sell commercial space on your blog or ad spots on your channel if your content is engaging and it sees ample regular traffic. You can sit back, relax, and reap sources of passive income after you put in the heavy lifting. The list of ideas for passive income could go on indefinitely. Never go for any passive income strategies that promise a fast return or require large sums of money upfront. Your other financial targets would be sabotaged by them. In this book, we will present ideas that are steady, profitable, and trustworthy.

CHAPTER 1: Understand Income and Importance of Passive Income

There are three main categories of income:

Active income

Portfolio income

Passive income

1.1 Active Income

Active income alludes to money made as a result of the provision of service. Examples of active income are wages, tips, salaries, fees, and income from companies in which there is material involvement. The owner must meet the criteria for "material participation," which is based on hours worked or other factors, in order for income from a company to be considered active rather than passive. The most popular example of active income is income earned in the form of a paycheck from an employer. "Money from business activities is deemed "active" for the self-employed or someone else with an ownership interest in a corporation if it meets the criteria of material participation by the Internal Revenue Service (IRS). That implies one of the following is valid, at least:

- The taxpayer works during the year in the corporation for 500 or more hours.
- The taxpayer performs the majority of the company's work.
- Over the year, the taxpayer works for more than 100 hours in the company and no other employee works more hours than the taxpayer.

However, income earned is treated as passive income if someone earns income from a company in which they do not actively participate. Meanwhile, portfolio income is income from investments, like dividends and capital gains. Depending on the legislation at the time, these various forms of income can be taxed differently. At present, for instance, portfolio income is taxed at lower rates than active income.

Example of active income from a business

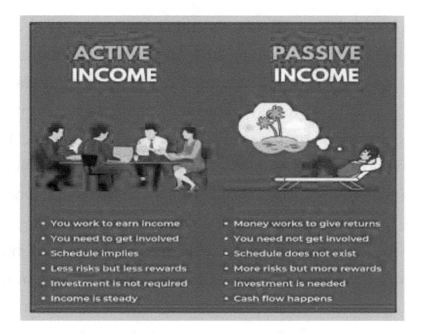

John and Laura are not married to each other. They have a 50% interest in an online business. John performs the majority of the day-to-day work in the business. Therefore, his income is considered active by the IRS. On the other, Laura helps with the marketing activities. She, however, works less than 100 hours a year in the business. It is for this very reason that her income from the business is considered passive income by the IRS. The material participation rule was established to prevent individuals that do not actively participate in a business from using it to generate tax losses which they, otherwise, could have written off against their active income.

1.2 Portfolio Income

Income from the portfolio is money received from investments, interest, dividends, and capital gains. Portfolio income streams are often known to be dividends received from investment properties. It is one of three main income groups. Active income and passive income are the others. Most income from the portfolio enjoys favorable tax treatment. Dividends and capital gains are charged at a much lower rate as compared to active income. Furthermore, portfolio income is not subject to Medicare or Social Security taxes. Income from the portfolio contains dividends, interest, and capital gains. Compared to active or passive income, portfolio income typically enjoys favorable tax treatment. Money from the portfolio is not subject to withholding from Social Security or Medicaid. One way to maximize portfolio income is to invest in an ETF that purchases dividend-paying stocks. Income from the portfolio does not come from passive investments. Moreover, portfolio income is not received from daily business activity. It is earned because of dividends, taxes, and capital gains or interest paid on loans. For tax purposes, the categories of income are important. Passive income losses can not necessarily be offset against portfolio or active income.

Ways to Increase Portfolio Income

Following ways can be employed for increasing portfolio income:

Purchase High-Paying Dividend Stocks

Investors can enhance their portfolio income by purchasing stocks that pay above-average dividends. Dividends can be paid directly to the shareholder. Moreover, dividends can also be used to buy additional shares in the company.

Purchase Dividend Exchange-Traded Funds

A cost-effective way to maximize portfolio income is to buy ETFs that explicitly track high-paying dividend stocks. For example, the FTSE High Dividend Yield Index is tracked by the Vanguard High Dividend Yield ETF. There are 396 stocks that have high dividend yields and are included in the index. For other dividend ETF options, the selection criteria concentrate on how many consecutive years the company has paid a dividend and/or on companies that have a history of raising their annual dividend payments.

Write Options

An investor can write call options against their stock holdings to enhance his portfolio income.

1.3 Passive Income

Passive income are earnings that come from a limited partnership, rental property, or another enterprise in which an entity is not actively engaged, such as a silent investor. Proponents of passive income tend to be boosters of the working lifestyle of a work-from-home and/or be-your-own-boss. Colloquially, it has been used on the part of the person receiving it to describe money being earned periodically with little or no effort. When used as a technical term, passive income is defined by the IRS as either "net rental income" or "income from an enterprise in which the taxpayer does not participate materially" and may include self-charged interest in some cases. Passive income is a source of income that may require some initial effort or investment but continues to generate payments in the future. Examples are music and book royalties and house rent payments. Passive income is the return on savings accounts. Passive income is created by a limited partnership in which a person owns a share of a company but does not engage in its functioning. Passive income consists of earnings generated from rental property, a limited partnership, or some other enterprise in which a person does not engage actively. Usually, taxes are charged on passive income. Portfolio income is perceived by a few analysts as passive income, and interest and dividends will also be considered as passive income. In order to earn and maintain, passive income needs little to no effort. When an earner puts in one of those little efforts to produce income, it is called progressive passive income. In many ways, a passive income investment can make an investor's life easier. This is true when a hands-off strategy is followed. Examples of passive income investment strategies include - Peer-to-Peer Lending, Real Estate, Dividend Stocks, and Index Funds. These four choices suggest different risk and diversification levels. As with any kind of financial investment, calculating the anticipated returns in relation to a passive income opportunity versus the loss potential is important. The main types of passive activities are explained below:

Cash flows from property income, including cash flows from a property or from any piece of real estate, capital gains, rent through resource ownership such as rental income, and in the form of interest from financial asset ownership.

Trade or business-related activities in which an individual does not engage in a company's operations other than investing during the year.

Royalties, that is, payments initiated by one corporation (the licensee) to another firm/person (the licensor) for the right to use the intellectual property of the latter (music, video, book).

Standards for Material Participation

The standards for material participation include:

- Five hundred plus more hours toward an activity or a business from which you are earning
- If the participation for that tax year has been "substantially all."
- Up to 100 hours of commitment and at least as much as every other person involved in the operation
- Material involvement in at least five of the past 10 tax years
- For personal services initiatives, material engagement at any point in three previous tax years

According to the IRS, there are two passive activity categories. Rentals, including equipment and real estate, are the first type; and businesses are the second type, where the individual does not engage materially on a daily, continuous and significant basis.

Examples of passive activities

The following are considered passive activities:

- Equipment leasing
- Limited partnerships
- Partnerships, S-Corporations, and LLCs where the individuals do not materially participate
- Rental real estate (some exceptions apply)

- Sole proprietorship or farm where the individual does not materially participate

1.4 Taxing of passive income

There are various forms of passive income, ranging from capital gains and dividends. Then the question arises whether the passive income is taxable or not. The brief response is, yes. Tax rates can differ depending on how long the assets are kept, the amount of benefit gained, and/or net income on each form of passive income.

Short-Term Passive Income Tax Rates

For assets retained for a year or less, short-term gains apply and are taxed as ordinary income. In other words, at the same rate as your income tax, short-term capital gains are taxed. The prevailing tax rates for short-term gains are as follows: 10 percent, 12 percent, 22 percent, 24 percent, 32 percent, 35, and 37 percent.

Long-Term Passive Income Tax Rates

Long-term capital gains (assets that are held for more than one year) are taxed at three rates: zero percent, fifteen percent, and twenty percent, based on your income bracket.

Taxing of real estate income

With lower tax rates, investing in real estate and high yield rental assets is now even more advantageous for individuals. The authorized business income deduction is now a twenty percent deduction on the taxable income while buying and holding real estate. This deduction of 20 percent now requires investors to subtract a portion of the real estate investment holdings, which may lead to a higher ROI.

1.5 Why Passive Income Beats Earned Income

income Earned is the income that you earn when you work the job full-time or run a business. Notice that, in most instances, "running business" doesn't require rent real estate corporate. Money gained from royalties, rents, & stakes in the limited partnerships is passive income. Income from the portfolio is the income from interest, dividends, and stock sales capital gains. Earned income would be subject to heavy taxation at all levels. Earned money should be utilized to rapidly create wealth, but your wealth must be transferred into the portfolio and passive income pools in order to reduce your tax position. Earned incomes are subject to FICA taxation and the full marginal income tax rate. There are undoubtedly ways of minimizing tax liability, such as operating an S-earned Corporation's revenue, investing in the firm and currently earning deductible expenditures, etc., but high marginal tax rates would also be subject to net income. The issue with earned money is that you still have to spend more cash in order to minimize tax liability. Passive incomes from the rental property aren't subject to the high operational tax rates. Rental property income is privileged by amortization and depreciation and contributes to a much lesser effective rate of tax.

Let's assume, for instance, you now own a rental property, which nets 10,000 dollars before the depreciation & amortization. Let's just say that $8,000 is the total amount of depreciation and amortization. It leaves with a taxable revenue of $2,000. You can pay a tax equivalent to 740 dollars if you fall in the 37 percent tax bracket. Yet you see an effective rate tax of just 7.4 percent as we equate the $740 with the amount raised ($10,000). If you made the same 10,000 dollars in the earned income, in order to minimize the amount available to tax, you would need to expend more. Otherwise, with $10,000 into taxable income, you'd pay $3,700, meaning you're in 37 percent tax brackets. With the rental real-estate, every year, you don't have to be paying for depreciation. It's a ghostly cost which you have to claim. That's why, from a tax standpoint, passive income knocks out earned income.

1.6 Reasons Why Passive Income Is So Important

It's no wonder passive income's, and for a good cause, one of the most thought about, sought after aspects of personal finance. Passive income will have an incredibly positive effect on only about any financial situation, from creating vast wealth to avoiding a paycheck-to-paycheck lifestyle. But that poses the question: why does passive income matter so much? In short, passive income's essential because in financial life, it provides flexibility, prosperity, and independence. In addition, because your time & resources do not limit passive income, it may have a beneficial and important impact on the ability to build wealth. Passive income, in different words, is 1 of the easiest ways to upgrade the financial condition. But if that's not compelling enough, we've listed the top reasons why passive income's important.

Improved financial stability

One of the most significant milestones you will hit on the road to prosperity is monitory stability. In different words, even if you really can see your financial position and realize, with certainty, that you're capable of coping with a powerful financial storm, so then you're on a very stable path. If you may count on the money rolling inside without having to fight for every cent of it, even more than that, so financial security is just a nearby corner. More money which comes in more you can be secure and comfortable in the finances. It helps you in relaxing, look at the bigger picture, & make smarter financial decisions because you don't have to grind for every dollar you earn, which, in turn, increases your financial health. This is a magnificent little cycle & one of key reasons why passive income is playing such a major role in personal finance.

Less reliance on a paycheck

The discomfort that comes with living paycheck to paycheck is not comparable by any means. And if it is your case, then one of the best moves you can take is to add a bit of the passive income in your life. There is no secret in that sometimes it may get a bit stressful as you trade time for dollars. And the more you will distance yourself from a focus on the next paycheck, the lighter it can be in your life. One of the greatest advantages of passive income is avoiding the paycheck-to-paycheck lifestyle.

It's easier to achieve your goals

Did you ever say to yourself, " only If I made extra money, then I could accomplish my monetary goals much more quickly..."? Well, that's just another explanation why the passive income's so awesome. It doesn't what financial targets you're trying to attain; you can accomplish your goals much quicker if you build certain passive income sources that enable you to make money all the time of day.

More freedom to pursue your passions

You will unexpectedly find yourself with the opportunity to pursue your passions or, for that matter, your ideal job, along the same line as avoiding the paycheck to the paycheck lifestyle, while you get some of the passive income flowing through the bank account. Remember that it's easy to end up trapped in a position you can't bear when you focus on the active income to make ends meet. It is tough enough to leave a career. But it is particularly tough to leave a job if you don't have sufficient money to pay the rent that is due in two weeks. On the other hand, you have the opportunity to do the things you really want to do when you have a stable stream of passive income running into the finances of yours. Passive income, to put plainly, offers you choices. & with those choices, independence comes.

Location independence

Likewise, in many ways, passive income encourages you to live and working from anywhere you like. Since you don't have to work constantly to earn a passive income, so you don't have to be working from a particular position either. You could tour the world if you like, as far as you earn passive income sufficient to support your lifestyle. And plenty of people do.

Early retirement

Retirement is, to some degree, for many people, that may only be done later in life. Although, if you're building any passive income sources, retirement may not be far away as you thought. Really, if you love the thought of retirement at a young age, so then your primary financial priority should be passive income. If it means creating a company that operates even without you needing to be present there, participating in real estate, or a mix of few different sources of income, if you desire to stop working at a young age, passive income is necessary.

More financial margin

 more financial margins you will build in life, better off you will be in personal finance. In different words, the more distance you've between the expenditures & your income, the better it will get for financial life. And when you produce a constant stream of the passive income per month, it becomes much simpler to build the financial margin. Let's say, for instance, that your monthly gross expenditures increase up to 3,000 dollars. Now, if you're earning $4,000 inactive household revenue, then the monthly margin is $1,000. Yeah, that's not bad. However, if you add an additional $2,000 in passive monthly income in to the mix, life just got a lot better.

Reduced stress

There's one unity between all, after everything we've spoken about so far. It's plain; passive revenue has a distinctive way to reduce the financial burden. A passive income life is considerably less difficult than a life deprived of it. Because your financial security, margin, independence, and too much more are improved by passive income, it's only logical that it will help alleviate your financial burden. So, if financial condition makes you feel a little tightened around the collar, you may just want to give passive income a little more priority.

It's exciting

Passive income is not constrained by the effort and time that you can put into it. In different words, at all the hours of night and day, passive income can be earned, including while you are sleeping. Yet, at the same time, making money is incredibly thrilling. There's nothing like waking up in the morning thinking that you've won a few hundred bucks while you're sleeping. And the more you are enthusiastic about the financial condition, the more probable you are to continue to improve it.

CHAPTER 2: Passive income ideas to help you make money in 2021

Passive income may be a wonderful way of helping you produce more cash flow, & global upheaval created primarily by the pandemic is evidence of the importance of having many income sources. Passive income lets you cross the gap whether you unexpectedly become jobless or even whether you willingly take the time from work away with the pandemic tossing the working condition of most people into disarray. You might get the cash rolling in from passive income even while you follow your primary career, or if maybe you can build up a good passive income pool, you may need a little to kickback. Anyway, you are granted additional protection from passive income. And if you are concerned about being capable of saving enough money to reach your retirement objectives, accumulating capital through passive income also is a tactic that could be appealing to you. Regular earnings from a party other than the employer or the contractor are counted as passive income. IRS (Internal Revenues Service) notes that passive revenue will come from 2 sources: a company or a rental property in which one is not directly participating, such as paying book royalty or dividends on securities. Most individuals agree that passive income's about getting more for nothing. It's got get-wealthy-quick charm, but it also includes work in the end. What you offer is work upfront. You may do any or all the job upfront in practice, but the passive income also requires some extra labor along the way too. To keep the passive dollars flowing, you might have to save your merchandise updated or well-maintained rental property. But if you're dedicated to the approach, it could be a perfect way to make income, and by the way, you'll build some more financial stability for yourself.

2.1 How many streams of income should you have?

"When it comes to generating revenue sources, there is no "one size fits all" advice. How many revenue streams you have can depend on where you are financially and what your potential financial targets are? But it is a decent beginning to get at least a handful. "With multiple lines in the sea, you'll attract more fish. Rental assets, revenue-producing shares, and company ventures are a perfect way to diversify your income stream, in addition to the earned income produced by your human capital. You'll want to make sure, of course, that bringing work into a new passive income stream would not cause you to lose sight of the other sources. So, you want your efforts to be aligned and make sure you pick the right options for your time.

2.2 Passive income ideas for building wealth

So, if you're considering building a passive income source, look at these techniques and absorb what this takes to succeed with them, whereas still recognizing the dangers involved with each strategy.

2.3 Selling information products

One common passive income approach is to produce information products, such as e-books, or video or audio lessons, and then kick back while cash rolls inside from product sale. Via platforms such as Skillshare, Udemy, and Coursera, courses could be distributed & sold. Otherwise, you may think of a "freemium model"-making a free content follow-up and only charging for the more comprehensive details or for the ones who wish to learn more. Language teachers or

/ & stock-picking guidance, for instance, can use the model. Free material serves as a demonstration of talents and can draw those who want to be going to the next stage. You may use advertising (or sponsor) to make your revenue as the third alternative for this concept while offering information or material on a free forum like YouTube to a growing audience. Take the love of music or video games, for instance, and transform it into the content.

Opportunity

The Information products will have an outstanding revenue stream, so after the initial time outlay, you quickly make money.

Risk

development of this product typically requires a huge amount of effort. And it needs to be good in order to make great money off it. There isn't space out there for trash. If you wish to be competitive, you must create a strong base, advertise your products & prepare for other products. Unless you get very lucky, one product isn't business. Generating more outstanding products is the easiest way to market an established good. You could create a strong income stream once you understand the business model.

2.4 Rental income

A successful way of earning passive income is to invest in rental properties. But more work is always needed than people expect. You could risk your money if you do not take the time to know how to create a profitable venture.

Opportunity

If you want to earn the passive incomes from the rental properties, then you must determine three things:

- Financial risk of owning property.
- Property's total expenses and costs.
- How much profit you need on investment.

For example, suppose your objective is to make $10,000 in a year in the rental income. At the same time, your property has monthly mortgages of 2,000 dollars and charges another 300 dollars in one month for the taxes & other expenses. In this scenario, you will have to cost 3,133 dollars in the monthly rent for accomplishing your objective.

Risk

few questions should be considered: Is there a marketplace for a property? How if you have a homeowner who pays off the property late or harms it? Suppose you cannot rent the property out? The passive income could be significantly impacted by any of the variables. And pandemic also has raised new threats. You could suddenly have occupants who could no longer afford their rent because of the economic crisis, although you may already have a mortgage of your own to be paying. Or, if earnings fall, you couldn't be capable of renting out homes for as far as you did before. So, to secure yourself, you'll want to consider these threats and have a contingency plan in place.

2.5 Affiliate marketing

However, with affiliate advertising, website owners, "influencers" on social media or blogs support the goods of third parties by including a link to the product on the forum or the social media network. The best-known associate partner maybe Amazon, but Awin, ShareASale and eBay, are all among the bigger brands. And for those watching to develop a following and sell goods, TikTok and Instagram have become major websites. To attract attention to the blog or else steer people to goods and services which they may like, you might also start growing an email list.

Opportunity

The site owner receives a fee if visitors click on the link and make a transaction from a third-party associate. The commission may vary from 3-7 %, so it would obviously need substantial traffic to the site to produce serious revenue. But you could be able to make some serious coin if you may expand the following or even have a more profitable niche (like tech, fitness, or financial services). Affiliate advertising is deemed passive, and, in principle, only by adding a link to your social media platform or website, you will gain money. In fact, if you cannot draw readers to the site to tap on the link and purchase anything, you won't earn anything.

Risk

You'll have to be taking time to develop content and generate traffic if you're just starting out. Building a following will take important time, and you'll need to discover the best formula to reach the crowd, a task that could take a while on its own. Worse, the audience might be likely to fly to the next famous influencer, topic, or social media site after you've expended all that energy.

2.6 Flip retail products

Make use of online sales sites like Amazon or eBay, and offer goods you find nowhere at prices of cut-rate. You will arbitrage the difference between the prices between your purchase & selling, and you will be able to create a following of the people who monitor your transactions.

Opportunity

The price disparities between what you'll find & what average customer will be capable of finding would encourage you to take advantage of them. If you've contact that may help you obtain affordable goods that some other individuals can locate, this might work extremely well. Or you might be capable of uncovering useful products which others have completely missed.

Risk

Although deals can happen online at any moment, you'll probably have to rush to find a reputable source of goods to help keep this strategy passive. And you're just going to have to know the competition so that you don't buy at a price that's too much. Otherwise, in order to market, you can finish up with goods that nobody needs. Moreover, you may be forced to slash the price drastically in order to make the product worthwhile for the buyers.

2.7 Peer-to-peer lending

Peer-to- peer (or P2P) loan's personal loan supports by the intermediary of third-party like LendingClub or Prosper between you & borrower. Funding Circle that targets firms & has greater borrowing caps, and Payout, which targets better collateral losses, are other players.

Opportunity

You generate income as a lender from interest payments made on loans. Yet, you face the possibility of default because the loan is insecure, implying you might end up with nothing. You must do two things to cut the risk:

By paying smaller sums on different loans, diversify the lending portfolio. Minimum investment for each credit is $25 at Prosper.com and LendingClub.

To make educated choices, evaluate old data on the prospective borrowers.

Risk

It takes time to learn the lending metrics of P2P because it's not completely passive, and you'll want to vet your prospective borrowers closely because you ought to pay particular attention to payments earned when you're engaging in several loans. If you intend to create profits, whatever you make for interest can be reinvested. Economic recessions may also make the high-yielding personal loans more likely to default candidates because if the COVID-19 manages to harm the economy at higher than historical rates, these loans will go bad.

2.8 Dividend stocks

The Shareholders in companies with dividend-yielding securities receive a payout from the company at regular intervals. The Companies pay the cash dividend out of the earnings on a quarterly basis, and what you need to be doing is to own stock. Per-share of stock, dividends are funded, meaning the more shares that you hold, the larger your compensation.

Opportunity

Since stock income is not linked to any operation other than the actual financial investment, it may be one of the most passive ways of money-making to own dividend-yielding securities. In your bank account, the money will simply be deposited.

Risk

Choosing the correct stocks is a tricky aspect. Without carefully researching company issuing stock, too many novices leap into the market. You have to study the website of each organization and be acquainted with their financial statements. 2 to 3 weeks you can spend researching each venture. That said, without wasting a massive amount of time analyzing firms, there are some ways to participate in the stocks dividend-yielding. ETFs, or Exchange-traded fund, are strongly recommended for income generation. ETFs are hedge vehicles containing collateral such as equity, commodities & bonds but trading like stocks. The ETFs are an excellent alternative for novices because, due to much lower prices than mutual funds, they are easier to understand, affordable, highly liquid, and offer much higher potential returns. Another key risk's that the stocks or the ETFs will decrease dramatically over short periods of time, particularly in times of volatility, such as when the financial markets were shocked by the Coronavirus crisis in 2020. Economic uncertainty may also cause certain firms to fully cut the dividends, while the diversified funds can experience less of a pinch.

2.9 Create an app

Creating an app may be a method to invest time in advance and then enjoy rewards over time. Your software may be a game or one that allows smartphone users to execute any feature that is difficult to do. Users download it once the application is public, & you can generate revenue.

Opportunity

There's a big upside to an app if you can create something that captures your audience's fancy. You'll think about how it's best to generate revenue. You could run in-application advertisements, for example, or else make users pay a small fee to use the app. You'll definitely add incremental improvements to keep the product current and popular as the app gains attention or you get feedback.

Risk

Perhaps the greatest risk here's that you spend your time unprofitably. You have no financial drawback here if you contribute little to no money to the project (and/or money which you'd have spent otherwise, for instance, on hardware). It's a competitive market, though, and genuinely popular applications must give consumers a persuasive benefit of experience. If your app gathers some data, you would also want to ensure that it is in accordance with privacy rules, which vary across the globe.

2.10 REITs

For a corporation that owns and manages real assets, REIT is a real estate investment trust, which is a fancy word. REITs have a special legal arrangement such that although they pass over any of their income to owners, they pay no or little corporate income tax.

Opportunity

In the stock exchange, you can purchase REITs much as every other business or dividend stock. You're going to earn whatever the REITs payout as a payout, and the strongest REITs have an annual record of growing their dividend, meaning over time, you might have an increasing supply of dividends. Specific REITs could be more expensive, like dividend stocks, than buying an ETF composed of hundreds of REIT stocks. Fund offers instant diversification, which is inherently much better than owning specific stocks & you can always earn a good return.

Risk

You'll have to be capable of selecting good REITs, much like dividend stocks, that means you'll have to evaluate any of the firms you might purchase, which indeed is a time-taking process. Also, while it is a passive activity, if you do not know what you're doing, you might lose a lot of money. And neither are REIT dividends safe from difficult economic times. If REIT does not produce enough income, this would possibly have to slash or totally remove its dividend. So just when you want it, most of the passive income could get hit.

2.11 A bond ladder

 bond ladder's sequence of bonds maturing over a number of years at various periods. The phased maturities help you to reduce the risk of reinvestment, which is a risk of locking up your cash as bonds offer interest rates that are too low.

Opportunity

bond ladder's a traditional passive investment that for decades has attracted near-retirees and retirees. You will sit back to collect the interest payments, and you "extend the ladder," transferring the principle into different package of bonds as the bond matures. For starters, you could start off with one year, three years, five years, and seven years of bonds. In the year that 1st bond matures, you have two years, four years, and six years of bonds left. You may use proceeds from the newly aged bond to purchase another one year or roll out an eight-year bond with a longer-term, for example.

Risk

 Bond ladder reduces one of the big dangers of purchasing bonds, the possibility that you may have to purchase a new bond as the bond develops when the interest rates will not be attractive. Bonds, too, come with the other risks. Although the federal government backs Treasury bonds, corporate bonds aren't, meaning you could risk your principal. And to diversify the exposure & eliminate the risk of someone bond harming your total portfolio, you'll want to buy multiple bonds. Many investors move to bond the ETFs because of these issues, which include a diversified fund of bonds that you may put up on a ladder, removing the possibility that a single bond will harm your returns.

2.12 Invest in a high-yield CD or savings account

Investing in an online bank's high-yield deposit certificate (CD) or savings account will help you to produce passive income and get one of the country best interest rates as well. In order to make money, you won't even have to leave home.

Opportunity

You'll want to do a fast check of the nation's great CD rates or the top savings accounts to make the most of your CD. Going to the online bank instead of the local bank is typically far more advantageous since you will be able to pick the highest rate available in the region. And if the financial firm is backed by the FDIC, you will also receive a fixed return of principal of up to 250,000 dollars.

Risk

Your principal is secure as far as the bank is backed by FDIC and under limits. So, it is just as secure a return as you'll find to invest in a CD or savings account. Nevertheless, though the accounts are secure, these days, they return even less than before. And with   Federal

Reserve aiming at 2% inflation, the least in the short run, you're going to miss out on inflation. A savings account or CD can, though, yield less than keeping your cash in cash or in a non-interest paying checking account where you will earn about zero.

2.13 Buy Property

Real estate can be a decent way to make a passive income, depending on where you invest and when. There has been a rapid growth in the value of property in common cities such as Toronto-44 percent in Canada alone in the last five years. You will find some lower-cost properties by purchasing pre-construction condos, which will rise in value by the time it is eventually completed, enabling you to sell the property once it is complete for a profit. Like for all investments, it can be dangerous, so if you're new to the market, it's better to talk to a real estate agent to help you purchase the correct investment property.

2.14 Rent out your home short-term through Airbnb

This simple approach takes advantage of space that you don't need anyway, and converts it into an opportunity to make some money.

Whether you're leaving for summer and/or have to be outside of the town for some time, or maybe even you want to fly, try renting your present space out while you're gone.

Opportunity

On a variety of websites, including Airbnb, you may list space and set rental conditions yourself. With limited additional work, you'll receive a check for efforts, particularly if you rent to a tenant who might be in place for a couple of months.

Risk

You do not have a lot of financial downsides here, but it's a gamble that's atypical of the most passive investors to let strangers stay in your house. Tenants can, for instance, even deface or ruin your property or steal valuables even.

2.15 Air BnB Business as a Passive income Strategy

Airbnb is an online website for selling and renting urban homes. It ties hosts and travellers and promotes the rental process without owning any rooms on its own. Moreover, it cultivates a cooperative economy by allowing private flats to be leased by property owners. Airbnb is an internet platform which links individuals that wish to rent the homes to an individual in that area who are searching for a room. It currently surrounds more than 100 thousand cities in the world and 220 countries. The name of the business derives from the "air mattress B and B." Engaging in Airbnb is a way for hosts to gain some money from their home, but with the possibility that it may be damaged by the visitor. The benefit could be comparatively cheap lodging for visitors, but with the possibility that property wouldn't be as advisable as the listing has made it look. For less than the cost of a hotel bed, travellers may also book an Airbnb. The traveler's biggest concern is that the property could not live up to its listing. The primary concern for hosts is that their property may be badly damaged by guests.

The Advantages of Airbnb

It offers the following advantages:

Wide Selection

Airbnb hosts list several different categories of properties on the Airbnb website, like single rooms, a suite of rooms, moored yachts, , whole homes, studios, houseboats, even castles.

Free Listings

In order to list the assets, hosts don't have to be paying. Listings may contain written descriptions, captioned photographs, and user profiles so prospective visitors can have the knowledge about hosts a little better.

Hosts Can Set Their Own Price

It is the host's prerogative to decide how much to charge per night, per week, or /and per month.

Customizable Searches

The Guests can filter the Airbnb database and not only through date & location, however also by price, property type, amenities, and the host's language. To further limit their search, they may also add keywords (such asclose to the Louvre').

Additional Services

Airbnb has increased its services to include events and restaurants in recent years. In addition to a list of available hotels for the dates they expect to visit, individuals searching by the venue can see a list of opportunities provided by nearby Airbnb hosts, like classes and sightseeing. Restaurant listings also contain Airbnb hosts' reviews.

Protections for Guests and Hosts

As a protection for customers, before transferring the funds to the host, Airbnb keeps the guest's payment for 24 hours following check-in. For guests, Airbnb's Host Guarantee program "provides security for up to $1,000,000 in damage to covered property in eligible countries in the rare incident of guest damage."

The disadvantages of Airbnb

It has the following demerits:

What You See May Not Be What You Get

Booking Airbnb accommodation is not like booking a space with a big hotel chain, where you have a fair promise that the property will be as described. Individual hosts, though some may be more truthful than others, create their own listings. Previous visitors, however, often post updates about their experiences, which may offer a more critical perspective. To make sure the listing is correct, review the reports of other guests who have stayed at the Airbnb house.

Potential Damage

The greater concern for hosts is potential that their property will be damaged. Although most stays go without incident, when the Airbnb hosts assumed they were renting to a peaceful household, there are reports of entire houses being trashed by thousands of partygoers. Some insurance is offered by Airbnb's Host Guarantee program, mentioned above, but it does not cover anything, like cash, rare artwork, jewellery, and pets. Also, hosts whose homes are destroyed can experience significant inconvenience.

Added Fees

A number of extra charges are imposed by Airbnb (just like, of course, hotels and other lodging providers). To cover Airbnb's customer care and other programs, travelers pay a guest management fee of 0 percent to 20 percent on top of the reservation fee. Prices are shown in the currency that the customer chooses, provided it is sponsored by

Airbnb. Banks or issuers of credit cards can, where applicable, add fees. And though listings are free, to cover the cost of handling the transaction, Airbnb charges a service fee of at least 3 percent for each reservation.

It Isn't Legal Everywhere

Would-be hosts need to review their municipal zoning codes before listing their properties on Airbnb to make sure it is legal to rent their properties. To receive special permits or licenses, hosts may also be required.

2.16 Advertise on your car

By merely driving your car across town, you can be able to raise some additional income. Contact a specialized advertisement firm to determine your commuting patterns, like when and how many miles you drive. The firm will "wrap" your car with the ads at no cost to you if you're a match with one of their advertisers. Newer vehicles are being searched by agencies, and drivers should have a clear driving record.

Opportunity

If you're still putting in the miles anyway, though you may have to get out and drive, then this is a perfect way to earn hundreds every month at little to no added expense. It is reasonable to pay drivers by the mile.

Risk

Be extra cautious about locating a reputable operation to work with if this idea seems good. In this space, many fraudsters set up schemes to try to bilk you out of thousands.

2.17 Invest in Stocks

When you look at the wealthiest people in the world, it's pretty fair to conclude that their deep, endless savings accounts are a result of their major investment in stocks. Warren Buffett reads 500 pages a day, but he doesn't read your usual mystery novel. He reviews the annual corporate reports. He better knows whether or not a company is doing well by reviewing annual reports each day, which helps him improve his decision to invest in stocks. While the act of investing in stocks is very passive, the analysis that goes into it is active. Nevertheless, investing in shares will help you gain passive income that goes well beyond what your value is worth at your 9 to 5 work. So, if you enjoy reading about the success of different firms, consider this passive income approach.

2.18 Make Your Car Work for You

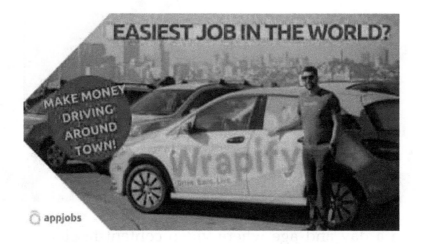

Driving is another everyday practice that you can translate into passive income. When you're just walking around, why not pick up a commuter or two to run errands? Uber can help you make money by taking people to their designated destination by driving your vehicle. You may also put ads on your vehicle to collect cash as you drive around. When your car is not used while you're on holiday, driving, or just during a normal workday, it will still make money. You will make thousands of dollars with an app like Getaround by renting out your car if you're not using it. Plus, drivers of Getaround vehicles get the best parking spaces in town, a $50 monthly rental credit on any vehicle they want, and one million U.S. dollars in primary insurance coverage.

2.19 Sell your Videos

We live in a day and age where video content fascinates hundreds and thousands of humans. You would want to take out your phone and hit the record if you still find yourself in the middle of drama and excitement. To allow you to make some passive income, you can sell stored content. Why? It is because the video can be sold to a news site. And you can make some recurring income for weeks, months, and maybe even years if the video takes off. Of course, being at cultural gatherings such as marches, rallies, and festivals is the best way to get in on the action. You'll find ways for your material to be sold anywhere there's controversy. And corporations will pay you to make viral videos along with providing a share of total earnings if you are successful at creating engaging content.

2.20 Create YouTube Videos

The passive income source that just keeps on giving is YouTube. You'll find that you can make a regular income from your YouTube channel, from funded videos to ad sales. Creating videos on a regular basis for a long time is the key to creating a profitable YouTube channel.   If you stick with it in the long run, you will finally start reaping the benefits of passive income.

2.21 Write an eBook

In 2009 and 2010, e-books came onto the scene and are now a hugely successful content medium. While they first became popular a few years ago, to this day, there is still a very decent chunk of individuals who make passive income from writing e-books. It's an insanely dynamic business, of course. Yet, you might find yourself with a nice slice of the profits if your writing chops are stellar. You could build a fanbase of loyal readers by designing how-to e-books on famous niches and marketing them.

2.22 Sell Digital Products

You can make digital goods if you're trying to create your own products rather than selling someone else's. You can sell your digital goods online using Shopify. From e-books, educational classes, PDFs, custom graphic templates, stock images, or some other digital goods, digital products will contain anything. Selling these items is the epitome of passive income, and with immediate updates, the whole operation can be streamlined on Shopify.

Car Wash

Car wash is a perfect way to earn a semi-passive income. Although a car wash will need daily cleaning, it is something you can either contract out or do once a week. We are talking about the very simple car wash that is cinderblocks, a pressure washer, and the powered coin, as a side note. It's certainly a corporation vs. a passive income stream if you're trying to run a drive-through car wash.

2.23 CPC Ads (Cost Per Click)

You get really paid whenever anyone clicks on your link and signs up for something or orders something through affiliate ads. On the other hand, show advertisements charges depend on the volume of traffic and eyeballs that you receive on their ads. On the other hand, for CPC advertisements, also known as "cost per click" ads, anytime someone clicks on an ad, you get paid no matter what they do after that. You don't have to hope or pray that they're buying anything or signed up for something. Any single click takes money into your account with the bank. Does that mean that all day long you can go to your own website and click on ads? It is not realistic since the corporation will inevitably find out what you are doing and cut you off. With all that in mind, it should not be a part of your plan here to click on your own ads. Instead, aim to build up traffic so that more and more viewers every day see the ads.

2.24 Minimize your taxes on passive income

A passive income may be a wonderful side-income generation strategy, but you can still create a tax burden for your effort. But by setting yourself up as a business and building a savings portfolio, you can reduce the tax bite and plan for your future, too. However, this solution will not work with all these passive strategies because to qualify. You will have to be a legal organization.

Register with the IRS to make your company receive a tax identification number.

Then call a broker, such as Charles Schwab or Fidelity, who will open a self-employed retirement account.

Determine the type of savings account that will fit well for your needs.

CHAPTER 3: Airbnb Offers The Best Passive Income Generation Strategy

rental vacation industry is rising quickly. It is real quick indeed as a matter of fact. The sector is currently generating 57,669 million dollars in sales, according to recent analysis reports from Statista.com. The revenue is awaited to grow to a market value of 74,005 million dollars by 2023 and is projected to see an average growth rate of 6.4 percent. This data illustrates just how broad & robust the holiday rental management industry is. And you should expect demand for Airbnb property management to pursue to grow over the coming years with the growth of Airbnb rental properties in recent years. Therefore, if one day you are aiming to become a manager of Airbnb property, now is a great time to be entering the business. But how are you able to get started? We will supply you with what you have to know regarding how to be an Airbnb vacation rental property manager. We're going to teach you what this takes to handle rental Airbnb properties, particular instruments you're going to be needing before you start, and stop points for the beginners for achieving successful property management. So, without further ado, over here are all six steps to beginning an Airbnb property management career in real estate.

3.1 Understand the Vacation Rental Industry

Just like some other business, without learning at least the fundamentals of this area, you can't succeed. However, no formal qualification is necessary to become an Airbnb property manager, and many find success with the only diploma of high school in this profession. Thorough knowledge of how the holiday rental industry

& Airbnb run is what you need to have. So, if you don't already have it, having this information now is the 1st step to being the manager of the Airbnb properties. Ideally, as Airbnb hosts yourself, you should have some experience. If you've already hosted your rental property on Airbnb, run it yourself, you can show to potential buyers which you know exactly what you are doing. Furthermore, this will allow you to be prepared better to predict challenges, recognize potentially troublesome travelers, and cope with common issues. But if you don't have the experience, through online guides and classes, you can empower yourself about the rental vacation industry & how Airbnb works. There are plenty of those out there that can help you create a good base on which you have to learn. For instance, you may take marketing coursework to know how to extend your scope and get bookings more and business courses to know how to manage a company, keep records, & file tax. As an Airbnb property manager, it'll help you improve your creditability. Before you start, another significant point to learn is where the Airbnb hosts invest in rentals for the short-term. You'll know the place to find customers looking for management support with this detail.

3.2 Create a Maintenance Management System

Managing rental of short-term rentals ensures that you'll get visitors checking in & out repeatedly. One of many duties of the property managers, of course, is to review property before visitors visit & after they depart. Every now & then, operators of holiday rentals must also conduct repairs to ensure that the properties are in perfect shape. This is vital to ensure the happiness of both your customer and guests. For instance, imagine having visitors who had parties and had rental property trashed before leaving. Nobody with such a situation is going to be happy to step into a rental. As a consequence, before addressing the issue, the manager of Airbnb property can never leave the maintenance as an afterthought or even wait for the property owner to receive several inquiries. In addition, to offer high-quality care on their behalf, great short-term property rental operators often work alongside a dependable maintenance team. Your staff should include, among others, plumbers, house cleaners, and electricians. For any check-in, these entities will ensure that Airbnb assets you handle are tip to top.

3.3 Put Together a Vacation Rental Marketing Strategy

The most significant tasks of property managers are promoting and selling holiday rentals to attract prospective visitors. Today, there are millions of listings on Airbnb & more rental sites for the short-term, which is creating rivalry among the Airbnb hosts. It is why one of the first things potential users would like to know is how you're going to get reservations and increase their occupancy rates for Airbnb. As a consequence, you must have a basic comprehension of tactics and methods for property marketing. Therefore, having a marketing campaign that will draw Airbnb visitors to the holiday rentals you run is the next step towards being Airbnb properties manager. Start by writing an enticing listing that will maximize the probability of retaining a high rate of occupancy & a positive flow of cash. To make rental properties under your management stand out, think about investing in advanced photography & videography facilities, also branding services. Moreover, selling holiday rentals suggests that you have to go outside the listing platform. It is why active rental managers of Airbnb use social media and also SEO to meet the target tenant audience. If you don't know how it works, before you begin handling rentals in the short term, we strongly suggest that you begin to read about real estate marketing.

3.4 Invest in Property Management Tools

You can handle them with hard work and a few spreadsheets as you become manager of Airbnb property for the first time when you have only some rental properties underneath your belt. This becomes difficult, though, as you continue to add more assets to manage. How are thirty check-ins & cleanings going to be done in 1 day? At an early point, it is best to begin thinking about it so that you're planning yourself & your company for success and expansion. Using real estate management of property software that allows to automate & remain structured is the best approach for this.

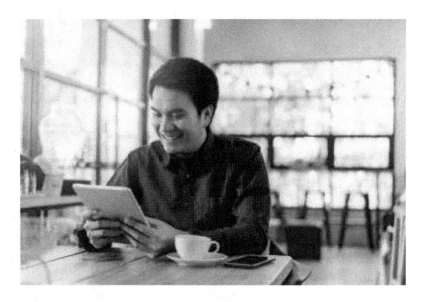

In order to operate their businesses more effectively, modern holiday rental property supervisors rely a lot on technology. There are several high-tech solutions that make it easy to handle Airbnb rental, from the smart lock to invoicing, pricing, and the guest screening software systems. You will even find holiday rental apps which will synchronize schedules and handle multiple Airbnb profiles for free from different platforms. Not only does the use of such instruments make your life more effective as a manager of real estate properties, but they can also give you the strategic edge to keep rising. Mashboard, for instance, is a software that lets managers of Airbnb property connect with their customers and find the right properties for those to expand their business.

3.5 Outline Your Guest Management Strategy

Amazing client care is one of the abilities that any manager of real estate property wants to provide when handling both conventional and holiday rentals. It is how effective operators of Airbnb assets set themselves away from the audience. A good selling point, particularly for Airbnb travelers, is customer service that goes beyond and beyond. Getting a guest engagement plan ensures that during their visit, the services can be open to visitors and their demands at whatever time. Expect the short-term visitors to have to inquire or inquire over something. You must be capable of responding in a timely way to such unannounced requests. How can you treat a case, for instance, where the visitor has misplaced keys to a holiday rental and can't get in? There will be a contingency in it and other cases for a successful Airbnb property manager. In addition, to manage communication with visitors, managers of top-performing properties also have automation tech systems in place. Airbnb guests really enjoy great customer service & show this by posting favorable feedback. This, in essence, helps to get more bookings & boost cash flow, that will surely make the customers happier. As you could see, one of the most critical skills for good management of Airbnb property is definitely customer service, so don't consider it as an afterthought.

3.6 Set a Reasonable (But Competitive) Price

To become a manager of Airbnb property, the only thing you need is a pricing plan. Usually, the holiday rental manager takes a percentage cut from the real host's secured rental fee. A selection of online outlets recommends anywhere from ten to twenty-five percent. At the same time, others believe that more consumers would be drawn by charging the lowest price; that isn't the case. Customers base their options on the quality o facilities rendered by property managers-not dependent on costs. Thus, providing the lowest price means that you don't have top-tier facilities for owners of Airbnb property. You need to take several factors into account in order to fix the correct price. First of all, as stated, is what kind of services you are providing. Naturally, for something that you don't sell, you do not charge. Look at experience instead, what distinctive points of selling you may give, and set rate accordingly. The local economy and what the other rental property (short-term) managers in the area charge, the seasonal demands, also current events, you will need to remember. Ultimately, you need to set a fair price which you are sure will be getting you back that your service is worth.

3.7 How an Airbnb Business Works

Nearly everyone has listened to Airbnb or has used it. It is the platform for online home rentals that helps hosts renting vacant private short-term accommodation from a single room to whole homes. Airbnb launched in 2007 & has expanded exponentially to have listings in further than 65 thousand cities in the world with more than three million available properties. Here is how to start a sustainable Airbnb company if you have sufficient rental space and are searching for additional revenue. Through uploading photographs and details of the room for rent, the first move is to be a host on Airbnb and register the home. When an Airbnb property's listed, travelers searching for a room in the host area will access it. Guests may use a number of requirements to check for Airbnb listings, like:

- Availability dates
- Destination
- No. Of rooms, such as bedrooms and washrooms
- Price
- Host language
- Amenities such as hot tub, breakfast, pets allowed, and etc.
- Facilities like air conditioning, parking,etc.

Prior to booking the chosen space through the Airbnb guest may establish a contact with hosts directly for gathering additional information through the Airbnb service of messaging.

Access

Along with browser access, Airbnb offers mobile applications for Android and Apple IOS devices.

Security

For security purposes, the hosts are expected to provide Airbnb with appropriate identification. Travelers should post the reviews of hotels to create a trustworthy group (and the hosts may review the guests). The Reviews aren't anonymous.

Guest Services

Airbnb offers a stable payment platform for the guest's calmness of mind, and fees to the hosts are deferred until 24 hr after the arrival of the guest. In the event that any difficulties are faced during the renting time, Airbnb has a 24-hour hotline for the guest.

Fees

Host sets the price for lodging. Moreover, Airbnb charges under-mentioned fees:

Host: Three % transaction payment fee

Guest: six to twelve % booking fee

The Hosts can also ask for a security deposit & could well charge a cleaning fee.

Taxes

Airbnb could apply provincial, state, or city taxes for guest bookings depending on the jurisdiction.

Travelers Prefer Airbnb Rentals

One of the best things about operating an Airbnb company is that, for several reasons, travelers choose Airbnb over motels, hotels, or hostels:

Cost: Usually, Airbnb rent is much inexpensive than a similar hotel room. In certain instances, an entire house may be rented through Airbnb for the cost of a single suite of the hotel, depending on the location.

Living locally: Living the life of a local person is the key advantage of the Airbnb service. Most guests of Airbnb choose to stay inside the community and explore the destination way the locals do, instead of renting a generic hotel room.

Privacy: customers of Airbnb are not continuously surrounded by visitors and workers at the hotel.

Peace & quiet: the Airbnb rents are usually more secure and do not suffer from loud hotel events, such as guest exits early in the morning, young children, maid service, and traffic.

Witness what you get already: Unlike a hotel where you can see a snapshot of similar rooms on their Airbnb page at best, you get full images and explanations of the real premises.

Diversity: From yachts and boathouses to castles and lighthouses, Airbnb has an immense variety of available accommodations.

Home comforts: Airbnb has a homey atmosphere of a real living space instead of generic hotel spaces (few have resident pets even). Kitchens allow the guests to cook their own food if they desire to save money on outside dining or have dietary issues.

Friends or Family: Through Airbnb, you may save a lot of money by renting a whole apartment/ house/condo rather than the multiple rooms of a hotel for family and friends.

Is Renting Your Space Permissible or Advisable?

Ensure you're legally permitted to be an Airbnb host into jurisdiction before you plan to start an Airbnb business, & you're prepared to respect local laws & regulations. Depending on the state/ city or regional rules, municipal laws governing the hosting of paid visitors will vary greatly; they are absolutely banned in some areas whilst they're subject to occupancy tax in others if space is condominium or apartment, check to view if it is allowed to sub-let the premises. There are also regulations in place for apartment landlords & condominium societies to prohibit an owner from renting the units out as Airbnb rooms. Renting your apartment out without the knowledge of your landlord will have you evicted. Neighborhood ties are also a significant concern. In the area, a few inconsiderate or loud Airbnb guests will easily turn you in a pariah. If none of the challenges are insurmountable, it could be an outstanding opportunity of home-found business to become an Airbnb host.

Are You Committed to Becoming a Host

There are a variety of additional concerns to remember prior to making a definitive decision to host Airbnb:

Would you like to start a business? Then Starting an Airbnb company is like establishing any business- that you need enthusiasm, entrepreneurial spirit, & the ability to make the required effort, starting off with doing relevant background analysis and developing business plans.

Do you've energy? It could take a great amount of time to be a landlord, particularly for the short-term rents. You'll have to:

- Manage reservations and reply to interactions with prospective tenants.
- Plan to meet the guests to give out or receive keys
- ensure the property, including fresh linen, breakfast supplies, is cleaned properly and ready for the arrival of the guest (if applicable)
- Fix some property maintenance problems such as plumbing and pest control, electrical & appliance repair
- Be accessible to the visitors on a 24 into 7 basis if the property has any problems.

Demand: The deciding factor in the popularity & price of rented accommodation is visitor demand. The highest places for rental returns are:

sought-after tourist destinations with high hotel rates (famous neighborhood ranks higher on the Airbnb searches)

situated Centrally, close to visitor attractions, shops & public transport,

Featuring panoramic views and facilities like parking, balconies, etc.

Seasonality: Demand for the property in the northern hemisphere will definitely drop drastically in winters (unless you're renting a ski chalet). In comparison, rental accommodation demand in colder southern locations (like Arizona) decreases dramatically in summers.

What are the marketing aims? Are you trying to earn a little cash or create a stable income on the side? The financial portion of the business plan must show target market analysis and reasonable forecasts of your property's future rental income. The income from the Airbnb contract depends upon:

Before you start thinking about leaving your job & making a living through running an Airbnb company, make sure that by seeing rental prices & booking regularity for comparing Airbnb listings of your area, you carefully examine the revenue potential of your property.

Extra costs: In addition to booking fees paid by Airbnb, there are extra costs involved with Airbnb hosting, including:

Insurance: Standard insurance plans for homeowners do not include the use of the property for commercial uses, including renting on Airbnb. Airbnb has a free host compensation insurance policy in Canada, U.K., U.S., and many other nations, offering up to 1 million dollars in guarantees against personal harm or property loss. If your place is not protected by Airbnb policies, please contact your insurance provider to see if there is sufficient coverage.

Business Licenses: Airbnb hosts are being required by more & more cities to hold a business license.

Repair and Cleaning: You want to keep rental properties in top condition all the time in order to keep your Airbnb host ranking at a high standard, which includes extensive cleaning during guest stays and daily repairs. The charges will contribute to your expenses if you have to sub-contract cleaning and repair duties.

Listing and Pricing Your Property on Airbnb

Accurately describe the place and make this stand out. Note that Airbnb is an online marketplace & you have to be thinking like a realtor to make listing stick out from the competition in order to optimize guest interest in your house. Start by looking at the same Airbnb listings inside the region and consider the amenities/features and prices listed. If this works, make a spreadsheet. The definition of your listing must be precise, comprehensive, complete, and highlight, which makes it special. Comprehensively define the facilities and functionality of your room also as any regulations or preferences of visitors. Providing high-quality photographs of the room is incredibly necessary. Airbnb has specialist availability of photography service in certain places if you are unable to do this yourself.. You don't want visitors to be upset because the room isn't as advertised or you've exaggerated amenities. Note that the guest rankings would be partially dependent on the accuracy of your listing description.

Price Your Listing Competitively

You should also get an idea of how to market your listing from your analysis of similar listings. It needs to be competitively priced to keep the property consistently booked (and increase profits).

Improving Your Host Ranking

Higher the property pops up in rankings, the more probable it's to be chosen by visitors, so having good rankings of Airbnb is crucial to the success of Airbnb business. Airbnb rankings are like internet search rankings. And by building confidence and offering a fantastic experience to your visitors, you will boost your rankings.

Build Trust

Airbnb community's based on trust and guests would be searching for hosts with contact information, credentials, and favorable feedback.

Verification

For the new hosts, verification is highly essential: change your profile and include other details like the email address, phone number, Facebook profile, and etc. For giving prospective visitors some confidence that you're a reliable host.

References

You should post the references from colleagues, co-workers, relatives, business partners, etc., to build more trust. For the other Airbnb users, you may even write references.

Provide Great Customer Service

Like any entrepreneur would tell you, the cornerstone of any successful business is customer care, and becoming an Airbnb host has no difference. Positive ratings, better search scores, and more bookings reward hosts of Airbnb who have the best experience of the guest. The hosts with the most popular are:

Responsive

The Hosts that can not be bothered for responding in a timely manner (or at some) to inquiries are a big turnoff for visitors. In reality, Airbnb keeps track and rates your replies to guests accordingly. With higher search rankings and improved bookings, the host who has the highest ratings of response is awarded. At all times, Airbnb mobile application will help you to keep connected. All the time when visitors are present, be available through phone and check up with them on extended trips and see if there's something more you may do to maximize the services.

Update Their Calendars Regularly

Keeping your calendar current, also enhancing the guest experience, boosts the Airbnb rankings of search.

Fix All Problems quickly

When a guest mentions problems like leaky taps or a burned-out lightbulb, it should be repaired promptly and render an apology to the guest. Sure ways to boost the guest rankings is to provide five-star service.

Act on Their Reviews

Fix the issue and benefit from the failures if a visitor writes a critical review. React to complaints all the time in a respectful way.

3.8 The Bottom Line

In real estate, there are many ways of earning profits. The growing success in the U.S. housing sector of Airbnb and other short-term rentals has created opportunities not just for real estate developers but also for property managers. Today, there is a great demand for vacation rental managers, and industry analysts expect that over the coming years, there will be national growth. Therefore, imagine being an Airbnb property manager if you're looking for a profitable means of generating passive income.

Conclusion

In a nutshell, passive income is money that comes at regular intervals without having to invest a large amount of work into generating it. By blogging, one method of producing passive income may be achieved. If you've figured out how to produce content that attracts sufficient traffic to the host advertising, you can make a product that your customers would want to purchase. From a basic e-book to a sophisticated app that produces sales for several years after it is released, passive income could be anything. Similarly, people have a lot of things, and they still look for cheap places to store this. What might be simpler than asking people to pay you for storing their things? An investment on a large-scale in purchasing storage facilities (with the cash) or anything simple like offering the basement or the shed might entail creating passive income by offering storage. All you'll need is to make sure their goods are clean and stable. You will make money by selling them to others against such charges if you've any things that you don't use at all times, which others will love to borrow. As rental items, useful items such as a tractor, trailer, kayak, trampoline, or your own lawn even may give you passive income. With the support of platforms like Airbnb, this also involves renting spare rooms out in your home. Upload the pictures of items, fix a date, and tell the world they're ready for the rent on your favorite social networking site. The reason why it is necessary to have passive income is that it will help increase your financial consistency. The more passive income you make, the easier it becomes to be consistent with your financial life, from consistently saving to consistently spending to consistently donating. One of the strongest and most relevant aspects of a sound financial condition is passive income. It is beneficial for you in several ways, from enhancing your financial health to reducing your financial burden.

The Golden Ratio Trading Algorithm

Discover the 9+1 Bulletproof Strategies that Helped 113 Dead Broke People Get Out of Debt

By

NESPY ONLINE MARKETING

Table of content:

Introduction:

Defining your corporate plan lets you make the best of your opportunities so you can accomplish your objectives. A successful business plan may be the difference between living and flourishing.

Some companies grow to a stage where the entrepreneur can no longer manage it themselves. Now is a perfect opportunity to start dreaming about a plan that can lead the company to accomplish its goals, e.g. by encouraging people to make choices. Getting a well specified approach to achieve your company goals will also help you clarify your plan to your staff, networks, sponsors, consultants, borrowers, accountants and investors. It's vital for moves like finding finance.

Overall, the effect of a successful plan is that you remain efficient over the long term, stop making typical errors, and stay ahead of the market. A plan provides a common understanding of your goal, making everybody in the company appreciate what you're working for. It will support you:

- Prioritise work

- Make the correct decisions

- Say 'no' to distractions

- Make the best of your place in the marketplace.

When you're experiencing loads of rivalry, developing a plan involves recognizing your benefit and your optimal place in the business. Then you should schedule things to reach you there. In this guide you can find lots of things to focus on so now it's up to you how well you select certain strategies and incorporate them in your business.

Working on a plan will help you discover your keys to progress, and set a course to follow towards reaching your goals. It may also help you grow into new goods or services. Without a consistent business plan, you might make choices that clash with each other, or end up in a bad financial and competitive role.

Chapter 1: Become a YouTuber

Until you even make a video that has viral value (making videos is not incredibly difficult if you enjoy what you do), you have to develop a platform that sticks out. It is also accurate that the videos you produce are the chemical X that will make your channel highlight. However, I have noticed that building a killer channel before releasing the first video is crucial. Let me also figure out that we shall not discuss how to build a channel; what we shall discuss is how to create your channel and make it stand out. Here are the ideas you need to accomplish this:

Create and design your brand

We will not cover, as I have indicated, how to create a channel. I should point out, however, that if you have a Google email and comment account or like YouTube videos, chances are, you already have a channel. It is important to note that your YouTube brand is at the heart of the channel you create. This is what's going to prompt viewers to sign up for your channel. What this means is that the proper attention it deserves must be given to your channel's name. The name of your channel should be memorable and relevant to the content you're going to share with your subscribers and the world. For example, you might create a channel under the name 'beauty within if you want to create how-to-make videos.

If you don't know how to build a channel, here is the link to the portal for creating a channel.

Exude professionalism

You will notice one outstanding thing, which is the quality of video and interactions if you take a second to wade through all the videos that attract many views and comments on YouTube. This simply implies that you have to be professional to create a killer channel and video that draws in millions of views. You need to be skilled in your presentation, how you make the video, and in particular, the technology you use to shoot the video. This means that you can use your iPhone (not recommended) if you do not have a video camera, but make sure to keep the phone as steady as possible. In addition, the audio on your video should be of excellent quality. It also suggests that you should seriously consider adding subtitles to your video if you are not a native English speaker or have an accent. I can guarantee that your channel will never come close to the status of stardom if your videos are out of focus. Visit some of the more popular channels to find out what is professional by YouTube standards and emulate their video presentation.

Create a video response

Despite the fact that they could generate high-quality sharable material, most YouTubers fail to get their channel noticed. This leaves the uploader with only the possibility that his or her channel may be found by anyone with a broad following. Here's a trick to make sure your channel is out there more easily. The trick is to produce a video answer to a famous video of high quality. In addition, to guarantee that other individuals click through to your platform without actually caring who you are, make your answers either informative or extremely divisive. Video answers that are divisive, fascinating, surprising, or informative can also guarantee you a few subscribers who believe your perspective or design appeals to them. On the other side, even though you don't receive viewers, the chances are good that a couple of your videos would be viewed by anyone who clicks through to your site. Using video responses is a caveat; make sure you do not attempt this trick until there are some really good quality, interesting videos on your channel.

Bait the crowd with reviews

The first thing you probably do anytime you want to purchase an object is to head over to Google to look for ratings. Video analysis is the quickest and more likely to go viral. As long as you make sure that the analysis is thorough and appeals specifically to the crowd of people involved in that specific thing, it really does not matter what gadget or item you review. All of us still search for product feedback (perhaps even you); as such, build a platform that gets many views and subscribers. The endeavor to create a few highly measurable review videos of some famous devices or items is well worth it.

Channel your energy on the channel

If only every three years your favourite musician produced a song, how would that make you feel? The word is Bored! A very similar approach is taken by a YouTube channel. If your commitment to the channel waivers, all the subscribers and subscribers you have gathered will drift off to another channel that consistently offers them videos if it takes you very long to upload. Uploading doesn't stop; you need to be active on the channel, interact with viewers, respond to their comments, and just make sure they feel appreciated and connected to you. If you do seem to keep your audience's interests at heart, they will move on by constantly interacting and uploading videos.

Key point/action step

To develop the mindset and routine necessary for creating an outstanding YouTube channel, fall into the habit of logging onto the site daily, watching a few videos and commenting on those that interest you. This is especially important because it will fuel your idea machinery and push you to create videos that people like.

How to Apply What You've Learned?

I am aware of the fact that too much information can work against you at times; the same applies to your journey for YouTube stardom. To help you out, I have decided that all we have learned will be summarized into an actionable plan that you can easily follow. Let it get to us.

Fuelling your idea tanks

Draw your ideas on YouTube from other videos that are doing well. I can guarantee you that there are other YouTubers in the field, regardless of which field or category you intend to upload to. Visit their channels, view their videos, and take away the best practices from their videos. Watch how they make their videos, voice-overs, etc., and then find out if you can replicate their style but add a flare of personality.

Viral does not come easy.

It is not easy, as stated earlier, to create viral videos. Sadly, to create viral videos, there is no trick or outright blueprint. There is only one definite way, on the other hand, to ensure that your videos are near perfection and closer to viral, and that is practice. Practice using various cameras, different lighting, and even different angles to create videos. You increase your video creation abilities when you employ this tactic. Make sure you don't look back in simple terms and say, 'I should have shot that angle differently.'

SEO plays a very central role

We looked at the numerous variables leading to the YouTube and Google rankings. Optimizing the video and platform is key to this rating. This suggests that to make the video rank higher, you have to read what you can about keywords and how to use them efficiently. Fortunately, the internet is full of tools you can use for SEO and keywords. You don't even have to use paying keyword queries since Google's free keyword analytics service works best.

Engagements make all the difference.

Through commenting, enjoying, and uploading their footage, you must actively connect with other YouTubers to push traffic to your channel and posts. When you create video responses to widely famous videos, this is particularly successful. In addition, commitment ensures that you have to interact with YouTube regularly by making and sharing videos as much as possible.

Chapter 2: Create an Instagram channel

What is Instagram?

According to Wikipedia, Instagram is an online mobile video sharing, social networking, and mobile photo-sharing service that allows different users to take videos and photos and then share them on different social networking platforms like Flickr, Tumblr, Twitter, and Facebook. As you can see from the description, it is a mobile app for smartphones and is available on Windows mobile, iOS and Android.

With the app, you can add captions and filters to your photos, get likes, and increase followers tremendously. You can also follow friends or whoever else you like to get their pictures on your Instagram feed.

If you are awfully talented in taking amazing pictures or want to turn your many followers into customers, there are many ways you can begin to earn money on Instagram.

A brief history of Instagram

Instagram was officially launched around 2010 and three years later became one of the largest and most engaging social networks. It's no wonder why Mark Zuckerberg, the Facebook CEO and founder, bought this photo-sharing app for a whopping amount of 1 billion dollars from its rightful founders (Mike Krieger and Kevin Systrom). Most people thought he was crazy. At the time of purchase, Instagram had only 13 employees had less than 22 million active users and no website. It has since grown so fast to currently have more than 300 million active users, definitely more than Twitter or Pinterest and over 100 employees. In fact, according to recent research, people are spending more time on Instagram than on Twitter or

Facebook. It's the fastest growing social platform in the world, and its future is very bright. Just as it has upgraded Facebook's balance sheet, it can upgrade your income. Instagram's social feeds and easy-to-use editing tools make everyone capable of creating and sharing nice edited pictures today. It has empowered people in unexpected ways, even those who don't bare Bieber, Hilton or Kardashian names. You can use it to share your interests, for instance, skateboarding, art, and other experiences, or just share your photos or videos and make money for such a simple effort. Many big companies are now using this platform to reach out to customers worldwide, and their sales have skyrocketed. Companies like Puma are even hiring Instagrammers with massive, profound, and engaging followings at more than $5000 a day to capture photos that display the respective company products.

Key Point

With over 300 million Instagram users, anything is possible. Think of it as a large billboard in a large intersection where over 300 million people frequent, and you will discover that this is an immensely big number of people. So, whatever it is that you might want to do, whether to gain in popularity or to make money, the potential is limitless.

Basic Tips for Making Money on Instagram

Like many people out there are doing, you can turn this so-called hobby to be a money minting cash cow by following the basic guidelines given below;

Build a follower base

Getting people to follow you is the first step to making money with Instagram. Without a very minimum of a few thousand followers, it will be hard for you to convince any brands to sponsor your posts. Even with the over 300 million users, it doesn't mean that being on Instagram automatically qualifies you to have access to this large number of users; you must strive to get a fraction of this number to follow you. Just like any other product, before you start making sales, you need a market, and this is your followers. Here is how:

1) Increase followers; Take all the time you need to expand on the number of your account followers by interacting with your followers and posting unique photos. You will learn more about this in the next chapter of this book.

2) Use hashtags to attract more people. For every photo you take, make sure that it has at least three hashtags that can add to your viewers. The hashtags should speak about the photo but should be broad enough to show up in numerous searches. Don't worry! You will learn more about hashtags later in this book.

Upload quality images

1) Master your craft; the fact of the matter is that if your photos aren't so good, people will not be willing to buy them. This may mean many different things to different people, but you need to take quality pictures if you want to end up selling them.

2) Use different cameras; avoid limiting yourself to your phone's camera. With Instagram, you can upload photos taken using other devices; all you need is to transfer them to your phone first.

Get yourself a nice camera and notice the significant difference in the quality of photos you take.

Set Up Your Store

Without an online store, you are almost doomed. You can't sell your photos via Instagram directly, so you have to set up an alternative way that people can buy your pictures. Here are some ways you can go about this.

1) Hire a store service; you can sell your photos directly through Services like Twenty20 and soon through their site. You get 20% of the sale, and they handle the printing and shipping for you.

If you want to avoid dealing with printing and shipping orders, this can be useful.

2) Get your own store; you can use your personal website to set up your own online store. You will definitely get more money than you would if you used a hired service, although you will have to take care of orders, as well as shipping and printing the images. For each image you upload to sell on Instagram, it should have a caption containing a link to its store page regardless of which method you use to set up your storefront. So that the link doesn't take up the whole caption space, use Tiny URL or Bit.ly to shorten the address. Take advantage of apps such as 'Hash Bag,' which automatically identifies and posts any items that have the hashtag '#forsale' on your Instagram account to their respective market.

Market your Products

After you gain followers and therefore in a good position to approach and convince any company, do this:

1) Contact companies; you need to explain and convince your target companies how you can help increase awareness for their brand through your Instagram account. Show them how often you update your Instagram feed and give details on the number of followers you have. Carry some sample shots to display and illustrate you know how to take clear, artistic pictures which can shed some positiveness to their product. Services such as Popular Pays and QuickShouts can connect you with companies, which hire aspiring Instagram marketers.

2) Work out a contract. You need to have a clear written contract indicating matters such as the expected number of pictures you are supposed to take and bonuses for the improved number of followers, if any. To protect yourself from being underpaid by the company you are marketing for, sign a contract.

3) Take quality pictures of the service or product. For sure, you wouldn't like to upload a mediocre or bad photo of a product you are supposed to be marketing. For you to keep the contracts coming in the future, you need to play your role as an ambassador for a given product effectively and uphold the expected standards.

You are free to add some personal touches to the photo, and in fact, you should. You don't want your followers to feel as if this is just one of those advertisements they would spam so easily if they weren't following you. Your followers need to relate to your image on a personal level.

Turn your many followers into Customers

1) Point followers to your blog or site; you should have a link to your company's or personal website or blog always on your Instagram profile. As you continue to gain more random viewers or followers, traffic to your site will also increase. Emphasize your skills. You can showcase your abilities and talents on Instagram, including fashion, web development, photography, and several other fields. Update your current projects and latest work on your Instagram feed always. Remember to use hashtags to attract potential buyers to your image.

2) Take your product's photos. If you run a business that deals with physical items like vehicles, cupcakes or whatever, one of the best ways to advertise your merchandise to new people are through Instagram. Take photos of some of your latest products, then make sure you use hashtags to entice more followers. Some hashtag examples include the product name and use, your company name or slogan. If you have a store page, make sure you link to the product's image comments. Remember to submit the nicest photos you got of the product and avoid those low-quality cameras at all costs.

Offer Brand Takeovers

You can earn some good money by doing an "Instagram takeover" as a substitute for sharing sponsored posts on your own account. It's exactly what it sounds like and is all about posting photos on another person's Instagram account. Either you can get temporary access to the person's or company's account, or you can be asked to supply photos, additional descriptions and hashtags to them. This works especially well for travel accounts, "We supply 5-7 amazing images to a company or tourism board and they feature our photos showcasing how we see the destination," says Bouskill, an Instagrammer.

Sell Your Account

You can sell your account for profit once you have a tremendously successful account. You can even get a six-digit for selling accounts that have 500,000 to a million followers.

Key point

Stay active on Instagram to get as many followers as you can, upload quality images of what you are selling, set up an online store, market your great skills to companies, and then turn your devoted followers to customers. Do "brand take over" or sell your account if you please. Don't forget to put the links and the hashtags on your Instagram images or comments. When you do that, you can watch your bank account swell in due time.

How to Post Memorable Content

You need to create posts that will stick in people's minds for a while. Here are some ways you can do this:

Take unique and interesting photos.

This may seem so obvious, but simply taking good pictures is one of the best ways to get followers on Instagram. Instagram is flooded with pictures of people's cats and meals, so have well-shot photos to set yourself apart. Let the pictures you take related to your audience fully. People are hesitant to follow you if you always post images they can't relate to. It doesn't have to be a "perfect" photo to be good. Good photos are more human, and any imperfections make them more so.

Put a boundary on "selfies." You can post some 'selfies' on Instagram, but don't let them dominate your account. Your followers don't want to see you but rather want to see your photos. You can seem narcissistic if you post constant selfies, and this can put off many followers. Sad as it may be, there is an exception to this if you are very attractive. Posting attractive pictures of your gorgeous self can drive many followers to your account. Still, don't let this take over your content!

Post Every Day

You need to have a new post every day and post reasonable several times if possible. Your presence must be felt all the time. With this, your follower's list will grow every day.

Add filters

Instagram became so popular because of the filter options. These filters fine-tune the colour of your photos and give them a more "real" feel. There is a variety of filters available on Instagram, so feel free to try out several until you identify the one that works well with your photo. Don't use the same filters too often, or your images will start to seem too similar.

#nofilter is a popular hashtag on Instagram; if the picture is too striking to even need a filter, use it!

Place captions on every photo

You will be amazed at how fast you can turn an okay photo into a remarkable one with a good caption. Your viewers' attention is grabbed by using a caption. The more people you make smile or laugh using a caption, the more you'll retain them as followers. Cute captions or jokes are particularly trendy.

Utilize apps for extended editing control

While you can slightly edit images on Instagram, there are many apps for both Android and iOS that can provide a lot more tools. Use these apps to darken, brighten, crop, add effects, text, and so much more.

Popular editing apps are Afterlight, Photo Editor by Aviary, Bokehful and Overgram.

Create collages

A fabulous way to show a collection of images or progression is to make a collage to post on Instagram. You can do this using several apps, including InstaCollage, PicStitch and InstaPicFrame.

Post your photos at a good time

Since Instagram is an extremely popular service, your followers' feeds are probably constantly updated. Post your photos at the right time for them to be seen by as many people as possible. Make sure you post photos in the morning and after the end of normal work hours. Instagram photos normally stay around a person's feed for 4 hours so if you want your followers to actually see your images, avoid posting them in the middle of the night.

Most Beautiful Photos

Not only do you need to post consistently, but you also need to post beautiful images, which are instrumental to increasing your Instagram followers. You can even be featured in media houses for outstanding photos. You need to inspire people through your photos and not shock them out of your account.

Avoid Posting All Your Photos at Once

The necessity to post photos regularly does not mean you post all the photos you have taken at one go. If you want to post more than one photo a day, make sure they are spread out in the day. Share one photo every three to four hours. You don't want to make your followers oversaturated with images-keep them yearning for more. Don't just dump all of your photos at the risk of making your followers start passing over them.

Pick up an Insta-Style

Like most successful Instagrammers, you need to develop a signature style for your photos.

Whichever technique or filter you choose, make sure your photos stand out from the crowd.

Chapter 3: Make money through binary options

What are the options?

Options are financial securities that give the consumer the opportunity, but not the responsibility, on or before a certain date, to purchase or sell an underlying financial commodity at a certain amount. Just as you know, with specified terms and conditions, options are like every other financial asset or instrument. It is important to note that options are not assets themselves, but their values are derived from other financial assets such as stocks, hence the name derivatives.

Two styles of choices are primarily available; call and place. Call options grant you the opportunity to purchase an underlying one at a given price on or around a specific date in the future, but not the responsibility. Call investors are betting that the value of the commodity will grow in the future and thereby allow them the ability to make market profits.

On the other side, placing options gives the customer an opportunity, but not the duty, to sell an underlying commodity during a specified time at a specific amount. Placement buyers conclude that rates are expected to collapse in the immediate term.

Why options trading?

Options have been branded as some of the riskiest investment ventures. However, over the past decades, participants in the options market have tremendously grown. Why would an investment vehicle think to be so risky to gain such popularity? There are several benefits that are attributed to this, but let us shift focus on the two main reasons why people use options hedging and speculation.

1. Speculation

Speculation is better understood if thought of as betting on the price of an underlying asset. People base their beliefs on what the security price will be in the future as the market adjusts itself and make a bet on the predicted market movement. The use of options for speculation is what makes options a risky venture. You not only have to be accurate in determining the direction of the market movements but also the timing and size of such movements. Let's say you predict that the price of Microsoft stocks will likely rise in the next three months; you can buy the call option, which will enable you to buy the stocks at a lower price and sell them at a higher price. If the market moves in your favor, you can make substantial gains. However, if the market movements do not favor you, you lose 100% of your investments (options price).

2. Hedging

Options can be an insurance policy for your investments. You can use options to hedge your investments against a downturn. For example, if you assume you wish to take advantage of the upside of technology stocks like Microsoft, you can buy a put option and take advantage of the upside keeping the stocks safeguarded against any downturn.

Key point/action step

Investing is all about determining the kind of investor you are and the goals you hope to achieve in investing. When investing in options, you have two main reasons for investing; to either hedge or speculate. It is important that you determine your reason for investing in order to invest wisely.

Types of binary options

There are many types of binary options available to you as an investor. Interestingly, the most common types of binary options not only confuse new traders but also experienced ones. I will go slow just to ensure that you get this information clear.

1. Digital binary options

Under this, we have call/put and up/down options.

Call options: You place a call option if you believe that the price will rise above the entry price.

Put options: You use this if you believe that the price will not rise above the entry price.

With up/down options, you only need to predict the direction of the price movements when you entered the market. Will it move *up/down?*

2. Touch binary options

These types of binary options come with predefined rates needed to win the trade as opposed to the trading participant just predicting the direction of the price movement. Here, you predict a level of decrease or increase it will reach (touch) and the level it will not reach (no touch). Please note that these types of binary options only trade when the market is closed, mostly during weekends. If the market touches or passes the specific level by 1700GMT on Monday, you get your returns. No-touch pays when the level defined is not reached.

3. 60 seconds option

Are you the type that gets excited by quick rewards? Perhaps this is your best bet. This option expires in 60 seconds. With this, it is easy to predict price movements. Basically, I usually recommend this option for traders who wish to profit quickly from a trending market.

4. Boundary options

This is sometimes also called range options. It differs from digital options in that two-level supper, and lower are defined. The asset must stay inside this boundary for a trader to receive any payout. This method is ideal for stable markets when trading inside the boundaries and volatile markets when trading outside the defined boundaries.

Key point/action step

As you have seen in this chapter, there are different types of binary options that you can invest in; hence, it is important to choose wisely. My advice would be to start small with binary options that are easy, for instance, the boundary options that give you more leeway when it comes to anticipating price movements. However, it is up to you to choose the most suitable option to trade-in depending on the returns you are looking for. If you are the adrenaline junkie kind of investor, then the 60-second option is most suitable for you.

Chapter 4: Social media advertising

There are a great many ways to earn money through social media. What we'll discuss for this chapter are the more straightforward methods of making money from your social media accounts.

More than 50% of all internet users all over the world go online for social media. This goes without saying that websites like Facebook and Twitter are huge opportunities for advertising and marketing, and many have taken advantage of the situation by allowing people to earn by displaying advertisements on their profiles.

This is especially profitable for people who have large networks and can be considered 'influencers.' Influencers are those who have a great number of followers and therefore have more powerful recommendations.

Earning can work in several ways. Once you display a Facebook ad, you can earn when someone clicks on the link, makes a purchase and leaves their mobile number or email address.

One can also go for paid tweets such as SponsoredTweets.com. As the name suggests, you get paid when your followers click on promotional links via Twitter.

Pros: Displaying Facebook ads can give you around two cents per click, depending on your arrangement with the advertiser. Sponsored tweets can earn you $6 for one tweet for 2000 followers and can reach up to $1000 for those with a massive following. Given the amount of time that you actually spend on your social media accounts, the rate is fair enough.

A good thing about displaying ads is that you are totally in control of the content that you wish to display. This is also an opportunity to help your followers by making quality recommendations while earning at the same time.

Cons: What seems to work for social media ads can also work against it. Most people really don't like ads, and so coming up with advertising links that are catchy enough to warrant attention may be tricky. Too much hard selling can also turn off some of your followers. It may not be as effective for people who have not yet established a large network of followers.

Social media advertising can be a very lucrative venture; however, it also highly depends on the extent of your social network.

Chapter 5: Stock trading

If you find yourself with more saved cash and an appetite for risk, stock trading may be a good venture for you. To describe it simply, stock trading involves buying shares of certain companies for a particular price, then selling them afterward for a profit when the value of these companies rises.

While it does sound easy, comprehensive research must be done before one engages in stock trading as it's not uncommon for people to lose their hard-earned money when the economy stumbles, and the prices of companies suddenly crash. Smarter traders can get profits of as much as 600% in three years, but this is backed by long years of experience and the 'feel' of the stock market.

Here are a couple of tips to earn extra money from stock trading.

Be in it for the long haul. Patience has always been a virtue, and the same holds true for stock trading. You will need to learn to apply the "buy at the low and sell at the high" law, and it requires a lot of patience to keep yourself from buying just because everyone else is buying because chances are the price maybe a little too high, and it will affect your profits.

You also cannot expect a 30% profit right away in your first year of trading, as it may take five years for you to truly realize your profits.

Buy great companies. One of the things that make stock trading a hit is a fact that your earnings depend on how well your company performs. That being said, a great deal of research must be done on a company before you decide to buy a piece of it. Does it have a good management team? Does it have years of experience to show for its stability? How profitable is it? Many experienced investors say that you should only buy a company that you truly know about for you to understand how it will be affected by key events.

Diversify. Another good tip is to not keep your eggs in the same basket. Do not focus all your investment on a single company to keep yourself from crashing with it when unexpected events take place. It is always a good practice to invest in various industries to create a buffer for your investments.

Chapter 6: Blogging and freelance writing

Blogging

Blogging is one of the most common platforms for web content on the internet and can be done by almost anyone. It is a form of social networking that allows you to create your own comprehensive content where you can showcase whatever you wish.

Blogspot and WordPress are some of the leading blog posts where people can sign up for free, and it allows anyone to publish their content online. If you have a knack for writing, this one is for you. You can post a wide array of content, from blow by blow accounts of how your day went, reviews of the latest movie you watched, opinions about current events, social commentary, book reviews, advice for mothers, shared experiences about pets and many more. Writing can be done for self-expression or to share experiences that you believe can help other people.

As fun as it sounds, establishing a blog isn't a walk in the park because you will need time and commitment to update it with quality content to keep readers coming back. Junk content that is simply copied from other web pages will easily be disregarded as plagiarized content and will not help the reputation of your site. It is also recommended to find a niche topic that you can focus on so as to target a specific brand of readers and establish a regular following.

A golden rule for web content: quality is king. If your readers find that your website offers something that they cannot easily find with other webpages, they will keep coming back. More readers mean a better reputation for your blog and, therefore, higher potential earnings.

Earning through blogging can be done by leasing your webpage space to advertisers, by writing sponsored reviews or blog posts about particular companies, or by selling actual products.

When you gain a following, people keep coming back to your page. The more traffic you get, the more attractive your page becomes to advertisers because they would want to take advantage of your page views and use it for advertising their product.

Using this concept, various sites offer bloggers the ability to display advertising banners on their webpage and get paid for them. There are hundreds of sites that offer these services, and some of the most popular are Infolinks, SiteScout (formerly Adbrite), and Clicksor.

You can get paid from $0.01 to $2 per click, depending on the value of the banner. The more traffic you get, the higher chances of people clicking on the banner link, and therefore the more money you get.

Other companies pay for impressions, meaning visitors really don't need to click on the ad for you to earn; they simply have to 'see' it. This has much lower payout rates but is also more convenient to use. Bloggers strategize on the placement of their ads to come up with more clicks and more impressions.

Google AdSense is one of the leading providers of blog advertising. They are the most popular; they provide the highest payouts but are also the strictest. It is recommended that you purchase a top-level domain (www.ebook.com instead of www.ebook.blogspot.com) for them to approve your request. They also go for top-notch quality as all pages with traces of plagiarism or copied content are immediately disqualified. They also strictly screen the nature of content that they approve to ensure that it only provides quality information for potential readers. If one passes through the rigorous screening of AdSense and keeps working on improving their blog quality and traffic, they can expect earnings of $0.15 to $15 per click, with most getting up to $48 for 1000 visits, the highest among all advertisers.

For those who have established a reputation with their blog—if you are a mom known for providing valuable baby-care advice, a girl known for fabulous taste in clothing, or a guy popular among bloggers for keenly observing gadget updates—some companies may want to bank on your influence in the blogosphere by sending you free products to review or by asking you to create a write up about their brand for a fee.

This can be a tricky line to tread, however, as some readers may get 'turned-off' when they find that you are being paid by companies to make positive reviews. A good way to work around this is by providing 'full-disclosure' to your readers by telling them if a particular post was sponsored by a brand. You may also want to keep your tone from getting too patronizing to keep your blogger's integrity intact. This way, the trust system between you and your reader is maintained. Another great thing about blogging is that the manner in which you create your posts and how you build your reputation is entirely up to you. Therefore, anything that happens is really under your responsibility.

Another great way to monetize your blog is by selling products. You may have some handmade crafts that others may find useful or a friend who knows a great supplier of accessories and clothing. Instead of renting an actual physical store, you can just post your goodies on your blog, advertise them on your social networking sites and receive orders from people. Selling with this method normally involves having the products delivered to your customers, so make sure that you also know the procedure for shipment.

A lot of people have earned a living by selling online products and relying on social media and word of mouth for their advertising. It's a pretty hassle-free method because your online space is mostly free, and you invest in your product and seller reputation alone.

Blogging is a great way to earn money online, but it takes passion and commitment to keep it going because the internet is flooded by all types of bloggers, and sometimes it takes a special flair to stand out.

Blogging is not as easy as it seems, but if you've got what it takes, it can also be the most rewarding.

Freelance Writing

Freelance writing is another way to earn online through the power of the pen—or in this case, the keyboard. Several bloggers venture to freelance writing and vice versa, while a lot of them actually juggle being both. The key difference between blogging and freelance writing is that with the former, you are in full control of the layout and content, and you write for your readers on your terms. Freelance writing, on the other hand, is pretty much like outsourcing your talent for their purpose, and therefore all articles are written on the client's terms.

It may be easier or harder, depending on which side of the fence you're on. But freelance writing will definitely give you a more reliable stream of income once you've got the hang of it. Beginners can start on sites like Odesk.com or Elance.com, where potential clients and freelancers can meet to discuss terms and gain an interface for communication. The more experienced ones eventually gain contacts of their own and can get projects for higher rates.

Articles can range from a simple 400-word description of products or 30-word description of hotels to 4000-word essays or long sets of blog posts. Formatting and tone of writing can also vary, which will require flexibility and good writing skills. A strong command of grammar and spelling is a basic requirement, along with the ability to consistently meet deadlines. This also includes the patience required for hours and hours of research.

Freelance writing can be as demanding as a day job or even more. However, it still allows you to manage your own time and decide which projects to accept and which to set aside for a later time, as long as you meet the expectations of your client.

Beginners can earn about $30 to $50 an hour, while the more serious ones can earn as much as $80 for an hour and even $2000 for a month.

While these sound like really good money, one must be aware that the life of a freelance writer is anything but easy. Here are a few tips that one should bear in mind when aspiring to become a freelance writer.

Get ready for rejections. Because of the increasing level of competitiveness that this industry requires, one must be ready to experience multiple rejections of their articles. Remember that they are not rejecting you as a person, only your work. Only when you are able to resist taking rejections personally will you be able to hope to make a living out of freelance writing.

Keep your reputation clean. Your reputation as a freelancer can either make or break you. Being able to consistently submit deadlines, work according to your agreement with the client and provide quality work are sure-fire ways to boost your chances of being referred to new clients.

Socialize. Go out, meet people and socialize. This is another way to develop networks and attract potential clients. Learn to market yourself.

Set your goals. Are you content with making $1000 a month, or would you like to earn $2000 or more? Set your goals according to your family situation; if you find that you can get a lot of more than 8 hours a day for freelance writing and that you would like to earn a significantly larger amount, then you should go for higher-paying clients and better writing gigs.

Seek help. Hundreds of websites are available for freelance writers who would like to improve their craft or would like to get the hang of the technical matters involved in the trade. Take advantage of these groups in order to meet fellow writers and keep yourself motivated.

Chapter 7: E-book publishing

If you are a book lover or enthusiast, at one point in your life, you may have dreamed of publishing your own book and being a world-renowned author. You might have sniggered at the thought back then because getting published seemed too far-fetched and ambitious. What if you learned that you can now be a full-fledged author of your own book for real?

The landscape for book-reading had changed quickly since 2012 when e-books outsold hardbound covers for the first time. More and more people have been turning to e-books because of their easy accessibility and portability. In no time, self-published authors gained popularity as well. Digital publishers are making it unbelievably easy for people to publish their own books, and many are taking advantage of this opportunity. Several authors are finding themselves easily selling a thousand e-books a month and are definitely outselling their hardbound counterparts.

If you have an idea sitting in the dark corners of your mind for quite some time, now is the best time to write that e-book, and who knows, it might just give you your first million! Here's a rundown of how:

Write. There's an initial draft that is basically your brain spilled over pages of chaos, a review draft that finally organizes your thought and develops what you really want to say, and the polished editorial draft ready for publishing.

This is, of course, the most important part of the process because, without publish-worthy content, your book will not sell a dime. Focus your thoughts and define your goal straight up — would you like to entertain, inform or inspire?

Formatting. This involves making use of the digital publisher format for your e-book and coming up with a cover. The design of the cover is critical for people to take an interest in your eBook. Take note that it also must be attractive even as a thumbnail because that's how your eBook will initially be presented.

A lot of self-published authors try to design their own covers with awful results. It is recommended to hire a professional cover designer to create a more polished look for your book. If you're going to earn thousands of dollars from it, you might as well invest, right?

Publish and Promote. Head over to your digital publisher, login to your account and follow the pre-defined steps to publish your e-book. You must have your tax info ready for royalties and legality purposes.

Pricing is a very important aspect. Most e-books are priced at $2.99 to $9.99. However, it is found that most readers buy e-books in the $2.99 to $5.99 price range. Price it too high, and no one will buy it, but if you price it too low, you may not gain enough profit.

There are many digital publishers out there like Nook, iBook's, and Smashwords; however, they have already established themselves as one of the most credible sites for online transactions. The intensive feedback system is top of its class, and they help to extend the reach of your book even to people who have no idea who you are.

Promoting the book is critical to the success of your e-book because no one will buy it if they don't understand that it exists. Make extensive use of social media, offer incentives for every purchase, or advertise it in online forums and blogs. Take advantage of the digital nature of e-books to spread awareness. It may take a lot of work, but it's definitely worth it.

Publishing e-books is a great way to leave a legacy on your passion or expertise. Now is the best time to do it!

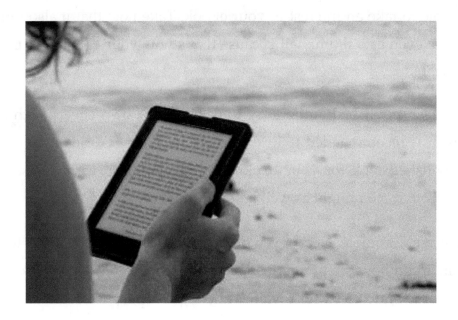

Chapter 8: Make your own video games

Your Debut into The World of Making Video Games

I am very tempted to tell you that the video game industry is a gold mine waiting for you to prospect, and indeed, it is. I am also tempted to tell you that video game creation is only a success story only for big game companies, but alas, I will not. Why? Because I would be telling you a lie. In the interconnected technology-driven world, which is where we live, anyone, and I mean anyone, can create a video game.

Do not get me wrong; I am not necessarily proclaiming video game creation success to all. I am merely stating the fact that thousands of people across the globe have been able to make their own games. Here is another fact; long gone are the days when video games had only two platforms: computers and gaming consoles. Today, with the advent of mobile technology, video gaming has gone mobile. With 98% of the world's population being owners of a mobile phone, it is only right that the video game industry would take advantage of this. Again, today, there are more mobile phone-based games than there are computers or gaming consoles in the world. What does this mean?

It means that the fruits are ready for the picking and that the pickings are in plenty. It means that if there ever were a time to get into video games production, now would be it. Contrary to popular belief and media hype, you do not need to be a geek with 'mad' coding or programming skills to create a video game (this does help, though). Anyone, even you, can create a video game. All that you require to create a game today is a bit of know-how, a lot of passion, and tons of patience. I am not promising that your video game will be an overnight sensation. I am also not promising that the journey will be easy. In fact, it may be very hard. What I promise you is that by the time we are through, you will be in a better position to create video games and well on your way to making some money from your video game creations.

Key point/action step

Although it is possible to make your own video games, you need creativity, passion, and patience if you are to become a success story.

After writing up your concept, hashing it out, and reflecting on it, it is time to fuel that enthusiasm train. Unless you are a serious video game creator with a few thousand dollars to fork out and some experience in pro programming, Unreal 4 Engine is not for you, albeit being one of the best video game creation engines. For the rest of us, who do not want to start from scratch, neither do some serious coding, we must rely on the help of software. Fortunately, the web is full of free and premium video game creation software. What I have found is that in a world of choice, most people are unsure of what to choose. It is important to point out that most of the software available each has different features, merits, and demerits. Your choice of software is entirely dependent on your game creation needs and level of expertise. I must also point out that you can do much using the available software that we will discuss shortly.

Before we move on to that, you are probably wondering why you should use an engine. Why not program the game by hand. I can give you a couple of reasons. However, I shall give you just one substantial reason. Engines provide a host of developmental tools, which aid and simplify the creation process. Furthermore, they are time efficient and less complex compared to hand programming. An engine also makes it easier to manipulate your AI (artificial intelligence), sound, and graphics.

Before I give you that list of software, I have to point out that some software is best suited for 2D graphics while others work best for 3D graphics. Above all, and regardless of your engine choice, most engines do come with tutorials to guide you in usage and creation. Here are the engines you can try to use.

Game maker: Platform-Windows and Mac OS X

The game maker engine is a product from YOYO games. It is a comprehensive engine well suited to help you create beautiful games without necessarily being a programming whiz kid. However, the program does require some getting used to (learning curve). Fortunately, the program does have a tutorial, manual, and a very vibrant user base and community ready and willing to provide you with answers to pressing questions. Unfortunately, only the light version, which does not allow for more robust features such as export, is free. For the premium version, you may have to pay up upwards of $500. Additionally, I have found the engine interface to be a bit lacking in terms of design. One of the more outstanding features of the software, both the free version and the premium version, is that you can port your game to different operating systems such as android, iOS, desktop, and HTML 5 (Web) with no basic knowledge of scripting or coding. This makes it an outstanding tool for a beginner.

Construct 2: Platform- Windows

If you liked Game Maker, then you will most definitely like Construct 2. Like Game Maker, construct 2 is also a premium engine that comes with its own user base, tutorials, manuals, and active community. Unlike Game Maker, construct 2 does not offer a free version. Instead, they offer a free 30-day trial of the full engine. Because the engine base is HTML 5, it is the best alternative to web animation tools such as Adobe Flash or Java. Using this engine, you can create beautiful 2D games that you can easily port to Windows, Linux, and Mac PCs, as well as Firefox Marketplace, Chrome Web Store, and the iOS and Android app stores. This means your games can be available on many different platforms. Unlike Game Maker, construct 2 has an appealing and robust user interface. Additionally, the engine has an in-built event system that allows you to instantly program actions and movements. The premium software costs about $120. However, if you want to use the commercial package of the engine, you will have to pay $400.

Stencyl: Platform- Linux/OS X/Windows

Stencyl is probably the most popular engine. More than 120,000 developers, with over 10,000 games published games across the globe used it. In its simple form, the engine does not require any programming skills. However, if you are tech-savvy, you can write code within the program to create more advanced features and functions. The engine has a drag-and-drop feature that adds to the easy use of the engine. Unlike all the other engines we have looked at thus far, Stencyl is not an all-out by. Instead, it works on a subscription basis; a $200 annual subscription basis; the $200 is for the most expensive (and comprehensive) package.

The engine offers cheaper discounts for students and game design experimenters. Because of the subscription nature of the engine, developers tout it as the easiest way to make some quick money (this means that the engine is commercially driven), rather than it being a fun way to experiment with video game designing. This does not mean that once you create your game, you have to submit it to them for sponsorship (which they offer)!

Flixel: Platform-Open source

Flixel is an open-source video game creation engine. This means that regardless of how you intend to use it (for commercial or personal purposes), it is completely free. This engine is very versatile. You can use it to create a wide range of 2D vector animations. The software itself runs on the backbone of ActionScript 3, an object-oriented programming language. ActionScript 3 adds a wide range of development tools to the program. These tools allow you to customize the engine. If you are looking to create filmstrip games or 'epic' 2D animation with side-scrollers, this is the 'it' engine. However, I have to point out that despite its versatility, Flixel cannot handle 3D modelling. On the other hand, I also have to point out that the tile-maps at your disposal in the engine are fulfilling and intuitive. Additionally, the engine has a plethora of camera functions; the in-built save game function and the pathfinding design all make this software one worth trying. Because the software is open–source, it has a bit of a C-style programming learning curve. I must point out that this should not stop you from using the engine. Why not? Because the open-source nature of the platform also means it has a wide user base and a thriving community.

Unity: Platform- OS X/Linux/Windows

If your aim is to make outstanding 3D video games on a budget, Unity is the choice for you. Unity is an outstanding fully-fledged design/development suite. The engine has a free version for personal use. However, for the commercial version, you must pay $1,500, i.e., if your aim is to create commercially viable games. Let not the money worry you, as the free version of the engine is something to behold too. The software, even the free version, can port to up to 10 different platforms, not limited to mobile and desktop. It is also capable of delivering crispy clear video and audio.

Key point/action step

Regardless of which engine/software you opt for, you will need to familiarize yourself with it fully if you really want to derive the most benefits. Therefore, I recommend you create your video game with a starter mentality. Additionally, if there are functions you are not sure of, turn to the online user community. They (community members) have a wealth of knowledge and are always willing to share

How to Publish and Market Your Indie Video Game

With more and more developers publishing games out to a hungry lot of gamers, generating downloads and sales for your games is harder than it has ever been. Do not despair; here are some tips to publish your game and get it noticed.

Publishing your game

Like any other store in the category of apps, your best chance for success in publishing your app is variety. Depending on the platform of your indie game, submit it to as many stores as you can find. This will ensure that more people get a chance to view or download it. Additionally, when publishing your video game, make sure that you fill out every single detail.

When you visit a store for submission, there is usually a game heading (what most of us call Meta tag), a game description, and an overview. Make sure to fill out all the fields. Also, make sure that you fill everything out correctly using keyword-rich sentences. What do I mean? If you are filling out the heading of your game, make sure it is something relevant to the scope of your game. If you are filling the description and overview field, view it as a marketing platform. It is your chance to tell users why they should download or purchase your game and what makes it different. Publishing your game is very standard and uncomplicated.

A key point you must note and a mistake that many developers make is that they fail to post their game in the right category within the store. If your game is a racing game, make sure you specify the category to increase your chances of discovery.

Marketing your game

Marketing your game is more difficult than it sounds. Moreover, it is the single most important thing to do if you are not creating video games for the fun of it. Therefore, you must create a marketing plan. A video game marketing plan is no different from any other product-marketing plan. You must set out well-defined goals and timelines by which you want to achieve those goals. You must also set out a marketing budget and resources (time, workforce etc.). If you do not have the money to hire someone to market the game for you, here are a few things you can do to enhance your total download and sales revenue.

Use social media- Social media is a vibrant marketplace that may have a great positive effect on the total sale and download of your game. If you have many friends on social media, share the game with them first and ask them to share the game with others. This is especially effective if the game is a free version. If your video game has a price tag on it, share the link to the video game with all your friends and ask them to download it. Additionally, social media also has very many developer groups. Join a few of them and contribute to topics. When you have racked up some points, tell the members that you just developed a game and you would love their support. In most cases, programmers are supportive of each other, and you will get some sales.

Use Forums- Forums are also another way to drive up your sales and downloads. They are especially effective because they provide a dedicated user base. For example, if your game is a racing one, you can join a developer's forum that caters to the racing niche. Here, you will find many people willing to download and try your game.

Create a website- This is very critical to your marketing. Most users will often time visit the website of a game they want to buy before they download it. They do this so that they can get more information on the game. Additionally, owning a website dedicated to your game sends a message of professionalism. Additionally, a website gives you more play with keywords and search engine optimization. This can be a gold mine for download and potential sales.

Key point/action step

If you are developing a video game for fun, you can simply publish your game and wait for users to try it. However, if you are doing it for a piece of the $97 billion, you must invest some money into marketing.

Chapter 9: Web industry freelancing and art of domain flipping

With almost all stores and transactions now going online, there is a great demand for people who are able to deal with the more technical aspects to securing their online presence. Web professionals are quite like the carpenters, civil engineers and architects of the online world. And so, if you have a good command of this field and would like to earn extra online, here are a couple of things you can do:

Create tutorials. There are a lot of web enthusiasts who would love to learn how to set up a website, create a good blog design or deal with servers. One can set up a blog and provide quality and targeted tutorials and earn by blog advertising, or readers can also pay a fee for your expertise. Just make sure that people get what they pay for. Earnings can range from $50 to $150.

Design web pages and blogs. The design of a website goes beyond what it 'looks like' but also deals with the interface and ease of navigation. It takes technical knowledge to correctly configure these. You can offer these services to aspiring bloggers or start-up companies.

Selling templates, patterns and icons. If you have a great eye for design and love tinkering with patterns and graphics, you can put up some of your designs for sale. Sites like Theme forest allow you to post your original works, and interested users can buy them directly from the site. This is a great way to produce passive income from your creativity.

Keep in mind, though, that coming up with profitable designs takes years of experience to pull off as it involves an intricate play of shapes, colours and lines.

Finding bugs. In an era of increasing cybercrime, larger companies realize the value of fool-proof software that can prevent hackers from taking advantage of their efforts. Because of this, they offer a hefty amount of cash for people who find vulnerabilities in their codes.

James Forshaw was rewarded $100,000 by Microsoft in 2013 for finding a potential security flaw in one of their software. Bugcrowd is a community of similar people specializing in finding coding glitches. It's pretty much positive reinforcement for people who have incredible skills in order to put their talents to good use instead of resorting to hacking.

The Art of Domain Flipping

Think of 'domains' as addresses to a house. This refers to the site address of your webpage, like www.ilovethisebook.com, for example. However, to get this address for yourself, you will have to buy it from a web host and domain providers so you could own it. This prevents someone else from the opposite side of the world from putting up a page named www.ilovethisebook.com because that domain name is already yours.

So, what if you have gotten so successful and realized that you would like to rename your site to www.ilovethisebooksomuch.com? You will have to buy this domain again and leave your former webpage address to expire. This will allow the happy lady from the opposite side of the world to finally own a website named www.ilovethisebook.com.

Domain flippers work in between these transactions to make profits. You can go through a list of the unregistered domain in sites like GoDaddy and look out for expired domain names that may be of great value for someone you know. You can purchase www.ilovethisebook.com for about $70, then send an email to a happy lady who would gladly pay you $200 for it. Bravo! The profit is made!

The key in earning through this method is being observant of current trends and insightful for things that may spark interest among people, purchasing domains while their value is still low, then selling it at a great price when you find it most profitable.

It definitely involves risk as you may encounter having to sell domains for zero profit. However, the rewards you get in the process may make this worth a try.

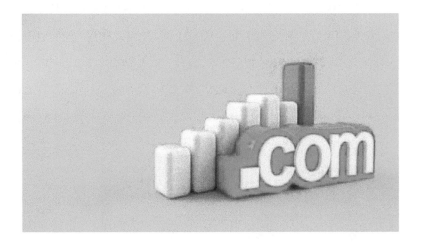

Chapter 10: Some other ideas

Turn Passion to Profit

" What do you really want to do?"

This is one of the most daunting life questions that hit us some time in our teenage years and stretches up until forever. Some people find the answer sooner, and others never really find out. Circumstances often lead us to do things that we'd rather not, and necessity tells us that we cannot always do what we want because the cool things don't always bring food to the table.

What if life finally granted you the opportunity to work on what you've always wanted?

The internet is a world without boundaries. It finds value in the smallest of things, reward your grandest efforts and grants you the possibility of reaching out to all corners of the earth. What may not work in your town may be a hit on a city that is miles away from you. This is a stellar opportunity to finally explore what you've always wanted, feed it to the world wide web and even earn from it! All in the comforts of your home!

Many people have followed their passion and have now gone on to become professional artists, writers, consultants and the like. Do not hesitate to explore your own.

Get Paid for Your Reviews

Do you remember spending a whole day debating with girlfriends on the phone on which makeup was better or what brand of shampoo was the best? Looks like you can actually earn from it!

Again, it all boils down to marketing and advertising. Companies would love to know what you think of their product and are willing to pay you for your opinion.

Vindale Research is an online shopping site that pays you for posting reviews about items that you have bought from their site. You can expect to get paid up to $75 both for answering reviews and surveys on their site. You can make withdrawals via PayPal to ensure the security of your information.

Other websites pay you to review other items like User Testing for website interface reviews ($10 per review), Shvoong for reviews about newspapers, academic papers, books and random articles (payout depends on revenue of the product).

Review Stream is another popular pay-for-review website that pays $2 for every review on hot topics and also gives additional points when people rate up to your review.

There are a great many legitimate sites that offer payment for each review you give their products; now, isn't that a better way to spend all that energy raving or ranting about various consumer products?

Pay-for-review is another targeted approach for earning extra money. It is a great feedback system that the common consumer can use to reach out to retail companies in order to improve the very products we use.

Getting paid for sharing what you think about your latest purchase seems to be a neat idea, yes?

The Era of Mobile Apps

The smartphone and tablet market are now saturated with apps of all shapes and sizes. While smartphone designs and capabilities are all the craze right now, mobile apps are quickly catching up because they allow you to use your phone for several functionalities that the manufacturer wasn't able to include.

There's an app that measures your heart rate, an app that reads your horoscope for the day, an app that gives directions, an app that plays dice and not to mentions the gazillions of games that are available both in Android's Playstore and I phone's Appstore. The most successful of apps are known to be earning thousands of bucks per month out of user purchases, and believe it or not, Candy Crush is actually earning $947,000 every day. Incredible!

What attracts a lot of people is that it is open to everyone with the right number of tools and knowledge. In spite of the saturated market, people still love to create something that others can use or have fun with, quite similar to publishing e-books. And there's always that hope of being the next viral thing and waking up a millionaire the next day. Remember Flappy Bird?

Creating a mobile app entails a complicated web of wireframing, data integration, user-interface development and design, server-side logic and user management, among others. But the bottom line is to create an app that can delight, entertain or be greatly useful for specific applications.

The interface of the app must be designed in an appealing and engaging manner following the modern laws of design and user-friendliness. It has to be comprehensively tested and refined with zero to minimal bugs.

Android will let your apps launch untested in the Playstore, while iPhone requires all apps to undergo a review process that takes about a week. Once it's out there, your apps will be tested through user reviews and purchases.

One thing that developers forget, though, is to advertise their apps. This is essential if you really want to earn.

Bookkeeping

Another technical skill that could be put to use is bookkeeping. This basically entails keeping a clean record of all the cash flow details of a particular company or individual. This includes keeping track of all invoices, receipts, earnings and payables. This is gaining increasing momentum in several countries because more and more entrepreneurs are trying to enter businesses without knowing how to streamline their cash flow. This is critical to businesses because it allows you to keep track of your collectibles and your deadlines. Unmanaged finances will only cost a business more money and a bad reputation in the future.

This type of industry is good for people who don't get bored with numbers, have an eye for detail and the integrity to keep records clean. Various online courses are now being offered for people who would like to get the hang of the industry, but one may require a couple of years of actual training before gaining enough reputation to work as an independent bookkeeper.

Armed with sufficient storage, reliable accounting software, and a great ability to organize, bookkeeping can be a great work-at-home job for people. The average bookkeeper earns $25 to $40 per hour but can also increase depending on workload and location.

Adding tax preparation services can also increase your value as a bookkeeper, and so does an accounting background. Having business cards and referrals from former satisfied clients will also boost your reputation.

Pay-to-Click Sites (PTC)

 Clixsense, Probux, Neobux and Fusebux are some of the most trusted online sites when it comes to pay-to-click industries. This is by far the easiest way to earn money on the internet. It basically starts with you clicking the "Register now" button and signing up for their services; then, you start to familiarize yourself with the website interface while earning. It will not require you to pay upon registration though some of them may require an optional 'investment' for you to grow your earnings faster, although you'll do just fine even without availing of this option.

The main mechanism of earning is by clicking and watching 30-second ads and quickly moving on to the next, depending on how much you intend to earn.

Pros: This is the easiest way to earn on the internet; no experience or necessary skill sets are required, and you decide how much time you are willing to allot. They also design the site and advertisements well enough to keep you engaged and entertained during the whole session.

The product also has a community forum where users can share ideas and help in navigating the site, which makes it all the more legitimate because you are confident that other people are really using and getting paid with it.

These companies also make use of PayPal, Payza, Perfect Money, SolidTrust Pay, and Ego Pay, which allow users to receive their payment without really revealing too much financial information.

Cons: In as much as they provide the easiest ways to earn money, they also have the lowest rates of payment. Clixsense has one of the highest payouts, which is $0.02 per click.

These sites also have a minimum payout threshold, meaning you have to accumulate a certain amount before you are able to withdraw to your account. Clixsense has a minimum payout level of $10, which means you'll have to click through the ads 500 times before you are able to withdraw. That's about four and a half hours of viewing ads! As you see, it may take a long while before you are really able to withdraw a substantial amount.

Other sites offer a smaller payout threshold like Neobux that only requires $2, and Probux, for only $5. However, the rate per click is also lower.

Earning PTC ads is a great idea only when you intend for this to be an additional activity while browsing the internet. You'll also need to be extra patient with it because it will take a while before you are able to really earn.

Value in the Smallest Efforts

Companies spend a great bulk of their budget on advertising and will go to great lengths just to extend their brand reach and to understand how their consumers perceive their products. This concept has driven an online industry that allows people to earn dollars by doing very simple tasks like clicking links, answering surveys, viewing advertisements and the like.

Many people are flocking to this kind of industry because of the promise of earning with very little effort.

As attractive as it is, this type of industry is also one of the most prone to abuse and scams and must therefore be examined carefully before getting involved. If you feel like the pay is way too large for the equivalent effort required, follow your gut feel and check if it is a scam.

Nevertheless, there are legitimate companies who really use these methods as part of their advertising, and it's a great deal for people who want to earn extra bucks for a couple of minutes. If you can spend a whole hour watching cat videos, then the idea of answering a 15-minute survey for five dollars shouldn't be a bad idea, yes?

No effort is too small for the internet. Everything has value.

Conclusion:

To conclude, business valuation, if done correctly, can work in your favor. That is also true for the intended buyer. Business valuation can be done in-house or through the help of certified public accountants and business valuators.

It is also very important to discuss matters about selling your business with people around you (business partners, workmates and family members) to help you cement the idea. Once a business changes hands, it is permanent until the current owner decides to sell again.

Placing value on your business and eventually selling it off is the culmination of all the years, tears and hard work of building the business and running its day-to-day operations. Some business owners are anxious about separating themselves from their own businesses. In the end, through proper business valuation, you will be able to see your business as it is. It is just an income-generating machine that you built and developed.

Remember that although this book provides you with the basic knowledge on how to place a value on your business' worth, the need for professional business valuators and certified public accountants are still necessary. The practical knowledge that they possess concerning this aspect of the business is one gained through constantly perfecting their craft.

This book aims to open your eyes to what goes behind the scenes during these transactions and help you understand the business valuation process. The simple action steps provided in each chapter and subchapters are there for you to perform on your own business.

Finally, it is imperative that you are keen on the details of your own business and are meticulous about keeping records. These records will help you find the true value of your business.

Deducting | The Right Way

Untangling Small Business Accounting and Taxes Based on Online Activities

By

LEONARDO BLANCO

Table of Contents

Introduction

You'll definitely have to do a lot of day-to-day daily duties, including accounting, when you first launch your small online business. Knowing how to track and forecast your business's income and expenses is a valuable skill for growth, so familiarise yourself with the basics of accounting.

And if you're willing to outsource your accounting and bookkeeping right now, learning the fundamentals can help you appreciate your finance professional's findings and correctly evaluate your company's financial wellbeing.

We've broken down all you need to understand about small online business accounting, including how to monitor and evaluate your business's main financial indicators, in the parts below.

Chapter: 1 Online Business and its importance?

There has never been a better or easier time in history to start your own business than now. Everyone is connected now, regardless of their income status or geographic location, thanks to the development and growth of easy-to-use website creation tools and social media.

Whether you are rich and powerful or impoverished, you can now freely share your abilities and connect with people around the world. It can also be very inexpensive and simple to get started for those looking to start an online business.

Many people have started online businesses for less than 200 dollars. (the cost purchasing a domain name, hosting service and professional theme).

You can start a business if you can connect with others and fill a need.

In fact, there are numerous advantages to starting and owning your own online business, ranging from increased income and freedom to assisting others in achieving their own personal goals; however, in order to keep things simple and to the point, I will only go over seven of the many advantages to starting and owning your own online business.

1.1 The importance of eCommerce

1. eCommerce Helps You Reduce Your Costs

To make your online store, it isn't essential that you have every one of your items introduced in an actual space. There're various organizations that work online where they just demonstrate all their stock through their electronic business.

This suggests not just saving by not requiring a purchase or rental of premises, yet besides all that includes electric power, the internet, and so forth or then again in the event that you need to have one, so clients have an actual space, it doesn't need to be just about as extensive as all that you offer. Regardless, you'll reduce your expenses.

2. eCommerce Helps Businesses Go Global

Straightforwardly identified with the previous point, this reality permits you to put your items available to be purchased anywhere on the planet. They won't have the express need to venture out to where you're to perceive what you've to bring to the table.

If you're running an actual store, it'll be restricted by the geological zone that you can support, yet possessing an eCommerce site will offer you the chance to expand your effort. It will offer your items and administrations to clients around the entire world, paying little heed to the time zone and distance.

Besides, this wipes out a wide range of topographical and etymological tango hindrances. Your online business converted into various dialects will permit them to purchase from various nations.

With eCommerce & mobile business also, the whole world is your jungle gym. Your services and products are accessible for many clients sitting on another edge of the world.

In this way, if you need to develop your online business worldwide, it is a good thought to begin making your online store & localize it in various dialects.

3. eCommerce Can Also Be Done through Fewer Overheads and Fewer Risk

Beginning an online store might mean essentially bring down expenses of a start-up contrasted with a physical retailer. The retailer or the online entrepreneur does not need to think about the shop rent high costs, employing a sales associate to facilitate the client, efforts, service charges, safety, and so forth. This, can empower you to sell them at good costs. Moreover, an online shop allows you to grasp expanded productivity with less danger.

4. eCommerce Can Broaden Your Brand & Expand the Business

Having some eCommerce store can be used to widen the scope of items or administrations available to be purchased, extending your business, bringing you a huge number of customers, and broadening your deals. It is the ideal method to take a personal brand from a conventional block & mortar store to a novice, all-around adored one.

With eCommerce, there's no compelling reason to have more than one branch, only one particular online store permitting you to completely arrive at clients without agonizing over moving areas; you can deal with your online business from home.

It's imperative to specify that eCommerce will be useful for Both B2B & B2C businesses to help personal brand mindfulness in the online market.

5. eCommerce Offers Better Marketing Opportunities

Your eCommerce website is the best advertising device that you could at any point have. On a web account, anybody can advertise via online apparatuses such as web-based media advertising, email promoting, web search tool advertising, pay per click advertisements, and SEO assists you in constructing valuable connections & contacts.

For instance, with great SEO, your online store will show up in the top searches of SERPs. Likewise, online media organizations will give you a stage to draw in and construct trust with your clients through audits and appraisals, just as keeping them acknowledged with normal posts about your items and offers.

6. Your Online Store Will Stay Open 24*7/365:

Additionally, one of the incredible significances of eCommerce that eCommerce merchants can appreciate is store timings are currently all day, every day/365 as the eCommerce stores are working 24 hours per day, 7 days per week, contrasted with the customary stores.

Along these lines, merchants can expand their deals by boosting the number of requests. Nonetheless, it's additionally useful for clients when they can buy items and administrations at whatever point they need, whether it's early morning/midnight.

7. eCommerce Is Easier & More Convenient

Individuals' lives are rushed; getting to an actual store implies taking a ton of time and exertion. In this way, beginning an online store implies you can find a way into your client's bustling lives, making the items they need available when they need them.

The agreeable thing about eCommerce is purchasing those choices that are fast, simple, helpful, and simple in understanding with the capability to move supports on the web.

"In web-based shopping, your product is consistently a single tick away instead of actual shopping where you might be compelled to hang tight for quite a long time or months before a product you requested is accessible," says Heritage House, who sell kid suits on the web.

On account of eCommerce's accommodation, shoppers can save heaps of time, endeavors just as cash via looking for their items effectively and making buying on the web.

8. Personalize Your Shopping Experience

In the event that there is one of the unmistakable favorable circumstances of having an online store, you will have the option to know what your buyer does. Genuinely, it would be entirely awkward for a likely purchaser to enter your store, and you were constantly behind him, inquiring what he needs or for what valid reason he doesn't accept your item.

Web-based business permits you, for instance, to know when in the process you left the buy midway and even recall that you left it in the center by sending an email. This, also, can assist you with improving your shopping experience for other events: shortening the means to finish the request or offering those purchaser items with comparable attributes.

9. Improve the Image of Your Business

Among the benefits of having some online store, there's no uncertainty that it likewise incorporates improving the picture of your organization. Offering a decent online deals stage to clients will give your organization an extraordinary corporate appearance.

Not exclusively will it end up being state-of-the-art; however, it will likewise show interest in encouraging buyer buys. For instance, it keeps you from making a trip to the actual spot of offer and permits you to analyze costs from home. Likewise, because of what we have referenced as devotion or input, you can even actualize upgrades in your items that clients will esteem emphatically

10. Easily Receive Feedback on Products

Have you generally needed to understand consumers' opinions about what you are selling to offer more or make it greater? Indeed, the online store will permit you to get that input to actualize enhancements in the business, through star appraisals, with the chance of leaving remarks.

Also, the client will feel heard after their buy. There could be no greater method to thank you for your trust in buying your organization's items. Besides, in the event that you offer the quality, you'll have nothing to stress over. Empowering an immediate channel where others notice what they can anticipate from the given resource is an extraordinary public illustration of trust in online business.

11. Maximum Security of Transactions

Today, working on the internet is practically more secure and dependable than doing this in an actual store. From home, without anybody watching on your mysterious number or Mastercard. The eCommerce site should have an SSL endorsement.

This testament not just permits safe perusing on the website. What's more, it keeps the information scrambled to be protected to add keys & passwords. This won't just be important for the client's business account yet to utilize much more touchy information, for example, Mastercard data with complete, true serenity.

It merits referencing that 33% of eCommerce specialists distinguished security, versatile installments, and portable applications as the main interests in 2019. Security will keep on being one of the best spotlights on eCommerce.

With changes in innovation, client practices, and shopping designs, dealers should give arrangements guaranteeing the trust and security of shopping measures.

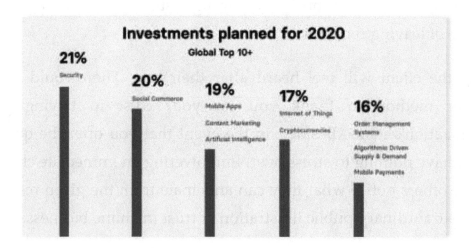

12 Ready for the Trade of the Future

It's another significant detail considering the long haul of the business. Search customer spending and patterns, the headway of innovation, and the most recent insights gauge that by 2040, 95 percent of buys will be executed through the web.

Along these lines, it's not just discussing a pattern of the present yet additionally about what the business relations of things to come will be. Furthermore, similarly, as though you are not on the internet, you don't exist; if your business doesn't sell on the web, it is monstrously restricting its deals.

13. Increase in Sales

Everything mentioned previously is centered around a certain thing: having the option to build your deals. At the end of the day, the business relies on selling more, and in this way, what it will be based on.

All the past focuses add to the way that the 10th and last bit of leeway are that there's an expansion in the acquisition of your items. Arriving at more clients, improving your items on account of remarks, or being accessible 24 hours daily will without a doubt add to the entirety of this.

As a rule, it's normally beautifully simple, with minimal risk and cost to begin an eCommerce business. As you choose your benefits/items incisively, have a suitable plan, got the right partner to help you construct your store, there is very much potential for automated revenue & high ROI.

Chapter: 2 Accounting and Its Purpose

Accounting is the structured method of defining, tracking, assessing, classifying, checking, and transmitting financial records. It shows a company's profit or loss over a specified time, as well as the value and quality of its assets and liabilities, as well as its shareholders' equity.

2.1 Why is Accounting Important?

Accounting is very important and necessary for small business owners because it requires owners, administrators, investors, and other stakeholders to determine the company's financial results. Accounting provides key facts regarding profit & loss, costs & earnings, assets & liabilities for decision-making, scheduling, and risk management within an organization.

Accounting's main goal is to document financial transactions in books of records in order to recognize, calculate, and transmit economic results. Furthermore, tax reporting authorities mandate you to maintain simple books that track profits and expenditures.

2.2 What Is the Purpose of Accounting?

Accounting is regarded as the "Language of Business." It is a system of communicating financial information to multiple uses for decision-making purposes. The major objects of accounting are:

1. Recording transactions

Accounting's primary purpose is to control a systematic, accurate, and full record of a company's financial activities. The accounting system's backbone is made up of these reports. When appropriate, company owners should be able to review and evaluate transactions.

2. Budgeting and planning

Business owners must prepare how they can distribute their limited resources, such as workers, cash, machinery and equipment to meet the company's goals.

Budgeting and planning, an integral aspect of business management, enable companies to prepare accordingly by forecasting requirements and resources. This assists in the coordination of multiple corporate segments.

3. Decision making

Accounting assists in a variety of decision-making processes and facilitates business owners in developing policies to improve business process efficiency. The price to be charged for products and services, the resources required to produce these products and services, as well as financing and business opportunities are all examples of decisions based on accounting information.

4. Business performance

Business owners may use financial records to assess how good their organization is doing. Financial reports provide a credible tool to evaluate important performance indicators, encouraging business owners to compare their output to that of their rivals as well as their past performance.

5. Financial position

The financial statements issued at the end of the accounting period represent a company's financial position at the time. It displays the amount of capital invested, the number of funds utilized by the company, the profit and loss, as well as the number of assets and liabilities.

6. Liquidity

Mismanagement of funds is a common cause of small business failure. Accounting assists in assessing a company's liquidity, which is characterized as the cash and other liquid capital available to pay off debts. Via the identification of bottlenecks, the information lowers the risk of bankruptcy.

7. Financing

Accounting assists business owners in the preparation of historical financial records and also financial forecasts that may be utilized while preparing for a loan or securing investment.

8. Control

Accounting assists in avoiding losses attributable to stealing, fraud, mistakes, injury, obsolescence, and mismanagement by enforcing different checks within the company. Internal monitoring secures the company's finances to eliminate long-term risks.

9. Legal requirements

Businesses must retain correct financial statements of their activities and disclose those records with shareholders, tax officials, and regulators, according to the statute. The financial statements and details are often needed for the filing of indirect and direct taxes.

Chapter: 3 Why Is Accounting Useful for Small Business Owners?

One of the most common causes of small business failure, especially in the first year, is poor financial management. Accounting plays a critical role in providing information that assists small companies in their growth and advancement when they have a restricted budget and other resources.

Accounting is important for small business owners for the following reasons:

➤ Maintain a careful watch on the cash balance. You should enforce strategies for effective record-keeping and a solid financial strategy to prevent the company cash flow from running dry.

➤ Cost management may help small business owners grasp the principles of fixed expenses, variable costs, and how to correctly cost a project. This way, you won't waste funds on a project you felt would be profitable.

➤ Accounting helps you to have a clearer view of the company's health. Learn to interpret a balance sheet, financial statement, and cash flow statement to do this.

➤ It helps you in identifying and avoiding consumer, employee, and supplier bribery and stealing.

➤ You'll be more able to tackle investigations if you grasp corporate accounts and transactions.

➢ When working with corporate leaders who have a strong grip on the company's finances and are mindful of the financial consequences, bankers are more comfortable.

If you're a sole proprietor or have workers, the trick to expanding your small company is to monitor your financial records on a routine basis and build a comprehensive budget that helps you to recognize operating inefficiencies. Saving a little money on a few things will add up to a lot of money in the long run.

Chapter: 4 Accounting basics How to Run a Successful Online Business

A painful task is accounting. It is the dull side of the business. But you can't ignore it if you want your business to grow. You could try to dump all your receipts into a drawer and hand them over to a stranger. Yet you are going to give them financial power. That means losing your business's future. You will hand them a sweet slice of change to do it all for you, too. I guarantee it isn't as hard as you may be afraid of, though. And, for day-to-day operations, you shouldn't require an accountant. You should still know the fundamentals yourself, even though you are paying for guidance. You may acknowledge and challenge what someone is talking to you in this context. It's your business at stake, after all.

The following accounting fundamentals help you need to know to grasp your money.

1. Get Accounting Software

Don't bother using excel or a calculator to piece it all together. Do yourself a favor and get software for accounting. FreshBooks are sold to clients that operate e-commerce businesses. Or there are a variety of accounting software apps you should get right in their app store if you use Shopify. Your business and interests would rely on the right choice. Make sure you choose a bookkeeping system while you're shopping in the app store. Look for software to monitor revenue, expenditures, and inventory. Keep away from programs that generate invoices only or include reports only. You want a tool that's able to do everything for you. Select one that can sync directly to your e-commerce store, whether you want apps like Shopify or go for something different. It would make things even better.

2. Monitor Cash Flow

Get one if you don't have a separate bank account with your business yet. You need to realize that making money is your job. And watching the cash balance is the best way to see this. When you've got more coming in than heading out, you actually do well, don't you? The timing of money going out and coming back can also be monitored. After all, what if, tomorrow, all your bills are due? When you have one million rolling's in next month, it won't mean a whole lot if you can't pay the workers by then. Bear in mind any investments on your accounts that you have. What ways of payment do you give your clients? Are some of them putting a grip on the money? From the moment a consumer spends to the time the money is in your accounts, is there a five-day delay? When you're finding out when you have resources to spare, you ought to remember this. For monitoring currency, Shopify offers a free template. With Excel, you can quickly build your own.

Per week, monitor what you plan to spend. Track the money that you plan per week to come in. You realize you're going to have a challenge if what you need to pay is more than the new bank balance and what's coming in. To improve to boost your cash flow, adopt these tips:

- Do not spend anything sooner than you have got to. If it is due within thirty days, compensate it within thirty days.

- To ensure revenue stays through, suggest selling recurring payment contracts or subscriptions to consumers.

- Hold a reserve 'just in case' in your company bank account.

- Do not overcomplicate yourself. You do not require massive statements of cash balance.

3. Determine how inventory should be counted

Ignore this step if you're selling a service. Inventory is the product that you sell or all the materials that you use to make that item. Do not forget to include any costs for your product being wrapped or packaged. Decide what minimum inventory volume you want to have on hand, and make sure you are tracking inventory before you pass this point so you can reorder. The last thing you want is for inventory to run out and lose sales.

Why does inventory form part of the basics of accounting?

Money equals inventory.

It is the money you spent buying that stuff. You will not make any money back until you sell your product. And while it is sitting in your warehouse, the money tied to your inventory can change (or store, or apartment).

If I purchase 50 items for 100 dollars each, and the price rises up to 150 dollars tomorrow, then immediately, my inventory is worth more.

So, if tomorrow's price falls to 50 dollars, the worth of my inventory is less.

And beware of 'shrinkage'!

That's why, unexpectedly, you have fewer inventory than you should have.

You know you've purchased 50 items. You understand that you sold and delivered 40. You should be left 10 items, right? What if you have only 8 left? This is shrinkage. Perhaps an item was misplaced, or robbed, or destroyed and had to be discarded away. There are plenty of explanations for why this happens. When you don't have a physical department location, the positive thing is the shrinkage is smaller. Currently, factory shrinkage is pretty poor. Less than 1% of the overall product is a normal shrinkage. It's also less probable that you will have shrinkage if you're running a business out of your house. After all, if you're the only person around it, you are less likely to see anyone rob the inventory. Compared with a large warehouse, it's also a lot tougher to lose stock in an apartment. Having said that, shrinkage will happen to everyone. This is why it's necessary to routinely physically count inventory. If you have missed 100 dollars worth of goods and factor it into your accounting, you ought to know.

CGS, which means cost of goods sold, is an expense directly linked to the goods sold by you. This is inventory sold, and also how much it costs to produce that inventory. Suppose say there is one widget you sell. The cost of goods sold for that widget should be whatever it costs you for the parts and also whatever it costs to build it. If the widget parts cost 60 dollars, the packaging cost is 15 dollars, and you paid someone 15 to put it together, that the total cost of the widget will 90 dollars.

MATERIAL COST	60$
PACKAGING COST	15$
LABOUR COST	<u>15$</u>
TOTAL COST OF GOODS SOLD	**90 $**

4. Calculate all Expenses

You already understand that the costs are directly tied to the volume of sales. Next, you need to know how much it costs you for anything else. Any costs that do not grow as you sell more or drop when you sell fewer are known as 'fixed costs.' Let's say If you pay a monthly rent, for instance, the price is set. If you sell one widget or a million, it won't shift. Such costs are not part of the cost of the goods sold, and the profit margin is not compensated for. However, they do control your earnings and your cash flow.

Some Common fixed expenses are

➢ Utilities

➢ Rent

- Interest on loan payments

- Property Tax

- Wages

These expenses are considered a fixed expense because even though you sell nothing next month, you have to reimburse them. Do not confuse this with an expense where every month is the very same amount. An expense such as electricity may be more than one month longer than the next. Or maybe there's more to it in winter than in summer. In accounting standards, it is always a fixed expense. You will use an average for budgeting if expenses change month to month.

5. Find out Break-Even Sales

Budgeting and planning are essential aspects of operating a business. Next, you are not only going to want to know if last month you made a profit, you are going to want to know if this month and next you want to earn more.

Your break-even sales amount is the amount of sales dollars you need to earn to cover all your costs.

Let's assume, for instance, all the fixed costs add up to 5,000 dollars a month. This ensures that you have to sell enough of the product to meet the cost of producing it (including labor cost) and also an additional 5,000 dollars only to break-even (no profit, no loss).

Break-Even Sale = _____Fixed Cost_____

Revenue per unit-Variable cost per unit

$$= \quad \underline{\text{Fixed Cost}}$$

Unit Margin

If your break-even number of units are 5,000 and you sell only 3000, then you are in problem. And if break-even 5000 and you sell 7000, then you are in a good position.

6. Schedule your right tax rates for customers

Here is the aspect for which most citizens groan: taxation. Taxes are necessary, and they may become very complex. At this point, you may want to contact a tax consultant specialist, if you sell a number of various goods & services to a lot of people around the world. Thankfully, systems these days are fairly smart. For you, the software can take control of much of this.

7. Prepare your Tax Payments

Now, if you are properly set up to collect tax, you also need to make sure you are ready to pay it. Your tax laws will rely on where you are located, actually. At a minimum, believe that as much tax as you have earned must be submitted. This suggests that it is necessary to consider that money of tax is set aside. If not, then when you submit tax return, you face some hurdles. Many online shopping platforms allow you to pay tax on your purchase price, such as Shopify.

For example, if you buy a product that price is 100 dollars and the tax rate is 20%, then you will pay the amount included tax.

Product Cost	100 $

Tax Rate (15%)	15 $
Total amount included Tax	**115 $**

8. Balance Sheet

At the end, you must understand your balance sheet. We have already addressed all as well as cash balance on the income statement. The balance sheet is the final thing to cover. This is what helps you watch the long-term performance of your business and see how your business is performing in general. An income statement is a timely overview. The broader image is a balance sheet. Assets, liabilities, and equity make up the balance sheet.

BUSINESS CONSULTING COMPANY
BALANCE SHEET
As at December 31, 2015

Assets		$	Liabilities & Stockholders' equity		$
Current assets:			Liabilities:		
Cash		85,550	Notes payable		5,000
Accounts receivable		4,700	Accounts payable		1,600
Prepaid building rent		1,500	Salaries payable		2,000
Unexpired insurance		3,600	Income tax payable		3,000
Supplies		250	Unearned service revenue		4,400
Total current assets		95,600	Total liabilities		16,000
Non-current assets:			Stockholders' equity:		
Equipment	9,000		Capital stock	50,000	
Acc. dep. - Equipment	3,600	5,400	Retained earnings	35,000	85,000
Total assets		101,000	Total liabilities & stockholders' equity		101,000

I have finally discussed all the accounting basics you should be practicing day to day and month to month. Start with simple accounting software. It can make your life a lot easier.

Then, note that cash is king, and keep a grip on your cash flow. You should be doing this on a frequent basis unless you have a large cash reserve built.

Next, you ought to consider the revenue, expenditures, and earnings. This is your income statement, which lets you know whether you are earning money per week, month or year.

Do not neglect to schedule for taxation. Set up the e-commerce platform to receive them if you need to. Place the money together to reimburse them should you need to.

Finally, construct the balance sheet. Or let the accounting software do it for you. This will help you exactly how 'healthy' the business is long term. It's a simple way to know if you have so much debt.

There are plenty of other accounting rules and methods that will help you save money at tax time.

There will also be reporting options that can be addressed whether you're seeking to get investors or a loan for growth.

But for running your company, don't get pulled into the complicated laws. It will only distract you from your crucial day job of operating your business.

An accountant will assist you with something beyond and above the fundamentals if you require to.

Chapter: 5 Common Accounting Mistakes and How to Avoid Them

Numerous new business visionaries handle their bookkeeping and accounting when they are beginning. Here are how to stay away from some normal DIY bookkeeping ruins.

When numerous business visionaries first begin, they attempt to deal with their bookkeeping to set aside cash. Notwithstanding, following each penny of pay, costs, charges, and seller installments are messy and tedious. Errors can happen effectively & they can charge your huge business loads of cash.

To help you forestall these monetary blunders, the absolute most regular bookkeeping ruins are below that entrepreneurs make and — all the more significantly — how to keep away from them.

1. Lack of organization

Accounting requires extraordinary association abilities. You'll need to record each exchange, digitize or store receipts for future reference, figure duties, and the sky is the limit from there. In case you're not appropriately following or putting away data, you'll probably miss a significant exchange or lose a receipt, which could get you into difficulty come season of tax.

2. Not following a regular accounting schedule

With the wide range of various duties, you have as an entrepreneur, refreshing your books may tumble to the lower part of your plan for the day. Notwithstanding, it's imperative to set a normal timetable for including late payments and costs. While every day refreshes are ideal, you ought to, in any event, enter your exchanges consistently.

3. Failing to reconcile accounts

While you are recording monetary information and income in your books, you need to routinely return and guarantee your ledger mirrors that equivalent equilibrium. In the event that there's a difference between the two, there's likely a mistake that requires quick thoughtfulness regarding keep the issue from deteriorating. Consistently exploring your business financial balances against your books can likewise help you get any fake exchanges that may have happened.

4. Ignoring small transactions

It's not difficult to disregard that little thank you blessing you sent to a customer or the ream of printer paper you got on your way back to the workplace. Regardless of how immaterial the exchange is, it's critical to record it & get some receipt. In case of an assessment review, you should have the option to give the IRS records of all your costs of doing business, even the little ones.

5. Not backing up your data

Envision if the gadget on which you put away your business' monetary data was lost, hacked, or taken — and you did not have it upheld up anyplace. These problems can emerge whenever, and you should be set up to reestablish your books. Luckily, there are numerous reinforcement alternatives accessible that will empower you to keep an extra, state-of-the-art duplicate of the business financials.

6. Not using an accounting software

In case you're monitoring your business funds in an Excel bookkeeping page or a paper record, you might need to consider moving up to programming. Putting resources into the correct bookkeeping programming can assist you with maintaining a strategic distance from botches and, at last, make it simpler to deal with your accounts.

Most bookkeeping programmings incorporate the financial balance, meaning less manual work. These projects likewise make it simple to back up your information if there should be an occurrence of a crisis. Also, if you wind up expecting to recruit a bookkeeping administration for your business, having unified programming will guarantee the bookkeeper has all the recorded information they require to deal with your books, finance, and assessments.

Regardless of whether you're taking care of your bookkeeping or moving to an expert, accounting mix-ups can cause significant issues for your business. It is ideal to forestall & face these problems.

Chapter: 6 Business Challenges & Solutions

Small enterprises experience a number of obstacles throughout their first few years of operation. Others are more challenging to resolve than others, and according to the U.S. Bureau of Labour Statistics, about 20% of small companies collapse during their first year. Fifty percent go under by the close of their fifth year, and that figure increases to 80 percent by the tenth year.

With so poor survival rates, it's clear to see why people are worried for their first few years of the company. In fact, though, many common market issues and problems are actually fixable. You can notice several moments when you need to take a step back, make an effort to understand the pressure points that you experience and re-think your plan.

Each small business faces some problems here, including some tactical tips about how to solve them.

1. Find the Customers

2. Increasing Brand Awareness

3. Designing Email List

4. Lead Generation

5. Delighting the Customers

6. Hiring Talented People

7. Managing Workflow

8. Financial Strategy

9. Scaling

1. Find Customers

This first one is not just an issue for small enterprises. Marketers of well-known firms such as Toyota, Apple, KFC, and McDonald's are not yet waiting for the leads to come in: Also, the largest, most popular firms have employees working tirelessly to attract new customers every single day.

Finding consumers may be especially challenging for small companies that are not well-known. It seems, for instance, like there are too many platforms you may choose to concentrate on. How do you decide what to prioritize and where money can be allocated?

How to solve it:

Seeking consumers begins by deciding who the target consumer is. It does not work for everyone to spray and pray — you need to ensure you distribute the message to the correct people.

By designing buyer personas, you will get a feel of what your potential buyers are like, what they are doing, and where they spend some time online.

It will significantly boost the market outcomes by producing very particular ones. When you have developed your buyer personas, you can start developing content and reaching out to your potential buyers in areas where they invest time online and with ads that appeal to them.

2. Brand Awareness

Customers can not purchase from you if they don't know who you are. Often it may seem like the largest brands of today seem to have sprung up from nowhere. When did it turn into a household name? Why did they continue to spread so quickly? Is it feasible for your organization to expand in the same way?

Of note, the hard work, mistakes, and rejections of each of these businesses existed behind the scenes. But there are tactics how you can begin right away to spread the word about your company and create a strong reputation.

How to solve it:

There are several approaches to increase brand awareness, but concentrate on three in this book about public relations, blogging & co-marketing.

- **Public Relations**

Public relations are less about competing for a place on a news site and more about concentrating your message on the consumer and discovering your location. I suggest reading First Round Capital's excellent research about what entrepreneurs and small companies often get wrong regarding public relations, which also provides some useful guidance about how to find out who reports the industry, develop relationships, and communicate with reporters.

- **Blogging**

Running a high-quality blog on a daily basis can also help you create brand recognition. A blog not only helps push traffic to your website and turn the traffic into leads, but that also helps you to build authority and confidence among your prospects in your industry. It will also assist you in the creation of an email list, which takes us to our next step.

- **C0-marketing**

Collaborating with another brand allows you to inherit some of their name and credibility while still producing brand evangelists outside of your immediate radius. It's an ideal opportunity to complement the organic marketing activities by acquiring a wide range of potential connections. More details about how to get acquainted with co-marketing can be found in our ebook.

3. Designing Email List

You must create confidence by being top-of-mind and continually delivering value to drive prospects down their buyer's path to finally becoming your client.

The first move is to link prospects to your email list.

As if creating an email list is not complicated enough, the typical marketing account degraded by 22.5 percent last year. That means you'll need to expand your email list by nearly a quarter just to hold it up to date, let alone develop it. Seeking opportunities to continuously introduce fresh, different email addresses to the lists is the task of the marketing staff.

Yet what many people term "making an email list" is simply purchasing an email list, and it is never a smart idea to purchase an email list. I repeat not a good idea. It is not only a waste of resources, but it'll also damage your email deliverability and I.P. credibility. If purchasing or renting email lists is your new plan, then it's time to rebuild and find appropriate ways to position certain tools.

How to solve it:

Develop opt-in email lists instead of purchasing or renting lists. Subscribers who willingly give you their email address so that you can send them updates make up an opt-in email list.

The process of opting in needs the accessibility of the website that catches their email address. This can be accomplished with a shape builder or other method to transform (more on that later).

Creating a market is the other part of the puzzle. Through making excellent blog posts, you will do this and make it convenient for people to subscribe, which can help you improve your web visibility, build up search credibility, and develop evangelists from your content at the same time.

Create an informative opt-in message and email it to your old list, inviting contacts to re-opt-in and pledging to delete any contacts that don't reply.

Rising your email list does not often mean growing your sales-qualified lead list, which leads me to my next stage.

4. Lead Generation

Lead generation is another concern most small companies share, namely, creating sufficient leads to maintain the sales staff satisfied.

However, the most critical goal of a marketing team is to produce high-quality leads in vast amounts. A decent lead generation engine transforms website users into future buyers and maintains a constant stream of sales leads flowing in as you sleep.

How to solve it:

To make the lead generation method function for your business, you must first increase the conversion rate of your current website. The most critical asset you have for converting opportunities into clients is your website. Look and question yourself from your website:

Do visitors specifically direct each of the webpages to take some action, or do they leave them uncertain what to do next?

Can you use a program, like HubSpot's free lead generation tool, that instantly pulls the inputs from your forms and brings them into your communication database?

For any single campaign that you manage, can you build custom landing pages?

Do you have CTAs for any of your blog posts for lead generation? (Have you got a blog at all?)

First, prioritize the most major blogs on your website. The homepage, "About" page, "Contact Us" page, and probably one or two of the most famous blog posts are usually the sites that pull in the bulk of visitors for most companies. Learn how to decide which sites to prioritize and how to customize them in this topic.

Then, utilizing conversion applications such as:

- Hello bars, hello

- Pop-up windows

- Diaposit-ins

Finally, free lead generation tools and applications for startups can be used. It is a huge obstacle in and of itself to afford ads in general, but it can be a game-changer to identify and incorporate the most effective free marketing methods.

5. Delighting the Customers

A perfect target is consumer loyalty, but much greater is customer delight. After all, the ones who purchase from you again, write expert opinions and accept case studies, and recommend you to others they trust, are delighted consumers.

You have to transcend standards and offer an unmatched service in order to gain true consumer delight such that your consumers become promoters of your brand.

How to solve it:

For your customer, it takes effort to begin solving in a fashion that converts them into crazed fans. Here are few moves that will bring you into the proper mindset:

➢ Realize why you were picked by your customers and what they want and need

➢ At the beginning of the commitment, set clear goals

➢ Deliver on certain requirements (and serve the wishes of your customers)

➢ Dream of innovative approaches to include unique extras that go beyond and above the call of duty.

➢ Continue to monitor consumer loyalty and allow changes.

6. Hiring talented workers

Without a great team who knows your mission and encourages your actions, none of the above will happen at large.

Hiring is one of the most challenging tasks for small companies, particularly when small corporate leaders are often under-resourced to start with. Hiring new hires is a huge deal and a difficult operation, and most businesses invest about 4,000 dollars per new hire on onboarding. Employee attrition can be very costly if you do not recruit properly.

Still, as Howard Bernstein, CEO of 2020 On-site Optometry, says, it is hard to recognize anything on your own. That's why it is crucial to identify and recruit the best people and others who are genuinely passionate about what you are doing.

How to solve it:

For a short-term recruiting approach, it is simple to send out a work description, screen candidates, and make a decision. However, owing to the high expenses of recruiting the incorrect employee, it's essential to dedicate a considerable amount of time to the hiring phase. When you may locate excellent workers, do not settle for decent staff, even though it takes more time. Good workers are what can drive the business to the next stage.

And when you build customer personas for your employers, for your career seekers, create nominee personas. For each new job you recruit for, the personas must be different, but they may share certain basic characteristics across the culture of the business.

Next, take care in drawing applicants to the name of your company and making them involved in knowing more. This would assist you in creating a recruitment pipeline that will have the same certainty in hiring as it does in revenue. Then translate certain opportunities into applicants.

7. Managing the Workflow

When you have the staff in position to make the magic possible, handling operations as you scale is the next obstacle. You want to make sure the staff has the procedures and resources they need to perform successful work fast.

Around the same moment, as a corporate owner, you will not be everywhere at once. So, how can you remain centered on the market but still ensuring that everybody in the organization gets everything they require?

How to solve it:

By providing opportunities for them to get suggestions, the only approach to diagnose the barriers the team encounters and improve productivity is to build ways to identify them. It is possible to do this via:

➢ Surveys on employee satisfaction

➢ Frequent discussions of immediate reports one-on-one

➢ Assuring the success of your direct reports Hold one-on-one conferences for their direct reports

➢ Occasionally, skip-level meetings are conducted.

➢ Asking regarding group risks and the things that cause them the most "pain" in their positions

➢ Seeking the similarities & the bottlenecks in the reviews you get

8. Financial Strategy

More capital (whether staff, resources or time) can ideally improve productivity and output. Providing all of the support you can to the staff is the first move in maintaining smooth operations.

In principle, it seems easy, but have you realized the caveat, everything. Can you? Unfortunately, corporate owners have revenue-based and margin-based spending constraints.

It becomes a struggle then to maximise productivity when operating under such limits, investing in the company without going overboard. By making sound choices focused on strong financial planning, this is solved.

How to solve it:

Each business is going to be different, so by remaining in front of invoices and bookkeeping, you'll need to use business credit carefully, reduce expenses where possible, and control cash flow. You will be assisted by corporate accountants and investment planners who evaluate the financial condition and help you to make sound choices.

9. Scaling

According to Nick Rellas, Drizly's co-founder and CEO, "There's this balance of creating power efficiency early, versus doing just what you have to do to get it all completed."

This is a complicated one, especially because every scenario is different. This topic can be seen in any aspect of the industry, including product growth, promotion, and content design, recruiting, and so on.

Most business leaders, for instance, would drive production at all costs. However, if you develop your business too fast, you'll find yourself trying to recruit staff quickly. Since preparation requires time, this can overwhelm the more seasoned team members. And if you wouldn't adequately prepare your staff, it might backfire.

How to solve it:

There's no right solution here, sadly. "The scale can tip one way or the other based on where you are in your business' lifecycle," Rellas says, "although I do agree you need both at various times."

Not obsessing about every aspect, but obsessing about the correct specifics, is what it comes right down to. For example, obsessing over product excellence may be less relevant than obsessing over customer care. It is easier to set away your worries and introduce a product that is not flawless so it can be changed and enhanced at all times. After all, you will understand a lot more easily what's effective and what isn't until the goods are in possession of your consumers.

Chapter: 7 Key Accounting Terms

The following are some standard accounting terminology that any small business owner should be acquainted with:

1. GAAP (Generally Agreed Accounting Standards)

2. Cash basis accounting

3. Accrual basis accounting

4. Accounts payable

5. Accounts receivable

1. Generally Agreed Accounting Standards (GAAP)

GAAP is a series of standard accounting principles that most American corporations are expected to follow. These guidelines detail how to keep track of, calculate, and report on the company's assets to third parties.

2. Cash basis accounting

Cash basis accounting is one of the two most popular accounting techniques, as it involves recording revenue and expenditures where they are earned and charged. Small companies like this approach because it is easy, despite the fact that it can offer a false impression of your cash flow (e.g., if you receive payment for a bill the month after you issued it).

3. Accrual basis accounting

Accrual basis accounting is needed for companies with a turnover of more than $25 million. You must log revenue as you charge it, rather than when it is paid, which implies you might be paying taxes on the money you haven't even received. However, opposed to cash basis accounting, it offers a more reliable long-term perspective of the finances.

4. Accounts payable

Accounts payable contains all unpaid payments for goods and services that you owe to suppliers. To accurately forecast cash flow, these liabilities must be considered against the company's assets and income.

5. Accounts receivable

Any of the money owing to the company by its consumers or clients is paid for in the accounts receivable. These accounts are normally monitored by invoices, which specify payment conditions (e.g., within a specified number of days of receipt) so you know when to expect incoming funds.

Chapter: 8 Common Accounting Reports

As part of their financial accounting procedures, every business must learn how to prepare a few main financial reports. Outside participants, such as owners, suppliers, and creditors, can use these documents to record the business's profits and expenses.

8.1 Profit & Loss Statement

When it is time to file your company returns with the IRS, accountants and tax preparers would most certainly ask for a (P&L) statement, but you will still need to share it with lenders if you apply for financing. Your profit and loss statement (P&L) outlines profitability of your company by listing gross margin, profit, sales, cost of goods sold and other primary indicators over a specific time period (monthly, quarterly and annually).

Profit and Loss Statement Template

[Company Name]

[Street Address], [City, ST ZIP Code]
[Phone: 555-555-55555] [Fax: 123-123-123456]
[abc@example.com]

Profit & Loss Statement
For the Period Ended _____

Income	$	$
Sales	0000000	
Services	00000000	
Other Income	00000	
Total Income		0000000
Expenses		
Accounting	0000000	
Advertising	000000	
Assets Small	000000	
Bank Charges	000000	
Cost of Goods Sold	00000	
Total Expenses		00000000
Profit/Loss		00000000

8.2 Balance Sheet

Balance sheet is a "snapshot" of the company's financial condition at any specific point in time. It includes a summary of the company's capital, assets & liabilities, both of which may be used to assess the valuation of your company.

ACCOUNT FORMAT

BUSINESS CONSULTING COMPANY
BALANCE SHEET
As at Date_____

Assets	$	Liabilities & Stockholders' equity	$
Current assets:		Liabilities:	
Cash		Notes payable	
Accounts receivable		Accounts payable	
Prepaid building rent		Salaries payable	
Unexpired insurance		Income tax payable	
Supplies		Unearned service revenue	
Total current assets		Total liabilities	
Non-current assets:		Stockholders' quity:	
Equipment		Capital stock	
Acc. Deal - Equipment		Retained earnings	
Total assets		Total Liabilities & Stockholders' equity	

8.2 Cash Flow Statement

A cash flow statement is a financial statement that records and categorises each actual cost and revenue line by line, helping you to maintain track of the company's financial operation. About any line item in the cash flow statement would be identified as an operation, investment, or financing task.

You will also be liable for making a stockholders' equity statement whether the business includes shareholders or partners with equity in the company. This declaration, which is part of your balance sheet, outlines all adjustments in the valuation of the stockholders' equity rights over time, normally from the beginning of the end of the year.

Example Corporation Statement of Cash Flows	All numbers in thousands	
Operating Activities	**$**	**10,100**
Net Income from Operations	$	10,000
Add: Depreciation Expense	$	100
Investing Activities	**$**	**(500)**
Purchase of Equipment	$	(1,000)
Sale of used equipment	$	500
Financing Activities	**$**	**4,500**
Increase in Long Term Debt	$	2,500
Issuance of Stock	$	5,000
Dividends Paid	$	(3,000)
Net Change in Cash Flow	**$**	**14,100**

Chapter: 9 Taxation

Taxation is the method of enforcing or levying a tax on individuals and corporate companies through a government or the taxing authority. Taxation applies at all levels, from corporate tax (GST) to goods and services tax.

9.1 What is Taxation

The federal and state governments have a major influence on how taxes are set around the country. The state and federal governments have enacted numerous policy changes in recent years to streamline the taxation mechanism and maintain accountability in the region. The Goods and Services Tax (GST) was one such reform that eased the tax system relating to the selling and distribution of goods and services in the world.

9.2 Purposes of Taxation

In the nineteenth century, the common assumption was that taxation could be used solely to support the nation. Governments have used taxes for more than just fiscal reasons in the past, and they do so again today. The differentiation between wealth sharing, income inequality, and economic prosperity is a valuable way to look at the function of taxes, according to American economist Richard A. Musgrave. (Sometimes global growth or progress and foreign competition are identified as distinct priorities, but they can be absorbed under the other three in general.) The first target, resource distribution, is reinforced if tax policy does not intervene with economic allocations in the absence of a legitimate justification for intervention, such as the need to minimize emissions. The second aim, wage redistribution, is intended to reduce income and wealth inequality disparities. The aim of stabilization is to sustain high jobs and market stability, which is achieved by tax reform, monetary policy, government budget policy & debt management.

9.2 Classes of Taxes

Taxes have been categorized in different forms in the theory of public finance, based on who pays for them, who carries the ultimate responsibility of them, the degree to which the burden may be transferred, and other considerations. Taxes are more generally categorized as either direct or indirect, such as the income tax of the former category and the sales tax of the latter. The requirements for discriminating between direct and indirect taxes are contested by economists, and it is uncertain which group such taxes, such as property tax or corporate income tax, should fall under. A direct tax is generally said to be one that cannot be transferred from the individual to anyone else, although it can be an indirect tax.

1. Direct Taxes

2. Indirect Taxes

Now we learn about direct and Indirect Taxes

1. Direct Taxes

Direct taxes are mainly imposed on individual citizens and are generally dependent on the taxpayer's capacity to compensate as determined by revenue, spending, or net worth. The following is a list of the most popular forms of direct taxes.

Individual income taxes are usually based on the taxpayer's gross personal net income (that might be an individual, couple, or family) that reaches a specified level. The conditions surrounding the capacity to pay, such as marital status, amount and age of the child, and financial pressures arising from sickness, are more widely tailored to take into consideration. Taxes are often charged at phased scales, which ensures that rates rise as income increases. A taxpayer's and family's personal exemptions can produce a range of income that is entitled to a zero-tax rate.

Net worth taxes are imposed on a person's overall net worth, which is proportional to value of assets less his liabilities. As in income tax, the taxpayer's specific situation should be taken into account.

Personal or direct consumption taxes (also referred to as taxes on spending or taxes on expenditure) are essentially imposed on all receipts that are not channeled into savings. In comparison to indirect spending taxes like the sales tax, a direct consumption tax may be customized to a person's financial circumstance by taking into account considerations like age, marital status, family status, and so on. This tax method has been implemented in only two nations, India & Sri Lanka, although it has long been appealing to theorists; both cases were short and ineffective. The "flat tax," which produces economic results close to those of the direct consumption tax by exempting many capital gains, came to be regarded favorably by tax analysts at the end of the 20th century. No nation has introduced a flat-rate tax base, while many have just one rate of income tax.

Inheritance taxation, in which the taxable object is the bequest earned by the individual inheriting, and estate taxes, of which the taxable object is the cumulative estate inherited by the deceased, are the two kinds of taxes imposed upon death. Inheritance taxes also take into account the taxpayer's specific conditions, such as the connection of the taxpayer to the beneficiary and his net wealth when the bequest is received. Estate payments, on the other hand, are normally phased depending on the value of the estate, although in certain nations, they include tax-free transfers to the partner and account for the number of heirs. Tax regimes which include a tax on gifts in excess of a certain threshold rendered by living individuals in order to avoid death duty from being circumvented by an exchange of property prior to death (see gift tax). Transfer taxes usually do not raise any money, if only because substantial tax collections can be prevented conveniently by estate planning.

2. Indirect Taxes

Indirect taxes, including imports and exports, are imposed on the output or sale of products and services or on transactions. Examples include general and limited excise taxes, VAT, taxes on some aspect of production or manufacturing, taxes on lawful purchases, and customs or import duties.

General sales taxes are levies that cover a large amount of consumer spending. The same tax rate may be extended to all taxable items, or separate rates can be applied to different products (such as food or clothing). Single-stage taxation may be levied at the retail level, like some states in the United States do, or at a pre-retail level (such as production or wholesale), as some developed countries do. At each point in the production-distribution process, multistage taxes are introduced. VAT, which grew in prominence during the second half of the 20th century, is usually collected by enabling the taxpayer to exclude from the sales debt the tax credit charged on transactions. At each point of the manufacturing and delivery process, the VAT has effectively substituted the turnover levy-a tax, with no tax relief charged at previous levels. Tax cascading, or the combined impact of the turnover tax, distorts economic decisions.

While they are usually applicable on a wide variety of items, sales taxes often exclude low-income families from the obligation to lower their tax burden. Excises, by contrast, are imposed only on individual products or facilities. Although almost all, including basics such as beef, flour, and salt, to non-essentials such as food, beer, cigarettes, coffee, and tea, to luxuries such as jewels and furs, taxes on a small category of goods, tobacco items, motor fuel, and alcoholic drinks, place excises and customs duties on most nations. Taxes on customer durables were extended on luxury items such as carriages, saddle horses, pianos, and billiard tables in earlier centuries. The car is currently a primary luxury tax item, primarily because registration regulations promote tax administration. Any nations also tax gaming & state-run jackpots have similar consequences as excises, with "take" of the government being, in essence, a gambling tax. Taxes on raw products, intermediate commodities (e.g., natural oil, alcohol), and equipment are imposed by certain nations.

Some excise duties and customs duties are particular, i.e., they are assessed on the grounds of the quantity, weight, duration, volume, or other particular features of the taxable product or service. Such excerpts, such as income taxes, are ad valorem, as determined by the price, depending on the valuation of the item. Legal transaction taxes are charged on the issue of bonds, on the selling (or transfer) of houses and land, and on sales on the stock market. They sometimes take the form of stamp duties for administrative reasons; that is, the legal or commercial paper is stamped to signify payment of the fee. Stamp taxes are regarded as an annoyance tax by many tax analysts; they are more often seen in less-developed countries & slow down the transactions on which they are applicable.

Chapter: 10 Small Business Tax Return

Most people are dreaming of holiday shopping, celebrations, and holidays as the year draws to an end. You're already worried about your 2017 tax return as a small business owner. Filing taxes, mostly as a small company, can be perplexing, daunting, and even cause you want to rip your hair out. It won't be too terrible if you take your time to make sure you have everything you need. Here's a short guide to filing a small business tax return in five easy measures.

1. Determine how to file

2. Collect all the documents

3. Find what forms you need

4. Make sure you are getting the deductions you deserve

5. Recheck your work with the help of a CPA

1. Determine how to file

The first step in planning for tax season as a small business owner is to know what sort of business you have. It would have an effect on the way you prepare your taxes. Are you a single proprietorship, an LLC, an S company, a general partnership, or a C corporation? When setting up your company, this should have already been known, but now it comes into play again. Different company forms have various criteria for tax returns, so it is necessary to consider what sort of business you are in order to understand what would be needed.

2. Collect all the documents

You've already learned that filing taxes needs a bunch of documentation, and this is true. Your documentation can be made up of real documents, or the documents might be digital. In any scenario, be-ensure you have them.

"The IRS says, "The company with which you are affects the kind of documents you need to maintain for federal tax purposes when it comes to what sort of documentation you can obtain. A list of your company activities should be included in your recordkeeping method.

Payroll, sales slips, bank slips, bounced checks, invoices, certificates, and cash register recordings are also exampling documents. Don't forget to keep track of travel costs, any sales, and records of items you buy and are using in your company, such as furniture or machinery. Last but not least, job documents are needed. Do the utmost to maintain track of these items during the year, instead of struggling throughout the tax season, to make it easy on yourself.

3. Find what forms you need

It's an unfair fact that while filing the taxes, there would be some filling-out of paperwork. The kind of small company you have may influence the forms to fill out, as described earlier. Every state may have its own types and specifications, so here's a short rundown on some of the federal income tax measures:

Form 1120 U.S. Business Income Tax Return-Form 1120 is for tax reports submitted by C companies. C businesses are organizations where the shareholders do not incur taxes on individual reports themselves.

Form 1120 S U.S. Income Tax Return – For S Companies, this is the form to use. S Company owners, unlike C Companies, pay income tax on their corporate income tax reports. As a consequence, each shareholder is expected to complete a Schedule K-1 Method.

Form 1065 U.S. Relationship Benefit Tax- You would need to plan one of these types if your small corporation is set up as a collaboration. Since partnerships do not incur income tax, this type is just for information purposes. Every participant may also need to fill out a Schedule K-1 Form if you are part of a relationship, which goes into specifics regarding the profits, dividends, and losses of each particular partner.

Form 1099 MISC-This is a form that is processed and issued as part of the tax return to any independent contractors you might have employed, and it is often submitted to the IRS.

You may still need to complete separate documents for the boss, such as Form W-2 Pay and Tax Declaration.

4. Make sure you are getting the deductions you deserve

Deductions are the one aspect of paying the taxes that may be deemed pleasant.

Taxes are not all about the government having its due, Drew Hendricks of Forbes points out. Some tax laws are loopholes that provide for deductions – which are simply opportunities for the government to get you and your company to use money the way it wants."

You have put in a lot of time this year because operating a small company is an expensive activity. Making the best of the tax deductions, but be mindful of what is and is not an appropriate deduction. The Internal Revenue Service (IRS) offers certain basic guidance in this regard. The deductible business cost must be "usual and essential." Supplies, car costs, corporate transport, contract labor, staff compensation, pensions, employee benefits, and employee investment systems are some of the most typical ones on a small business tax return. Be vigilant not to combine personal expenditures with work expenses and be mindful of what company costs are 100% deductible versus a lower percentage.

5. Recheck your work with the help of a CPA

It may be confusing to submit a tax return as a private citizen, and filing as a small businessman is much, much harder. It's important to consider the measures involved in processing a small business tax return, as well as the criteria. It is advised, however, that you enlist the assistance of a licensed CPA to ensure that everything is properly and accurately filled out, particularly if this is your first filing as a small business. A CPA will help you manage all the forms, locate deductions, and advise you what reports and documentation to gather are required.

Chapter: 11 How to Audit Your E-commerce Business

E-commerce is one of the fastest-growing business markets nowadays, so make sure you are prepared with an online business audit to help you develop the site. To boost traffic, make profits, and create a long-term consumer community, e-commerce companies need great material.

➢ How is the content performing?

➢ Is there anything that you should be doing?

➢ What was the last period you performed a comprehensive e-commerce audit?

It is important to take a step back and audit the material on a daily basis and ensure that it is fulfilling your company objectives. Continue reading to learn how to audit (and improve) your e-commerce material.

11.1 Review your current vision

Before you start your e-commerce business audit, you can do some deep thinking. This involves having a good, hard look at the new plan and finding some places that you might be falling short.

Do you really have any editorial calendar for the company's site and social network, for example? An editorial calendar is an important and basic function that many e-commerce company owners ignore.

➤ Take into consideration if the material is advertised. Are you making the best out of your email & social network accounts?

➤ Do the landing pages have well-defined objectives?

Prior to implementing some modifications or improving your approach after an e-commerce market analysis, you must first recognize existing issue areas that need to be resolved. You are already mindful of where (and why) you've been deficient in strategic guidance. Tackle certain places with passion, and bid farewell to your strategy-poor past.

11.2 Be critical

Now it's time to get back to work for the content auditing.

Create a list of every website on the e-commerce platform, beginning with the home & landing pages and making your way down to specific blog posts and product pages. Now go to each page and ask yourself the following questions:

➤ Is the website producing as it promises? Are your headings in line with your text? Do the call-to-actions execute on their promises?

➤ Is anything current? Since search engines don't value old material as much, it's crucial that the connections, items, and material are accurate and up-to-date.

➤ Is there a conceptual framework for each piece? Examine the organization on the website. It should sound normal and not haphazardly placed together.

➤ Is it easy to find? Internal links should be plentiful in your material, linking it all together. It's not just SEO-friendly, but it's still user-friendly.

➤ Is it efficient? Using the site analytics to see if any specific piece of material gets a tonne of traffic or converts. Don't forget these metrics if you want to expand your e-commerce business.

When undertaking an e-commerce company audit, don't be delicate with yourself: a stern eye on each material feature can sound harsh, but it will deliver the best outcomes.

11.3 Use tools to source the accurate data you need

Since an e-commerce company audit involves effort and time, it's a smart idea to use one of the numerous free or low-cost tools available to assist you to organize and quantify data easily. You have access to a wide variety of content resources, each of which is customized to a particular target.

➤ **Google Analytics:**

Google Analytics is helpful for finding issue areas and assessing the success of content by indicators.

➤ **Screaming Frog:**

Screaming Frog is an SEO tool that crawls your site and returns valuable (and actionable) details.

➤ **Site Analyzer:**

Site Analyzer offers a thorough review of the site, as well as an overall rating dependent on criteria such as speed, style, and copy.

> **Yoast:**

Yoast, a wonderful WordPress SEO plugin that offers a fast rundown of keyword targeting for blog posts and websites.

But be careful: with so many auditing tools at your hands, it's possible to get too dependent on them. To get the best out of the e-commerce quality audit, invest just in a handful and use them wisely. Don't get paralyzed by research paralysis. There are many resources that will assist you.

11.4 Get into auditing to maximize the value of your business

Finally, don't feel too cozy. Auditing is a constant phase that necessitates daily focus. Your content isn't a stand-alone entity; it's up against a slew of other products in a saturated sector, and standing away requires effort.

A content audit is a valuable practice that will help you keep on top of things. It's also a particularly rewarding talent to practice. Flipping websites is a popular route for aspiring entrepreneurs, and a content audit will make it simple for you to acquire an online company, transform it around, and then market it for a profit — it's a talent that can pay off again and again. It all comes down to providing outstanding web content in terms of profitability, performance, and market resale value.

Chapter: 12 The impact of Covid-19 on eCommerce

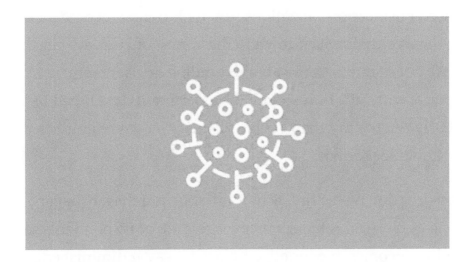

2020 was a difficult year for almost all individuals. Simultaneously, the online business developed more than ever. What would we be able to anticipate from 2021? SearchNode distributed another report on the most recent web-based business patterns and the effect of Covid-19.

A year ago, SearchNode distributed a report on online business patterns in 2020. Obviously, in those days, there was mostly secret about the Covid that would spread all over the globe. In the overview, there were loads of discussions with Magento, an improved spotlight on personalization and natural manageability.

2020 was, of course, all about Covid-19.

What has changed in a year? You should discover, as the Lithuanian tech organization distributed another report on online business patterns. In October 2020, the organization interrogated 100 internet business leaders from Europe and North America.

12.1 Six% eCommerce revenue decreased during the lockdown

There were inquiries concerning Covid-19. It appears to be that most web-based business organizations saw their online income increment during the worldwide lockdown in the spring of 2020. As per the study, 90% of organizations saw their online deals increment at any rate a piece, with 50% of respondents asserting it developed by more than 100%. Yet, 6% say their online business income diminished during Covid lockdown.

After the lockdown was finished, numerous purchasers began shopping at physical retailers once more. 86% of respondents say that their online incomes expanded, and just 4% say it diminished.

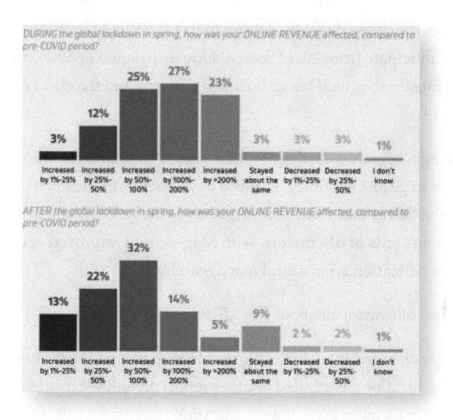

12.2 Online profit margin increased by 38%

Producing on the web deals is a certain something; the entire Covid-19 circumstance has additionally prompted things like disturbed inventory chains, inadequately staffed client assistance, and the sky is the limit from there. This straightforwardly influences the online net revenue. It appears to be that for 38% of internet business leaders, their online net revenue developed during the worldwide lockdown, while for a comparative rate (40%), the circumstance expressed about the equivalent. Just 15% asserted that it diminished.

12.3 The impact of Covid-19 on the workforce

The pandemic has, obviously, additionally prompted a few changes in organizations' labor force. Around 44% said they needed to move staff, while three out of ten recruited more individuals. The opposite side of the coin is that 26% needed to terminate a few groups, and 15 percent say they needed to lessen their workers' pay rates. Also, perhaps somewhat amazing for a few, yet 5 percent figured out how to expand compensations. What's more, much astonishing: 21% of organizations didn't change their labor force by any means.

21% of organizations didn't change their labor force.

23% of omnichannel players observed disconnected deals increment

Another intriguing finding from the investigation is that for retailers on the offline and online stores, 23% say their disconnected deals expanded, and 16 percent figured out how to keep it comparative. Lamentably, for 43%, their disconnected deals endured a shot.

12.4 Measurements for physical retailers

Numerous physical retailers needed to change their business on the off chance that they needed to maintain a strategic distance from to leave the business. In this way, numerous new practices were presented a year ago. Among the members, 31% presented in-store pickup, while 26% decided to present home conveyance. Sadly, around one of every five needed to close down some actual stores for great.

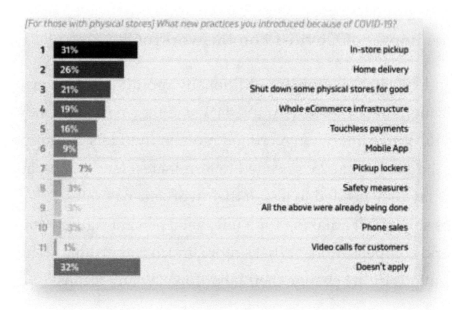

Covid has vigorously affected online retailers on various levels. Among the fundamental difficulties for internet business organizations, upset stockpile chains and satisfying interest for items were the, for the most part, referenced ones. Yet, restricted tasks because of the lockdown, overseeing stock, and the general absence of representatives were likewise vital difficulties for online retailers.

What's more, 17% said it was testing since they need to shut down their actual stores.

An upset store network was the primary test for some online retailers in Europe.

12.5 Shifted strategies

A year ago, numerous respondents said they would generally execute, improve or change personalization, site-search and omnichannel. This year, the essential vision has moved because of Covid-19. The majority of the organizations (45%) will presently have more spotlight on the advanced piece of their business by changing the combination, putting resources into new online business programming or emphasizing additionally on internet advertising channels.

One of every five said they would increase activities, which means they need to execute their methodologies and act quicker. One out of ten says they are currently centered around actual store changes, and 8 percent went for inventory network changes, from minor ones to new store networks or coordination's.

12.6 Financial consequences

Notwithstanding all the terrible things occurring because of the flare-up of the Covid, monetarily 2020 wasn't so awful for some web-based business organizations. The greater part of them (63%) say the year (up to October) was effective. Furthermore, 28% case their web-based business was progressing nicely, while their actual stores didn't. What's more, an astounding 2% said the inverse!

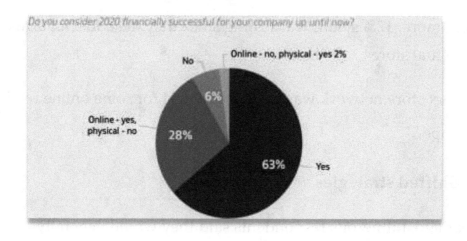

Chapter: 13 What is the Future for Online Business?

With the online world changing apparently from one day to another and an expanding number of sites (today, there are just about 2 billion sites out there), the future for organizations working on the web consistently appears to be unsure. From the finish of unhindered internet to the limitations on YouTube adaptation to progressing computerized innovation and that's just the beginning, the inquiry is the thing that patterns will be generally noticeable for online organizations within a reasonable time-frame.

Right now, with the US economy extending, it appears to be that the not-so-distant future for online organizations is splendid gratitude to more noteworthy customer certainty and ways of managing money. What follows are new patterns in online business that have all the earmarks of growing as buyer propensities change over the following, not many years, which will significantly affect how web-based advertising is being performed.

Expansion of Cryptocurrency

While there has been impressive information about the inconveniences related to bitcoin, digital money itself has all the earmarks of being extending quickly and turning out to be standard. With more organizations and governments going to cryptographic money as an alternative, the exchanges will turn out to be solidly advanced. This implies an adjustment in the manner purchasers purchase across all business sectors, which implies that online organizations should be set up to acknowledge this type of cash soon.

The advent of Machine Learning

This type of innovation is ready to venture into deals and client service, implying that how organizations work with clients will be improved. AI will be through utilizing discourse examination, which better aids client assistance divisions in how to react to every one of their clients. This improves connection which means assembling a more grounded brand and enduring fewer misfortunes because of mistaken assumptions.

Increased Security Spending

In light of ongoing hacks and break-ins that have uncovered the individual data of millions of clients, more organizations are venturing up their security conventions to keep it from happening to them. This has implied a move in accentuation from avoidance towards recognizing interruptions and reacting in like manner. Better security implies more costs, which may tremendously affect the monetary situation of little and medium-sized online organizations.

Personalized Marketing

With such countless online organizations attempting to arrive at similar clients, it can get hard to get over the clamor. This is why individual promoting patterns have been developing and will keep on extending as more organizations spring up around the planet. Effective online organizations will zero in on brilliant showcasing that arrives at the individual, not simply the ideal buyer gathering. On account of new advanced innovation, specific Artificial Intelligence (AI) (web-based business organizations are now confronting this test), the progressions are now occurring and will keep on developing.

Rise of the Sharing Economy

The blend of the sharing economy, which is most broadly addressed by ride-sharing administrations like Uber. It has additionally dug into retail with monsters, for example, Google and Amazon getting into this pattern. For online organizations, the sharing economy addresses an incredible pattern ready to attack medical care and monetary administrations, which may change how numerous online organizations work.

For online entrepreneurs, the extension of the web to world business sectors implies a new wilderness of clients just as contenders. The individuals who succeed will be adaptable to the inescapable change that happens and finds a way to remain one stride ahead to guarantee their future.

Conclusion

Accounting is described as "the processing, review, and systematic documentation of numerical business transactions, the preparation of financial reports, and the examination and evaluation of these reports for management's knowledge and guidance."

Accounting is an accounting mechanism that observes, tracks, and communicates an economic entity's monetary activities.

It is the method of defining, evaluating, and communicating economic data in order for consumers of the data to make educated choices and decisions. Human life is evolving in this ever-changing environment.

Accounting has taken on a different form as a consequence of technical advances, such as holding records mechanically.

With the widespread usage of electronic accounting tasks, a modern arena has arisen. As a consequence, it is obvious that the concept of accounting will evolve in the coming years.

CPSIA information can be obtained
at www.ICGtesting.com
Printed in the USA
BVHW012325150321
602550BV00004B/419